My Family
is All I Have

My Family is All I Have

A British Woman's Story of Escaping the Nazis and Surviving the Communists

HELEN-ALICE DEAR

With Andrew Crofts

EBURY
PRESS

1 3 5 7 9 10 8 6 4 2

Published in 2007 by Ebury Press, an imprint of Ebury Publishing

Ebury Publishing is a division of the Random House Group

The Random House Group Limited Reg. No. 954009

Addresses for companies within the Random House Group
can be found at www.randomhouse.co.uk

A CIP catalogue record for this book is available from the British Library

Penguin Random House is committed to a sustainable future for
our business, our readers and our planet. This book is made from
Forest Stewardship Council® certified paper.

MIX
Paper from
responsible sources
FSC® C018179

Printed and bound in Great Britain by Clays Ltd, Elcograf S.p.A.

Interior designed by seagulls.net

ISBN 9780091912239

For all my children, especially my eldest daughter Gloria: she went through all the years of fear and struggle by my side, and has been a second mother to her siblings. I would also like to thank Roza, my youngest daughter, and my great granddaughter Yana for all their care and support.

Introduction

It is hard for today's young people to imagine how different the world felt seventy years ago. Where now the greatest fear is caused by the bombs of anonymous terrorists, at that time the fears were that foreign armies would march across borders and subjugate their neighbours.

The fears were very real, and in many countries they came to pass. In some countries, like the one my family happened to find themselves in, it happened twice. First the German army invaded, and then the communists took over, dividing us from the rest of the world.

Today everyone in Europe can move freely from one country to another, but at that time millions of people were imprisoned behind walls, both real and ideological. We – myself and my family – became trapped in exactly that way. This is the story of how we survived cruel entrapment in an alien culture for nearly half a century, until one day the whole world changed.

Chapter One
A Foreign Adventure

Big city railway stations seethed with life in 1935. Few people could afford to travel anywhere by air, and cars were not up to long transcontinental journeys, so the train was the main mode of transport for anyone wishing to travel abroad. Arriving anywhere new, soot-stained and disorientated from days of staring at passing scenery, hearing different languages being spoken, always felt like an exotic adventure, especially to a sixteen-year-old girl from a sheltered background.

My brother, Octave, being five years older, was busy being the man of the family, trying not to stare in quite such an open-mouthed fashion. Looking out at the crowd as we struggled to alight from the carriage with our luggage, I was a little disappointed not to see my grandmother among the sea of faces waiting on the platform in Vienna to welcome friends and relatives. All around people were greeting one another with cries of delight, hugs and kisses and torrents of questions and news, but there was no one there for us. In her letters Granny always seemed so anxious to see us.

Despite having no one to meet us, our mother was in high spirits, mainly at the thought that our long and uncomfortable journey from England was over at last. She must have been looking forward to seeing her mother as much as we were. She led us confidently through the city, pointing out well-known landmarks, as we headed towards Granny's house to find her. Excitement and anticipation at meeting my grandmother for the first time soon displaced my initial disappointment. Infected by my mother's good mood, Vienna struck me as a happy city. Looking back now, it seemed to me there was music coming from every door we passed.

When we reached my grandmother's house, we rang the bell several times, but there was no reply. Still undaunted, Mother borrowed a key from a neighbour and we let ourselves in. The stillness settled over us like a dust-sheet. Something didn't feel right. Everything was too tidy, like no one was living there. It gradually dawned on us that Granny had gone away without telling us. Octave and I couldn't think what to say. She knew we were coming to see her, so how could she possibly have gone away? We gazed around the neat, dusty rooms and watched as our mother burst into tears.

We both knew how much she had been looking forward to the reunion, not having seen her mother since the end of the First World War, nearly twenty years before. The strain of the journey had exhausted her and this disappointment was just too much.

When we investigated the quiet house more closely we found a letter in Granny's handwriting addressed to us and lying on the table. Mother opened it and read it with wide-eyed horror. A childhood friend of Granny's, who had married a Bulgarian student some forty years earlier, had written to say there was a terrible shortage of midwives in their newly opened maternity hospital in Bulgaria and had asked our grandmother to come and help out for a few weeks. Granny had immediately packed her bags and gone, leaving her dressmaking workshop in the hands of her employees for a while.

'She suggests we join her in Bulgaria for an extra holiday,' my mother sighed. Instead of reaching our destination, as we had imagined, we had actually arrived at the start of an unexpected adventure.

Three days later we were on the train to Budapest, where we changed to another heading towards the Orient. The carriages were even more crowded than they had been on the way to Vienna and the unfamiliar stench of garlic was almost unbearable as everyone around us tucked into home-made sandwiches and talked at the tops of their voices. It was as if they were at a big family gathering, rather than on a journey. From the window once more I watched the scenery passing, staring at the pretty houses and tiny farmyards filled with geese, ducks, turkeys and chickens. I'd never seen so many animals, coming as I did from the north London suburbs.

Although this was my first real taste of travel, my family had long been seasoned travellers. I'd heard my father's brothers telling tales of their journeys around Europe as children, when their father, my grandfather, had been an engineer working on the Orient Express line. They had lived in railway wagons originally intended for carrying livestock. Their mother had insisted they travelled everywhere as a family and so they were allocated two wagons by the railway company, one for their carefully fixed bunk beds and wardrobes, the other to be their kitchen, dining and sitting room. Water came from barrels on the roofs. My grandfather's office was a smaller wagon attached to the engine.

'The instructions on those wagons said "eight horses or 52 people",' my uncles used to joke.

As well as their five children, my grandparents had also taken with them a recently orphaned French student who kept a strong grip on the elder children and acted as their tutor, and a young Austrian widow who helped with the housework, cooking and sewing. She also taught them German. My father, their sixth child, was born when they reached Constantinople and ended up speaking twelve languages, seven of them to official standards. It seemed strange to be travelling along the very same line so many years later, like a link to my currently absent father.

As we passed from Hungary to Yugoslavia the houses began to look poorer, the farmyards and gardens less tidy. Most of the women wore headscarves; the men had round sheepskin hats with the woolly side on the outside. Everyone wore sleeveless sheepskin jackets, and pigskins on their feet, tied together with string.

We arrived in Sofia, Bulgaria's capital, in the middle of the night, eight hours late and exhausted. Once again we searched the platform in vain for any sign of my grandmother. My mother's spirits sank even lower. The station was dark and ugly, the crowds much less prosperous-looking than in Vienna, and the few other passengers who had alighted with us soon disappeared, leaving us feeling exposed and a long way from home. As Octave and I gathered up the luggage, our mother sought out the stationmaster, her hand shaking as she held out the address which Granny had left for us, and asking if he knew where it was. He didn't.

'If you take a carriage,' the stationmaster suggested, 'maybe the driver will know the address.'

A porter was dispatched to find a carriage while we hauled the luggage to the front of the station, which opened on to a gloomy, unlit square. In the darkness I heard approaching hooves and a one-horse carriage appeared beside us. The shabbily dressed driver grumbled at the sight of so many suitcases but agreed to take us. My mother didn't seem sure she could trust him, but my brother and I were now too excited at the prospect of riding in a horse-driven carriage to worry about any possible danger. Octave climbed up beside the driver while my mother and I sat in the back, clutching the cases, which threatened to topple out at every corner. In the following two hours we met three people, each of whom the driver asked the way, each sending us in different directions. The final man and the driver talked for ages and I could see Mum was becoming increasingly nervous. Only later did she tell us that they had been speaking in a gypsy language.

Dawn was breaking when we finally found the address and a landlady let us in. There was still no sign of Granny.

'This seems like a bad start to me,' Octave muttered under his breath, so only I could hear.

The woman assured us that our grandmother had been to the station twice but had been told the train was going to be eighteen hours late.

'That is quite normal in this part of the world,' she assured us. 'So when she was called to the hospital late last night she thought it would be safe to go because you would not be here until the afternoon.'

At least we had arrived and there would be no more travelling. Our first concern was to find a bathroom so we could clean up. We asked the landlady where it was.

'Well,' she said, looking flustered, 'the local council promised to build one just two streets away, but because of some financial difficulties it hasn't even been started yet.'

'So where do you bathe yourselves?' my mother asked, with a look of mounting horror.

'We go to the mineral bath in the centre once a month.'

'Only once a month? And on cold winter days?' Mum asked.

'Oh no,' the woman assured her. 'We don't go in the winter.'

The excitement of the trip was beginning to wear off as I struggled with tiredness and discomfort. At least, I reassured myself, we would only be in Bulgaria for a week or two, then we would be able to go back to London before travelling to Canada and to the comfortable house that our father was preparing for us there.

When Granny finally came home it didn't feel like I was meeting her for the first time because of the many letters and photographs we'd exchanged over the years. My mother wept tears of joy and Granny went first to my brother, whom she had met when he was small, then she and my mother hugged and kissed. Finally she stood back to take a long look at me before throwing her arms around me and covering me in kisses.

Granny was originally English, but had married an Austrian who had been studying in England, and had gone back to Vienna with him. Her visits home had become less and less frequent, particularly after my Austrian grandfather died young. Widowed in her early twenties, she had declined to stay in the large, six-bedroom marital home with its many memories of her beloved husband and had

instead moved, with my two-year-old mother, to the house
we had gone to when we arrived in Vienna.

Once the excitement had calmed, Granny began to sing
the praises of Bulgaria, saying that what my mother really
needed was a good rest.

'Bulgaria is the ideal place for you,' she said. 'I'm being
well paid for the work I'm doing and life is much cheaper
here than in London or Vienna. The climate is healthy and
you won't have a worry in the world while you're here.'

'But Mama,' my mother tried to interrupt, 'I still have
quite a few things to arrange in England before we leave
for Canada.'

'Oh, those things won't go anywhere in a few weeks,'
said Granny, brushing aside her protests. 'Look at yourself,
you're so pale and run down, you need to be looked after
properly. God knows what kind of life is lying ahead of you
in that far-off land.'

'Dad is waiting for us,' I tried to explain, 'we need to
leave as soon as possible.'

I was under the impression that we would soon be on
our way to Canada to join our father, who had been out
there for the previous two years, starting a new job with
his bank and finding us a suitable family home. His last
letter had informed us how happy he was with his job and
that he had high expectations of being promoted very
soon. The house he had found, he told us, was just as nice
as the one we were leaving in England and even had a few
more rooms.

I dearly loved our house in Camrose Avenue, Mill Hill, but I was sure being reunited with my father would compensate me for any sadness at leaving the family home.

'I don't mind staying and having a look round for a while,' Octave chipped in, always ready for an adventure. 'But we shouldn't stay too long.'

'Aren't you going back to Vienna soon?' Mum tried again. 'I'd rather stay there.'

'Not for the moment,' Granny said. 'My girls are managing quite well in the workshop without me. I need a bit of a change myself.'

Mum's resistance was weakening. 'We have travelled here to be with you so, if the children don't mind ...'

'Oh, they'll find it very interesting here once they start exploring the town.' Granny seemed to think the matter was settled. 'Now let's have something nice to eat.'

The next morning the landlady's son took us around town. He, like us, had learned a bit of French at school and so we could communicate as we wandered the clean, yellow-paved streets, watching the picturesque horse-drawn phaetons trotting down the avenues of chestnut and lime trees. I began to feel like I was finally on holiday.

A few days later Granny took Mum to see the maternity hospital where she worked. As soon as the head doctor met her he began begging her to stay and work for a while.

Mum had been a nurse, working for the International Red Cross during the First World War.

'We're desperately in need of staff,' he explained. 'We've been promised more but they haven't arrived. If we have three or more women coming into labour at the same time we just don't have the people to care for them.'

Like her own mother, Mum was always easily swayed by anyone in need of her help and we could see that she was beginning to bow to the pressure. At supper that evening Octave pointed out that our return tickets would expire if we stayed too long.

'Oh, I'll give you the money for the fare back to England,' Granny said, airily brushing aside his worries.

'But Dad is waiting for us,' I muttered, trying to sound a bit sulky, even though it didn't really come naturally to me.

'Your dad has waited so long, another two or three weeks won't harm him.' There was an edge of irritation to Granny's voice now, which I didn't understand.

After a few more minutes of our protests Granny started to sound close to tears. 'Oh well, I suppose all these things are more important than staying with me a few days longer. I thought you would all be so pleased to see me after all these years.'

She eventually confessed she had already told her friend and the head doctor that Mum would stay and help in the hospital.

'Now I don't know what I'm going to say to them tomorrow,' she sniffed.

'Well, I'll come with you tomorrow,' Mum tried to lighten the tense atmosphere, 'but I can't stay, really I can't.'

While Mum and Granny were at the hospital the next day the landlady's son took us for a walk up the Vitosha Mountain, to a point where we could see the whole town spread below us. After eating our picnic of home-baked bread and white goat's cheese, washed down by cold water from the mountain streams, we ran all the way down through the beautiful pine forests, our shouts of laughter startling the hares and deer.

The next morning Mum said she was going to go into the hospital to help out for a few hours again because there was a difficult case.

'I'll be back by two o'clock,' she promised.

Octave and I were back home by half past one and Granny met us in front of the house.

'Where's Mum?' we both asked at once, expecting them to have come back from the hospital together.

'She's had a slight mishap,' said Granny. 'She's had to stay in the hospital, but don't worry. There was this young man whose baby couldn't be saved and whose wife was in a critical state. He was running down the stairs in despair just as your mother was coming up. She fell and broke her leg and now it's in plaster.'

'Oh my God,' I shouted, 'we must go and see her.'

Octave agreed. I noticed he had turned very pale. 'Please take us there.'

'Let her have a little rest,' Granny said. 'I'll take you

there before supper. She must sleep a bit now. She was very brave.'

'But she's all alone there!' My tears were flowing freely now as Octave tried to comfort me. It seemed Granny was going to get her wish after all to have us stay for a bit longer.

Three months later, after contracting jaundice in the hospital, Mum finally came home. Her leg had mended but her heart seemed to have been broken. Whatever had happened in the hospital had frightened her badly. She was weak and pale and constantly fearful, a condition that communicated itself to us although we didn't feel we could talk to her about it. Looking back now, I suppose she must have realised that the Germans were approaching and we needed to get back to England as quickly as possible; but such grown-up matters didn't enter my head, I was just glad to have her out of hospital. I'd had enough of our adventure and wanted to get to Dad in Canada.

Octave, being five years older than me, read the papers and mixed with other young men, talking politics and listening to the rumours. He told me there were stories of a new war starting. He said borders were being closed between countries and food was getting scarce, clothing even more so. There was no news from either our father or uncles. I was missing Dad so much and I just wanted to know when we would be able to travel to Canada to join him.

'Don't ask your mother so many questions,' Granny cautioned when I tried to find out what her plans were. 'This constant crying is not helping her health.'

One afternoon we all went to the British Embassy, hoping to get some news and to ask for help in returning to England now that our return tickets had expired. The embassy was closed to all visitors and a notice informed us that 'temporarily' no visas would be given. I could tell from the expressions on the faces of the grown-ups that this was bad news. It was puzzling and frightening because no one seemed able to explain to me what was going to happen to us next.

We went back home and Mum started writing letters to the embassy every day, explaining our predicament, but only ever received one reply. The grammar in the letter was bad, suggesting it had been written by a Bulgarian secretary. The letter informed her that the embassy couldn't give her any positive news at the moment. After that there was silence.

Chapter Two
Becoming Bulgarian

Until the moment we set off from Dover to visit Granny, I had led a very sheltered life. Shortly after my father's departure to Canada two years before, my mother had left me at a convent, St Francis of Assisi, run by some very strict nuns. Life there had been run like clockwork: getting up, making beds, standing in queues for washrooms, getting dressed, marching downstairs to a breakfast of porridge before going to the classrooms. Lunch (mostly meatless and always tasteless), was followed by afternoon school, one 'free' hour for knitting or needlework, during which we were allowed to talk quietly, then supper, evening prayers in chapel and back to bed. We had to wear long-sleeved, black, coarse dresses, and long black stockings. The nuns handed out no smiles, no gentle words of comfort. There were no games, no sport and no laughter. The sun did not shine through the windows that overlooked the flowerless gardens. It all seemed more like a punishment than an education. If anyone had told me that for most of my life I would look back on those days with nostalgia and affection, I would never have believed them; but then, I had no idea of what was about to befall us, none of us did.

My first taste of the Continent, when we alighted from the boat at Ostend, had been promising. The houses were tidier and more colourful than I was used to in London. The windows were all spotlessly clean with pretty, snow-white lace curtains. Brightly coloured flowers stood on every windowsill, around every doorway and along paths, everywhere.

As we tried to find our way around we met two young girls dressed exactly like a Dutch doll I had at home, white linen starched hats with turned up ears, white pinafores, knee-high red socks and clogs which made a funny noise as they walked. Turning to watch them as my mother and brother walked on, I bumped into a stout gentleman who patted me on the head and handed me a small bar of chocolate.

'Good Dutch chocolate,' he said.

Stunned, I thanked him and ran after my mother, who scolded me for straying too far. Although I had just turned sixteen, I really was still a child.

That exciting arrival began to seem a long time ago as we fell into the rhythm of life in Sofia. Both Octave and I learned to read and write Bulgarian with the help of a neighbour who was a professor, so we could follow what was happening in the newspapers, and make ourselves understood. It no longer felt like a holiday; it felt like our lives had changed and taken an ominous turn for the worse.

'Now look, dear,' Granny said to Mum one evening. 'It can't go on like this for ever. Everything smells of a new war. The children need winter coats and shoes, and so many other things. Why don't you come and work for a while in the hospital, to bring in some money?'

'Mamma, please!' Mum protested. 'I'm so mixed up. William doesn't answer my letters, I can't get in touch with the embassy, our permission to stay abroad has expired and I have no money to go back even if I could get permission. The Bulgarian authorities seem to be deliberately making things difficult for us. The children should be going to school. What am I to do?'

'If you go to work at least they'll see you're being useful,' Granny insisted, 'you'll be working exactly where they need you the most.'

'I've been offered a job as a hotel receptionist,' Octave interrupted. 'Because I can speak English, German and Spanish they said I could be helpful.'

'Good for you,' Granny beamed proudly.

'You're too young to work,' Mum's voice rose. 'You have to finish your education.'

'I know,' he answered calmly, 'but where shall I go? And how are we going to pay for it?'

Mum stormed off to the bedroom, looking as if she might be about to faint, and refused to let any of us in until it was time to sleep.

Octave took the job, at one of the best hotels in Sofia, and started working twelve to fourteen hours a day. A lot of the foreign authorities used the hotel, so he learned what was going on around us as Europe prepared for war. The more he learned, the more silent and withdrawn he became. He found my ignorant girlishness increasingly irritating and I realised that I was losing not only my brother, but my best and only friend as well.

Octave was the product of Mum's first, tragically brief marriage. His father had been a Romanian consul who Mum had met in Vienna. Octave was born in Bucharest a year before his father was killed in a train crash in 1915. Mum went on to meet my father, an Englishman, during the First World War and he took her back to London to marry her.

Following Octave's example, Mum summoned all her energy to go back to work while I spent my time improving my Bulgarian and Italian with the help of teach-yourself books. Every day I heard the grown-ups worrying about how we were going to get permission to leave the country and go back to our homes in Vienna, London and eventually Canada. The embassies all refused to respond to any letters and we weren't allowed by the guards to go near to their doors. Everyone talked and talked, but still the situation seemed hopeless.

Granny's friend, Gretel, who had suggested she come to Bulgaria in the first place, had managed to get permission to go to Vienna on leave and tried to get in touch with the British and the Canadian embassies for us while she was there, with no result. The situation in Austria, it seemed, was just as uneasy as in Bulgaria. The whole world was gearing up for catastrophe and the fate of our small family was not a priority for anyone.

Suspicion and hatred seemed to be simmering all around us; no one knew who to trust. One evening I was alone at home when there was an impatient hammering at the door. I heard raised voices as the landlady talked to the callers. Then the door was forced open and several young men barged in, carrying a limp Octave. They threw him on the couch and left, giving some sort of explanation I didn't understand. I ran over to him, thinking he was dead. Every muscle in my body was shaking. I discovered he was breathing but he was unconscious and blood was running from somewhere on his head. His clothes were all muddy and torn. The landlady and her son helped me to take his clothes off and wash his wounds, and then she went in search of bandages.

By the time Granny returned he had regained consciousness, but didn't seem able to talk, as his mouth was swollen and his jaw was obviously hurting. Granny examined him and decided he'd had a beating but nothing was broken. We carried him to his bed, where he passed out once more.

He couldn't manage to stand for four days, during which he was obviously in terrible pain. It was frightening to think that such violence could come from nowhere, with no reason. I couldn't understand what was happening and Octave didn't want to talk to me any more, lost in his own thoughts and plans. As soon as he was well enough, he left the house without saying where he was going. Hours later, when he hadn't returned, Mum began to grow restless, imagining the worst. At about half past ten that night the landlady's son brought us a letter Octave had given him to deliver.

'I'm all right,' the letter read. 'Please don't worry about me. I'll write soon. Take care of yourselves, love Octave.'

My grandmother said nothing as my mother wept. I was so stunned I couldn't think of a single question to ask. What could have happened to him? There was no one to go to for help, no one to ask. We just had to sit and wait and worry. The days turned into anxious weeks of silence as my mother tried to cope with her sadness at losing her son. At work she was able to distract herself with her duties; at home there was nothing, and she hardly spoke.

One evening, a few months after Octave had left, and when Mum was working a night shift, a middle-aged man knocked at our door. Over a cup of tea he told Granny and me that he was a businessman and travelled a great deal. He had bumped into Octave in London.

'He asked me to come and tell you that he was all right,' the gentleman went on.

I couldn't believe that Octave was in London without

us. Why couldn't we have gone with him? I could picture my home city so clearly as I listened to the man talk and longed to be back there.

'Apparently,' our visitor told us, 'after leaving Sofia he hitchhiked to Burgas, a port where he knew British ships docked. He travelled for three days to get there and then waited for a British ship to arrive. When one did he made himself known to the captain and asked for help. The captain gave him a porter's uniform and told him to carry on passengers' luggage just as they were about to set sail. The crew then hid him while the customs officers made their final check. He performed the same trick at Dover, walking off under the noses of the English customs men.'

Hearing the story I could understand why he'd had to travel alone; he would never have been able to smuggle all of us on to the boat. Perhaps now he was safe he would be able to get help for us from England. News that he was alive lifted all our spirits, because things were not getting any easier for us and we needed him to do something to get us out.

Prices were rising every day and many shops were closing down because they had nothing to sell. It was becoming hard to find clothes and even food. Only 'government ship-ments' were allowed in and out of the ports, and ordinary people never knew what those shipments contained. When war is imminent the authorities have the perfect excuse to start being secretive and taking control of everything. Soon only the better-off could afford to buy fresh produce and the black market began to thrive, increasing the prices of even the most basic essentials for people like us who had no connections and no influence.

My job, when the others were at work, became to wander from shop to shop, market to market, finding out what they would be selling the next day and where things would be cheapest, so that I could be sure to be the first in the queue whenever there was anything available. I noticed that I was hearing more and more German voices in the streets, which quite pleased me since it meant that at least I could understand what people were saying. My Bulgarian was improving, but I was still struggling and often found my attempts to speak it being laughed at, but my German was fine. I had been used to hearing different languages spoken all my life, so it didn't seem strange to me to swap from one language to another. What I didn't realise was that at a time when there was so much uncertainty about the future and about who could be trusted, people who can speak more than one language immediately fall under suspicion. Where do they come from? Where do their loyalties lie? Are they spies?

Pining for England, and Octave, I decided to have another try at speaking to someone in the British embassy while Mum and Granny were at work. The guards didn't even let me near the entrance, shooing me away with angry shouts as if I was a dangerous enemy. I returned home feeling humiliated, and hoping that Mum wouldn't find out. The next day a man from the district council arrived and ordered me to accompany him to the council offices. I could see Mum was frightened and she insisted on coming too, even though the man protested. I felt sick with apprehension as to what was going to happen to me and on the way I confessed to her about my little adventure.

Once we reached the offices the councillor himself met us and started firing questions about how and why we came to be in Sofia, making me feel frightened and confused and angry all at once.

'Who gave you permission to work?' he demanded of my mother. 'And you, what were you trying to do at the British Embassy?'

Mum started to stutter, making it sound as if she wasn't sure of her answers, making him become angrier and angrier. After an hour of interrogation he gave us his orders.

'You must immediately apply for new, separate identity cards, and for temporary Bulgarian citizenship. Times are getting hazardous, we must know everything about everyone. It's for your own safety. You must understand that.'

'But I'm expecting news from my husband any moment,' Mum insisted. 'And we shall leave Bulgaria as soon as we receive it.'

'As soon as you get the news come and tell me and I'll see what can be done. But until then you must do as I have told you. Tomorrow bring me three photographs each and we'll get you legalised before you get into any more trouble. And,' he turned to me, 'if I were you I wouldn't go too near that embassy just now.'

We were escorted home by a policeman, arriving just as Granny got back from work. Mum gave her a discreet sign, telling her we were all right, worried that she would attack the man before waiting to hear what had happened.

Once we were alone Mum laid into me for my stupidity and disobedience in trying to get to the embassy on my own. Granny tried to calm her down but she went on and on, pouring out all her grief, fears and worries. I said nothing, although I felt like screaming with frustration. Everything was going wrong and I could see that she had no more idea than I did how to put it right. The longer we were trapped in Bulgaria the harder it was going to be to get out, especially now they wanted us to become citizens. I didn't want to be a Bulgarian; I'd only come to the country to visit my grandmother. Eventually Granny persuaded her that it would be best if she went to lie down. It seemed we had no choice but to do as we were told and get on with it.

Becoming Bulgarian citizens was not easy; we had to supply fingerprints as well as photographs, since many Bulgarian citizens could not even sign their own names, and officials could not understand our foreign-sounding names. Not only were they hard to pronounce, they couldn't understand why our surnames were not the first names of our fathers and grandfathers, like theirs were. They didn't believe that in other countries surnames went down from father to son.

'No,' they shouted at us, 'only nicknames are passed on! You must have proper Bulgarian names.'

'All right, all right,' Mum was trying not to show her uneasiness in the face of their aggression. 'Do it according to the law, although it doesn't seem right that we should change our names.'

'It doesn't matter what it seems to you. Now what is your Christian name? You are christened aren't you?'

'Rosa,' Mum answered with a trembling voice.

'Second name?'

'Dear.'

'Don't try to make fun of me. There is no such name!'

'Look, this is my marriage certificate.'

The clerk took the certificate and pretended to be reading it, holding it upside down. I forced myself not to laugh.

'What's your father's name?' he demanded.

'Anthony.'

'See, now that's sensible. So you are Rosa Antonova so far. So what is your husband's name?'

'William.'

'No, no, that doesn't fit in, and you might get into trouble identifying yourself with such a funny name. We'll leave it as Rosa Antonova for now. Sign your name here.'

Mum did as he instructed and he turned to me.

'What's your name?'

'Helen Dear.'

'Well, I suppose the best name for you would be Elena. Plain, clear, the whole world will be able to pronounce it and accept such a nice name for such a nice girl.' He tried to smile.

'But that sounds Russian,' as I raised my voice I could see my mother looking uncomfortable.

'You are quite right,' he said, 'and to make it easy and understandable you will be Elena Antonova.'

'But that has nothing to do with my real name. I must have my own real name written down there!'

'Well, nothing can be done, I've already written it down. Just sign here and you will be free to go home.'

There was no alternative but to do as I was told. I could see from the looks Mum was giving me that she was willing me not to make any more fuss.

'A letter, a letter from Octave!' My mother was overwhelmed with joy. It had been nearly a year since he had vanished from our lives.

She opened the letter with trembling hands. It was short and to the point. He informed us that he had married a girl a few years older than him, who stood to inherit quite a fortune from an uncle. He had gone back to university to finish his studies, with her financial support. He assured us he was very happy. He had not yet had any luck in contacting Dad.

I was dismayed. Of course I was glad he was all right,

but I had trusted him to come to our rescue not to just get married and continue with his life as if we didn't exist. He had promised to do everything he could to get us out of Bulgaria, but he didn't seem to be doing anything. The war was even closer now. Friends of Granny's who had connections with the Austrian embassy warned her to stay put, that it might be safer in Bulgaria than in Austria, where it was rumoured Hitler would soon invade. We had to get back to England if we were to be safe.

The next piece of news we received was that the maternity hospital was to be turned over to the Ministry of Defence. Some of the staff were being sent to other hospitals. Being temporary workers, and foreigners, Mum and Granny were told to find work somewhere else. We were also instructed to leave our flat. It seemed that anyone with any authority at all could tell us what to do with our lives.

The head doctor advised my grandmother to move to a suburb which until recently had still been a village, but was now part of 'Great Sofia'.

'The people there are simpler but good-hearted,' he said, as I listened from a nearby chair. 'They will look up to you. The elderly women who assist at births in these places can hardly sign their names.'

'What if there's a problem?' Granny asked.

'Call it fate,' the doctor shrugged. 'You may survive there if you can give people medical advice.'

It seemed to me that this was going to break Mum's fragile spirits altogether.

Chapter Three
Early Interrogations

The doctor had been right, Mezdra was more like a village than part of a capital city and seemed very primitive. Most of the houses had been built by the villagers themselves, with the help of neighbours and relatives. They were still doing it. I admired their courage and skills as I watched them making bricks by hand out of earth, straw and water. It was hard, heavy work. Every member of the family took part, even the small children. It was as if we had stepped back in time.

The surgery was a small, whitewashed building in the centre of the village. Granny and I waited until the last patient left before introducing ourselves to the doctor, a pleasant middle-aged man who greeted us heartily.

'There will be plenty of work for you,' he assured my grandmother, 'because the woman who usually attends births is growing old and doesn't always come out when she's called, especially during the night. We've asked around about some lodgings and have a few for you to look at.'

His nurse offered to take us around. All the people she introduced us to were friendly, but all the rooms we were shown were in terrible states of repair.

'I dread to think how your mother will react when she sees where we're going to be living,' Granny said.

We didn't have any choice now that the police were pressing us to leave our flat in Sofia. The government was registering the number of rooms every private household had, allowing them to keep only as many as were considered necessary.

We chose the best lodging we could find and a few days later we moved into one room with a small kitchen attached. The room contained two double beds, a big, heavy table, probably made by the landlord himself, a few hand-made chairs and an iron stove, which was also our source of heating. In the kitchen were an old cooking stove and two small tables. On one table were two basins, one for washing the dishes and one for washing ourselves.

'Do you bathe sometimes?' I asked our landlady.

'Oh yes,' she said. 'In the summer we go to the nearby river. The water there is very soft and pleasant, our hair simply shines afterwards.'

'But where do you bathe now?' I persisted, already guessing the answer from what we had discovered in Sofia.

'I don't think anybody takes a bath in the winter,' she replied. Mum went pale while Granny swallowed hard.

We were told we could draw water from the well in the yard, but for drinking and cooking we had to go to the marketplace, where there was a fountain with constantly running cold water coming from the mouths of two iron lions' heads. On the top was an iron crown.

'The king himself came to the inauguration,' neighbours told us. 'That's why it's called the king's fountain.'

My mother was given a job at the convalescent home while my grandmother went straight to work delivering babies. The local people were grateful but could never pay as much as they were meant to. Instead they brought produce: eggs, flour, vegetables, fruit, meat from freshly killed pigs, sheep or chickens. We needed everything they gave us because we too were growing poorer by the day. Living in a nice house in London seemed a million years ago. Now every waking hour was spent worrying about how to survive, how to get enough food to stave off the hunger pangs and enough fuel to keep us warm. I wanted to make a contribution in any way I could.

I discovered that some of the girls of my age in the area were working in the wool factory producing yarn and thought I would see if they would employ me. I went in with a neighbour's daughter and knocked shyly on the director's door, asking the group of men inside for work.

'We don't need any new workers,' one of them said. 'We're soon going to be sacking some of the girls we have got.'

Disappointed, I turned to leave.

'Where do you come from?' one of the men asked.

'England.'

'How long have you been here?'

They all stopped to listen as I told my story in halting Bulgarian.

'Come with me,' one of the men said. 'Don't be afraid.'

He led me to another office and introduced me to the owner, a Mr Klein, who invited me to sit down and repeat my story in English. It turned out that he was from Manchester. He'd come out on business and when his first wife died he had married a young Bulgarian.

'Well I never,' he said when I'd finished. 'You know, it isn't really allowed for anyone under the age of eighteen to work, but I'll see what I can do.'

A few days later the girl from next door told me to go to the factory. I went straight away and was taken to Mr Klein's office.

'This work isn't easy,' he warned, 'the wages are low, and the conditions are pretty miserable. The Germans are on the doorstep and I don't know how long we'll be able to keep up production, but if you like you can start on Monday.'

I nodded enthusiastically. It didn't matter how bad the conditions were, anything was better than starving.

'All right, be here at five o'clock on Monday morning. If inspectors arrive you'll have to hide with the other underage girls until they've gone, and please don't tell anyone you're working here, and try not to tell anyone you're English.'

That evening my mother cried as my grandmother issued a string of warnings: 'You must be alert at all times, working with machines is always dangerous. The people there are rough and rude and fights will often break out, so keep out of the way, and never tell anyone how nice it is in England. These are dangerous times, remember that!'

It felt like the middle of the night when she woke me on Monday morning, making me put on some clothes she'd worn to work in the hospital and a warm knitted jacket. She gave me some sandwiches and walked me to the gate where other girls were waiting. There were some adults there who assured Granny they would take great care of me, although I didn't feel too confident from the look of them. All the way to the factory everyone talked at once at the tops of their voices, so that I hardly understood a word. As we walked the four kilometres more workers joined us, all dressed very poorly, their shoes worn to shreds. Would I soon be looking like them?

It was still dark and cold when we reached the factory and 'the master' showed me what to do and where the dangerous places were. For eight hours I would be arranging the unpleasant-smelling fleeces that had just come out of the washing basin on the floor to dry. The smell was overpowering and I was afraid I would faint as I tried to watch what the others did. Within a few minutes my back was aching unbearably. Now I realised why my grandmother had sounded so worried, and why my mother had cried so much. It was all I could do to hold back my own tears. Was this really what my life was going to be like from now on?

After about four hours the others started to open their lunch packs, revealing plain lumps of bread sprinkled with salt and red pepper. Some added a few drops of sunflower oil and called it gypsy pie. They ate with one hand while continuing to spread the wool with the other. The air was full of fluff, which stuck to the bread. Some tried to blow it away but most just swallowed it. I was nervous about how they would react when they saw my sandwiches. I knew they would be curious.

'You can get a quick bite now,' our next-door-neighbour told me, 'because the master has left the area.'

My hands were dirty and sticky and smelled vile. I'd never before eaten without washing first. The thought of it was too terrible and even though I was hungry I shook my head.

'Maybe later,' I said.

The master soon returned and didn't go again until the end of the shift when everyone rushed towards the room where we were to leave our overalls. Trying not to get crushed, I stood aside and was the last to leave, running to catch up with the others, not wanting to walk home alone. I found my neighbours waiting for me.

'You must be quicker in future,' they said. 'We have a lot of things to do at home before the end of the day.'

I was relieved to find Mum wasn't in when I got home because I was dreading her face when she saw the state I was in. She'd been called out to replace one of the nurses. Granny gave me some warm soup, which tasted like the most wonderful food in the world, even though I was too exhausted to be able to eat much. She had prepared a pail of water for me to wash myself in the foul-smelling lavatory which was about twenty metres away across the yard, past the cows which wandered around loose, terrifying me. I had a tin cup to pour the water over myself and a bit of old towel to rub the soap on with as I shivered in the cold, desperate to get the grease and dirt off my skin. I was always terrified the priceless soap would fall through the wooden slats and be lost forever. After rinsing as best I could I dried myself on another scrap of towel. All the time other people were queuing outside for their turn.

I missed my dad so much at times like that. He had always been so anxious to make our lives as comfortable as possible in London, buying any new innovation that came out, jokingly calling them 'cultural acquisitions'. Even though he never had much time to show his love for us, I always felt he was a caring, loving father and adored him in return. But where was he now? Why didn't he answer our letters any more? When would we see him again? First we had lost him, and then Octave. I felt so helpless, dreading the next day but knowing I had no option but to keep going.

All the adults were talking about the approaching war: those old enough to remember the 1914–1918 war were frightened of what was to come, while the younger ones seemed to look on it as some kind of adventure. I kept telling myself we would be safely in England or Canada by the time it happened, but in my darker moments I couldn't imagine how that would be possible, now we were living miles from anywhere.

An Italian family, the Fontanottis, who had like us been thrown out of their home, came to live nearby. The father and three sons were all some sort of specialists who had been sent to work in a factory in Bulgaria and two of the sons' wives worked in the same company. I got to know them because I spoke a little Italian and had helped the mother when she was in difficulty in a local shop. Through them we met a French family in a similar position who had a daughter just a year younger than me and a Hungarian woman with two daughters. We were all foreigners together.

The Italians had a wonderful way of always finding something to laugh at. They were all good singers, accompanying themselves on guitars and mandolins. The men built some boats for us from whatever wood, screws and half-empty tins of paint we could find, to use on the nearby river.

When the boats were finally ready that spring we planned a Sunday outing to launch them, about twenty of us in all, with everyone bringing something to eat; tomatoes, green peppers, onions, white sheep's cheese, melons, apples and plums. Some brought home-baked bread. The men pushed the boats to the river on wheels taken from old prams, while the women carried the food, blankets, guitars and an old, patched, home-made tent. We were in high spirits and started singing once we were safely out of the town.

The elders sat in the shade of the trees while the Italian boys tested the boats to make sure they were safe for the rest of us. The young children and older women gathered wood and built a fire, brewing up tea and coffee and starting to cook in a big copper pot suspended on a chain, like in the old cowboy films. It reminded me of the picnics we'd had with our father in London but I made an effort to cover up my sadness for my mother, who was sitting peacefully beside the fire talking to the other women while they cleaned the vegetables to make a soup. To hide my tears I jumped into the water for a swim. As well as the soup we had salads and some freshly caught fish, which we skewered on sticks and baked in the embers of the fire.

A couple who lived in the small house on their vegetable farm during the summer months allowed us to leave the boats with them, in exchange for a small rent which we collected between us, so that we could return for the next couple of weekends. The outings raised our spirits so high that some of our neighbours noticed and complained, feeling it was inappropriate to be so 'light-minded' at a time of impending war.

'God knows what they're doing out there,' they gossiped, 'out of town and so far from everybody.'

Their jealous words spread until they reached the ear of the local chief superintendent, who decided he should investigate this suspiciously cheerful bunch of foreigners. He started with a visit to the Fontanottis.

'Why did you come to Bulgaria?' he asked Mr Fontanotti.

'I came with my family because we were invited by the Bulgarian government to help improve the work in the factory for the production of spare parts for the assembling of airplanes,' he replied.

'For how long?'

'Until the board of the company consider they don't need our advice any more.'

'What will you do then?'

'I suppose we shall go back to Italy, or maybe some other country if we're invited.'

At the end of the interrogation he was allowed to go, once he had promised never to use the boats or go to the river again unless it was some national celebration, and there were other people there. The Hungarian woman was then called to the police station and told the same, although she never seemed to want to talk about exactly what happened there, withdrawing into herself and rarely being seen in public afterwards. Everyone in our merry company got the same warning. My turn came when a policeman approached me as I came home one Saturday evening, exhausted as usual from my day's work and looking forward to my one day off.

'You must come with me to the police station,' he instructed.

'Can I just tell my mother where I'm going?' I asked, feeling frightened of what might be about to happen.

Without a word he grabbed me by the arm and marched me all the way to the station, pushing me into the police chief's room.

'There she is,' he announced, before leaving the room, slamming the door behind him. It must have been obvious how scared I was.

'Don't be afraid,' the chief said. 'I won't harm you, just sit down and answer a few questions.'

I lowered myself on to the edge of the chair opposite him and tried to stay calm.

'How did you get to know all these people that you go to the river with?'

'They live near us, that's all.'

'And what happens at these meetings by the river?'

'We just go for a swim if the weather's hot.'

'So, so, and what else do you do?'

'Well, we sit in the shade of the trees, spread out our sandwiches and eat them.'

'And what do you talk about all day long?'

'Some of us tell a joke or two, or we sing songs, or tell stories.'

'Sing songs, ah. What kind of songs? Special ones? Who taught them to you?'

'Nobody really, they're the ones you hear on the radio, or on gramophone records.'

'I see, and what about the boats?'

'We only used them three times. Nobody goes there any more, not even to swim.'

'Right, you can go now, but be careful who you talk to and what you do.'

When I left I felt embarrassed and frightened, and unsure if I should tell anyone where I'd been. Mum had been so nervous recently I didn't want to give her any more to worry about. Only Granny was there when I got home so I said nothing and we ate some supper before going to bed. The next morning Mum was back and I still hadn't plucked up the courage to say anything. When one of the Italian children came knocking on the door I realised my mistake.

'Today is my aunt's birthday,' he told us. 'We're going to take our gramophone to the park to celebrate and dance, all our friends are coming, would you like to come too?'

Remembering the chief's warning I hoped Mum would say no, but she accepted immediately and I realised it was now too late to tell her about the interrogation. Granny gave us some biscuits and a bottle of wine that a grateful new mother had given to her and we set off. Mum was in a good mood and even danced a few times. I guess she must have missed being able to go out dancing with my father as she had done when we lived in London.

At about half past ten we noticed that other groups in

the park were gathering their things up and leaving in haste. Grandpa Fontanotti and one of the sons grabbed the gramophone and records and shouted for everyone to go home. I'd been playing with the other children and looked for my mother, feeling alarmed, but someone had already dragged her away. Policemen appeared from out of the darkness and surrounded me and about seven other children. They arrested us and escorted us to the police station, telling us to sit on some benches in the backyard and stay silent. The place was filthy, stinking of rubbish and the boots of the snoring policemen who were on duty during the night.

At about seven the following morning one of the senior officers arrived and interrogated us. Unable to prove we had committed any offence he let us all go.

'Don't do this any more,' he warned. 'It's dangerous nowadays and you could get into real trouble.'

On the way home I whispered to one of the Italian boys about what I'd been told by the police chief. 'What should I do?' I asked.

'I'll ask my father,' he said, 'and let you know.'

Mum and Granny were waiting for us, worried out of their minds.

'We came down outside the police station with Grandpa Fontanotti,' Granny told me, 'but as everything was quiet he advised us to go home'.

We avoided meeting people after that, staying indoors most of the time, and my mother's nerves became much worse, making her jump at every little sound. Two weeks later I was taken back to the police chief's office.

'I hear you were mixed up in that illegal meeting the other night,' he said.

'I don't know what you mean by "illegal meeting",' I replied, mustering all my courage despite being able to see I was making him cross. I didn't want him to know how afraid I was of him. 'I didn't know it was illegal to dance in Bulgaria. There were other young people there as well.'

'Of course no one says you mustn't dance you silly girl, and don't try to be cleverer than me.' Spit was flying out of his mouth, as his voice grew louder. 'You were there to discuss your communistic ideas, and most probably you were given some other tasks. Don't think I don't know what's going on behind the government's back!'

I didn't know what to say and my face must have changed colour.

'See?' he shouted triumphantly, 'I've caught you.'

A satisfied smile spread across his ugly face and I was unable to stop myself from crying.

'Stop that or I'll get really angry,' he warned.

'Please,' I sobbed, 'I've never heard of such people, let alone got mixed up with them. We were only celebrating a birthday.'

'Yes, yes, that's what the others said. That's the excuse.'

I couldn't stop crying or shaking and he seemed to realise he'd gone too far and calmed down a bit. After listening to a few more stupid questions that I didn't understand I told him my mother would be worried and asked if I could go.

'All right, you can go now. But you must come back here again at four o'clock on Saturday.'

'Why? What have I done?' I felt my fears rising up again.

'For now, nothing. It's an order.'

By the time I got home my mother was beside herself with worry. 'Where have you been all day? Who have you been with? You'll drive me mad with your irresponsibility. You don't care how worried I get.'

Granny tried to calm her and her voice grew higher and higher.

'But Mum,' I tried to explain.

'No buts, go and wash yourself and change. Look what you look like!'

Granny nodded at me and I obeyed without saying a word. At supper I didn't even dare ask for another bit of bread. When Mum eventually went out to the lavatory I explained to Granny what happened in a whisper. She was immediately furious with Mum for not having given me a chance to explain.

'Wait till she comes back,' she fumed.

'Please Granny, don't say anything till she's calmed down.'

'No Helen, this is serious.'

At first Mum didn't want to listen. When Granny mentioned the police station she jumped up and looked like she was going to slap me, but Granny was quicker and came between us.

'Whatever have you done now? I've told you not to go anywhere near that embassy!'

'Stop shouting at the child and listen. She was taken for questioning, but that's not all. She's been told to go back on Saturday. So let's calm down and try to work out what they're aiming at. We're foreigners here. We can't leave until things get settled so we have to live by their rules if we don't want to get into trouble. I'll go to the doctor tomorrow and ask his advice.'

The next day I bumped into the youngest Fontanotti boy in the bread shop and smiled a greeting. He immediately held up his hand to silence me, looking around guiltily. 'Not now, please,' he said quietly and hurried from the shop. He had always been such a friendly, polite boy; I couldn't understand it. Had his family been ordered to present themselves in front of the police chief as well? Maybe I shouldn't talk to any of our friends. But why not? We were only singing and joking and being happy. Was that a crime now? I was soon to find out that it was.

Chapter Four
Becoming the Enemy

'I've talked to the doctor,' Granny told us over afternoon tea the next day. 'He's moving to another hospital more than a hundred kilometres away.' I could see how upset and worried she was. 'Soon the Ministry of Defence is going to mobilise the clinic where your mother works too. Without work we will have no money and no food.'

Granny had also received a message from her Austrian friend saying she was ill and needed help.

'I must go to her,' Granny said, 'it will only be for a few days.'

Mum didn't like the idea of being left alone, but Granny couldn't be dissuaded. The house seemed deathly quiet once she'd gone. There was no one to cook when Mum was at work so we lived on sandwiches and salads. I missed her soups. I didn't dare to say anything to Mum or ask her any questions. She would pretend to be reading in the evenings but I could see she was crying. I finally plucked up the courage to speak.

'How long do you think we will be trapped in Bulgaria?' I asked. 'Is there any chance we'll be able to get back to England?'

My words made her inconsolable, crying and shaking. I tried to comfort her but nothing helped and she wept all night. I had to get up at half past three to go to work with the neighbouring girls and I was worried about leaving her alone.

Each evening that week I would hurry home to see how she was, wishing Granny would return, and then the worst happened and the same policeman as before grabbed me at the gate and took me to the police station again.

'Just let me see how my mother is getting on,' I begged.

'These tricks won't work,' he laughed.

'Why do you look so frightened?' the chief wanted to know when I was bundled into his office. 'Have I ever hurt you?'

'My mother is ill,' I began.

'Oh, come on,' he interrupted impatiently, 'I saw her yesterday, she can't be that bad.'

'But she is.' The tears were rolling down my cheeks.

'I don't like it when somebody lies to me and takes me for stupid. If she was so ill you wouldn't be strolling around the streets.'

I was just about to say I was on my way back from work when I remembered I wasn't supposed to tell anyone. I stayed silent.

'Actually I've been thinking,' he went on, 'instead of roaming around the streets you should be doing something useful. For instance, you could come and cook some supper for me from time to time.'

'I can't cook,' I protested.

'Oh, I'm not fussy, anything simple will do. Fried eggs, maybe. And we could have some fun as well.'

I had an unpleasant feeling about the way he was looking at me, although I couldn't quite understand what he was getting at.

'No please, I can't cook and I prefer to stay home with my mother in the evenings.'

'Oh, I see,' he sneered, 'you don't want to become friendly with me because I'm not as handsome as some of your Italian friends.'

'No, it's not that. My mother never lets me go out in the evenings.'

'Now listen to me, young lady. Do you realise I have the power to intern you and your mother to any place, whenever I wish? And those commie Italian friends of yours will soon be interned or imprisoned. If I see you with them once more you may be following them. Stupid foreigners, you think the world belongs to you. We are the rulers here!'

Once he'd had his rant he let me go, but a cloud of fear and danger hung over us all the time, even in the following days when nothing else happened. One evening, on my way to the lavatory, I saw the two youngest Fontanotti brothers on the other side of the fence. I opened my mouth to call out a greeting when I noticed they were making signs for me to remain quiet. They beckoned me close.

'We had a talk with our father,' the eldest whispered. 'The situation is becoming very dangerous, maybe we shall leave this place soon. Be very careful, all of you. We'll try to keep in touch. Good luck.'

Somebody came out of the house and they disappeared as quietly as they had appeared.

A few days later I was ordered to go to the police station again.

'So, where have your dear friends gone?' The police chief demanded as soon as I walked in.

'I have many friends, which ones are you talking about?'

'You know very well who I mean, the stupid Italian commies,' he roared. I realised if I wasn't careful I was going to get myself into serious trouble.

'I don't know. I haven't seen them for a long time.'

'You don't know? You little bitch, do you think you can deceive me? I'm not as stupid as you think I am. Remember that. You try to act like a saint but I know more about these tricks than anyone else in this region.'

His fist was banging on the table, emphasising his words. The spit was flying from his mouth and some landed on my face. I wiped it off in disgust.

'Tell me where they've gone or that holy mother of yours will never see you again.'

Tears came to my eyes and I begged him to believe me. A policeman came in and interrupted his flow.

'What do you want?' he demanded.

'We've arrested a group of suspicious citizens,' the policeman told him.

The chief turned and hit me round the face with the back of his hand, sending me reeling.

'You,' he said, 'go. But I'll be calling you back again.'

I ran home, my cheek bleeding and my head bursting with pain. I had never been hit before and I felt humiliated. I couldn't understand what I was guilty of. Mum was out and Granny put some cold compresses on my face, making me lie down. She kept blaming herself for bringing us all to Bulgaria.

'But I came to help them,' she said, 'I'm still helping them, so why are they treating us like this?'

The next day she decided to confront the police chief and we went together to the police station and asked to see him. I felt terrified, even with her there to protect me. He made us wait a while before inviting us into his office. I was on the verge of fainting when I saw that it was a different man. This man was much younger and better looking.

'Look what you've done to this child,' Granny launched into her attack, showing him my bruises. 'What right do you have to beat her? What was her offence?'

Not surprisingly the man looked astonished.

'Granny,' I said, 'this isn't the same man.'

Not to be put off by such details Granny went on

shouting how she was going to complain to the ambassador about this attitude towards us.

'I was invited here to help in the maternity hospital and I'm still helping expectant mothers, and this is the thanks I get?'

When she finally fell silent the superintendent assured her he knew nothing about it and promised to look into the matter. My grandmother strode from the station as dignified as ever, pulling me behind like a puppy she had just rescued from drowning.

When the wool factory was closed down most of the workers got some unemployment help, but I couldn't apply for it as I'd been working there illegally. We desperately missed my wages, even though they were so meagre, and a few weeks later I heard that the silk factory was looking for female workers since most of their men had been mobilised. A few of the neighbours' girls and I decided to try our luck and were told to start the next week. The wages were low and the work was hard but at least it was something. We also had to walk the four kilometres to and from the factory four times a day. We worked from five till nine in the mornings, then one till five in the afternoons. If the weather allowed, some of the older workers simply laid down in the yard and slept between shifts rather than make the journey home.

The war was now well under way in Europe and posters were up all over the factory depicting a soldier with a bayonet in one hand and a finger to his lips. 'Be careful,' the words warned, 'the enemy is listening'.

Some of the older workers had found out I was a foreigner and I noticed them standing in front of the posters whispering and looking at me. I felt humiliated and offended, but I knew better than to say anything in case I lost the job or got into trouble. I didn't want to lose my income again and I certainly didn't want to end up being interrogated again for being an enemy agent.

At home we never talked about the past any more, never went anywhere and had no friends we could trust. We just existed from one day to the next. The money I earned was hardly enough to buy us a daily loaf of bread. Granny earned almost nothing from delivering her babies and my mother hadn't been able to find work for some time. We heard nothing from Octave, my father or the embassy. It was as if the whole world had forgotten that we existed. The only good thing was that I hadn't been called back to the police station for several months.

Returning from work with two other girls one day we came across a crowd being rounded up by the police. Some of the youths tried to escape and ran towards us. Startled, we turned and ran ourselves but the police were too fast and caught us all, along with another passing couple, and there I was back in the yard of the police station. Some of the others had been locked up in another room and the couple were allowed to go free before the brutal police chief finally got round to interrogating my workmates and me. We tried to explain what had happened.

'You must have known those young men were going to be there exactly at that time,' he roared. 'What did they want you to do for them?'

One of the other girls started crying.

'Stop that immediately,' he bellowed, 'or do you want a few slaps?'

She tried to stifle her sobs and the other girl put her arm round her friend's shoulders.

'Leave her alone. Get away from her,' he yelled, and then seemed to lose interest. 'You can go now, but if I find out you've been lying you have no idea what will happen.'

Unable to believe our sudden change of luck we turned quickly to the door.

'No, not you,' he said, 'I haven't finished with you yet.'

I froze as the other girls left.

'Sit down,' he instructed. 'You've complained about me, although I haven't done anything wrong to you.'

'You hit me,' I said quietly.

'That was just to teach you some manners, as a father might do. By the way, where is your father?'

'He went to work in Canada.'

'Aha, and he sends you money to keep the organisation going. That explains everything.'

'What money? What organisation? I haven't heard from him in ages.'

'Don't try to make a monkey out of me. I know everything.'

'Please,' I said, 'if you know where he is, tell me, or at least tell me how I can get in touch with him. I've written so many letters and haven't had any answers at all so I've given up.'

There was a lot of noise coming from the room where the youths were locked up and a policeman came in to ask the police chief to speak to them.

'You are really lucky,' he told me, 'but I haven't finished with you yet. You will come back again as soon as I send for you.'

Mum and Granny were talking with one of the other girls' fathers when I got home. I didn't know what they were saying but when he'd gone Mum burst into tears over supper.

'How could he say such a thing? She's still a mere child.'

'Stop getting into a state,' Granny said, 'pull yourself together.'

'What do you mean I'm a mere child?' I wanted to know. 'What were you talking about?'

Granny answered as Mum went on sobbing. 'Oh, just stupid things like you getting married so as to get rid of that awful pestering police chief or whatever he is.'

I dropped my spoon. 'What about us returning to England?' I asked. 'Or even Canada? Are we really going to stay here all our lives without doing anything to escape? How would things improve if I got married?'

Mum let out another wail and looked like she was going to faint. I was so confused I couldn't find the right words.

'Why don't you make things clear to me, tell me what I can do, what you expect of me? But making me get married ... ugh!'

It was the first time I'd ever raised my voice to them or protested about anything and they both fell silent. That night I cried all night and must have looked terrible when I dragged myself out of bed to go to work.

'Whatever happened to you?' my neighbour, Maria, asked. 'Are you ill? Did your mother and grandmother beat you because of your visit to the police station last night?'

'No, no, of course not. It's only ...' I burst into tears.

None of them had seen me cry before and I could tell they were shocked, always believing I was happy and brave. They all kept asking me what was wrong as we walked.

'It's because we're foreigners,' I explained, 'some people treat us as if we're the worst people in the world.'

'Oh, take no notice, they're just jealous because you're nice and intelligent, and ...'

'Please stop that,' I cried, 'it's just ... sometimes it's too much.'

I pulled myself together in time to start work and through the day I realised that I now had responsibilities. Mum's health was getting worse and Granny was getting older. There didn't seem to be any hope of us returning to England or getting in touch with my father. What should I do? I couldn't afford to go to a lawyer. All I could do was keep working. A few weeks later the policeman was waiting for me again at our front gate and grabbed my arm as I tried to walk past as if he wasn't there. 'Come on, you've got to come with me.'

'What have I done?'

'You'll find out soon enough.'

'Let me at least tell my mother.'

'They'll tell her you're all right.' He was already dragging me away.

'Who will tell her?'

'Your landlady.'

Now I knew the whole street would know, and their imaginations would be adding to the picture, pitying my poor family. In the end I would probably be found guilty of being the death of my own mother. My fear was mixing with a seething anger as I was pushed into the police chief's office once more.

'Well, here we are again. I hope you've seen some sense and will listen to my advice this time.'

I said nothing.

'You still haven't explained what you were doing at the time those youngsters were stirring up trouble.'

'Nothing,' I snapped.

'If you were there you must have been doing something.'

'I was with the other two girls from our neighbourhood.'

'Don't go involving them. I know them well and I know their families. It's you I'm talking about.'

I fell silent again.

'Haven't you anything to say?'

'Whatever I say you never believe me.'

'Now that isn't true,' he purred, changing his tack. 'I've always tried to advise you but you're very stubborn.'

Still I said nothing.

'Now look, I could turn a blind eye if you were to come some evening and cook dinner for me.'

'I've told you I can't cook and I never go out in the evenings.'

'Oh, trying to play the saint again, eh?'

My self-control reaching its limit, I burst into tears.

'Stop that immediately, I haven't even touched you yet!' he shouted, making me jump. 'Don't you realise that if you don't do what I tell you I can make you sorry for even being alive? You dirty foreigner, you'll come crawling to me, begging for mercy, and I won't even look at you then!'

There was a lump in my throat and my ears were thumping. The telephone rang and he barked into it, then suddenly he caught hold of my ear and pushed me out of the room.

'And don't you dare tell anyone about our conversations here.'

I didn't tell a soul. Some days later I was in the baker's shop and noticed that Maria's father was waiting to walk home with me. On the way he brought up the question of marriage.

'Believe me,' he said, 'it's the only way out of the terrible mess you're in. I know this police chief well and know what he's done in the past. He's a real monster. But I'm sure that if you were married to a Bulgarian he would stop harassing you and your mother.'

'My mother?' I was shocked. 'Has she been there too?'

'She's never said, but I have a feeling that she has.'

The thought had never crossed my mind. I felt so ashamed to think that Maria's father must have been talking about us with his family. How would I ever be able to look at them again? My thoughts must have shown in my face.

'Don't worry,' he reassured me, 'I haven't talked to anyone about all this; nobody else needs to know about our conversation. At times like this we should all hold our tongues as much as possible.'

Chapter Five
Talk of Marriage

My grandmother received a letter from her sister, an actress who had her own travelling theatre group with her husband, who was also a playwright and a popular children's poet.

'They've been in Hungary and Yugoslavia,' Granny told us excitedly, 'and they're coming to Bulgaria. She's rented a flat and wants me to go and look at it.'

The news brightened my mother up too, despite the fact it meant Granny was going away again.

While Granny was away preparing the flat for my great-aunt's arrival, our neighbours invited us to their daughter's name day. If you had the same name as a saint it was the custom to celebrate on that saint's day. The family were very hospitable, offering us the best chairs and separate plates filled with food that everyone else was helping them selves to from the middle of the table. Everyone was talking at once at the tops of their voices, then they started to sing with wonderful voices. Feeling overwhelmed, we tried to excuse ourselves as more and more people arrived, but our hosts wouldn't hear of it. Then a young man sat down beside me and started talking as if he'd known me for years.

He told me his name was Vladimir. He was very good looking, smiling and joking all the time. He seemed to fancy himself as a real 'town boy', although he spoke in the local dialect of the villages. Although I wasn't a particularly shy person, I had no experience of talking to boys and wanted nothing more than to escape, even though I was flattered by his attentions.

'Would you like to go to the cinema with me?' he asked.

I saw my mother watching me and refused him politely. More people arrived and we were able to make our excuses and leave. I had so many things to worry about in my life; I didn't feel I had the energy to worry about dating a young man as well. The effort of working so hard and helping my mother exhausted me and left me with no spare time. But still, I found myself thinking about him once the party was over.

My grandmother and her sister were the last survivors of thirteen siblings. They had all been well educated, becoming a lawyer, a doctor, a musician, an officer, an artist and teachers. One died of a heart attack on her wedding day when she heard that her brother had been killed falling from his horse on the way to the ceremony.

As there were no babies due in the village, Granny stayed to help her sister settle all her actors into accommodation. My mother couldn't wait for them to come to visit us, although she became increasingly worried about how we would feed visitors when they did arrive. Such things had been important to her in England, with her fine clothes, beautiful furniture, and beloved dinner service and tea sets. She hated the idea that anyone would see us living in our reduced circumstances, that we wouldn't even be able to offer them decent hospitality.

'Will auntie let us into the theatre through the back door, do you think?' I asked, excited at the thought of meeting glamorous theatre people.

'Maybe,' she said, 'but what would we wear, especially you? You haven't anything decent enough even to wear to the local cinema.'

'Oh well,' I said, remembering the invitation from the young man, 'you and Granny could go and tell me all about it afterwards.'

'Don't be silly,' she protested, 'you know I would never do that.'

It wasn't long before I was back in the police chief's office.

'Sit down and tell me what you've been up to,' he said with a snakelike smile.

'Nothing.'

'So, you have nothing to say?'

'No.'

'But I've been told you've been out and about.'

'We only went to a name day party.'

'Who's we?' He was becoming irritated with my coolness.

'My mother and I.'

'Aha, having some fun, meeting lots of people and getting into mischief. So, where will your next secret meeting be?'

'I don't know of any secret meetings, and I haven't been anywhere else.'

'Of course, a young girl like you doesn't go anywhere. Do you think I'm that stupid?'

'Maybe other girls are allowed out on their own, but I'm not and I don't want to anyway.'

'You don't wish to, but you will have to, because I'm taking you to my home this very evening, whether you wish to or not.'

'But my mother isn't well,' I pleaded, my coolness deserting me. 'I can't leave her alone. Even now she'll be worried to death because I haven't come home on time.'

He seemed pleased to see that he'd managed to frighten me again. 'Don't worry so much, she's not going to die that soon.'

'Please, please let me go home, I haven't done anything wrong. I don't understand what you're accusing me of.'

The door was pushed open and a younger man came in. He seemed to be senior to the police chief. 'What's going on here?' he asked. 'What has this girl done? Is she a prostitute?'

I couldn't believe what I was hearing.

'Well, er ...' the chief mumbled, 'we haven't caught her yet at the actual crime, but I've heard some rumours.'

'Who is she? Do you know her?'

'I know her all right, she belongs to that midwife ...'

The younger man held up his hand to stop him and turned to me. 'Go straight home and don't talk about this interview to anyone.'

I ran out, then noticed that my shoelace was undone and stooped to tie it, taking long enough to hear the younger man shouting angrily at the chief and accusing him of acting improperly. As I hurried home I heard a passer-by saying my name softly. I turned and saw Maria's father.

'I'm sorry,' he said, 'I didn't mean to startle you. I want to have a serious talk with you.'

'Please, let me go now. I'm late as it is.'

'All right, I can see you're in a rush, but find a little time tomorrow. It's very important.'

Why did everyone think they had the right to give me advice when they weren't even anything to do with our family? I could hear loud voices as I crossed the yard to the house and opened the door.

'There she is at last!'

'Hasn't she grown?'

'How pretty she has become!'

The two strangers and my grandmother were all trying to cuddle and kiss me at once.

'This is my sister,' Granny told me, 'Rosa Popova, famous all over Europe, and this is her husband Stoijan Popoff, better known as the author Chicho Stoian (Uncle Stoian).'

My great-aunt was tall with wonderful dark, expressive brown eyes, her voice gentle, clear and strong. She looked a lot like my mother and grandmother. My great-uncle had laughing, good-natured eyes. They had brought all sorts of treats to eat and I was sad to hear that they were going to have to catch the last bus back that night because they were starting rehearsals the next day.

All the next day at work my thoughts were spinning as my fingers worked mechanically. If we had never come to Bulgaria I would probably have been at university by now, able to mix with people who could talk about art, music and literature and other interesting things. How could things have gone so badly wrong? My childhood was over so abruptly with all the cares of the world arriving at once.

I was woken from my dreams by Maria. and another neighbour waving goodbye. The shift had finished but I couldn't leave yet because the woman taking over my machine hadn't arrived. We were obliged to keep working until our replacements came. It had happened to me before, but never this late at night. I began to feel nervous at the thought of walking home in the dark on my own.

When the woman arrived twenty minutes later she didn't even thank me or offer an explanation. I hurried out to the iron gates, knowing they were usually closed and locked once the shifts had changed over. The porter was standing with the keys in his hand.

'Come on lass,' he said. 'You're lucky to have such good neighbours. They told me you might be late.'

'Thank you so much,' I said. 'It wasn't my fault.'

'I know, but run along and don't talk to any strangers.'

'I won't,' I promised.

I wasn't even half way to the nearest highway inn when I noticed someone walking ahead of me at the side of the road. I stopped running, not wanting to draw attention to myself. As I drew closer I saw he had a uniform and my heart began to thump. Should I go on or should I turn back to the factory? He was walking slowly and didn't seem to have noticed me coming up behind. I hoped he would go into the inn for a drink and I kept walking, keeping a safe distance.

But it was getting late and he was walking more and more slowly. I was going to have to overtake him or it would look as if I was deliberately following him Plucking up my courage I increased my pace, hoping I would at least be able to get to the safety of the inn. I prepared myself to run if necessary.

As I drew level with the uniformed figure he turned suddenly and laughed.

'Caught you this time, haven't I?'

I froze in my tracks. It was the chief of police.

'I'm going home from work,' I said, trying not to tremble, and keeping on walking.

'At this time?' He caught me by the arm, his voice sarcastic. 'When everyone else has gone home ages ago? Maybe even safely in bed already?'

He gripped me tightly and I could smell the alcohol on his breath.

'The woman who takes over from me came late.'

'Oh I see, so you pass your clients over do you?' His fingers were hurting me.

'No. I mean at work. Let me go, you have no right to hold me here.'

'Even if you scream nobody will help you. If someone does come I can prove that I've caught you doing something ...'

'What can you prove she has done?' a voice asked from the darkness. I hadn't noticed Maria's father coming up behind us. 'Let her go, you're hurting her.'

'You again,' the chief spat, as if they were old adversaries. 'Where did you come from?'

'I came to meet the girl and take her home.'

'Who sent you?'

'No one. We work on the same shift and when I found out the woman replacing her was late I took the other girls home and came back for her. Thank God I came in time.'

'I wouldn't have done her any harm,' the chief slurred, 'I was only having fun frightening her.'

'Come on, girl.' Maria's father led me away. 'The sooner we get away from here the better.'

It was a while before I found the voice to thank him as we walked.

'That's all right,' he said. 'I'm sorry I didn't get back earlier.'

I burst into tears.

'The swine,' he whispered, 'I'll get him one day.'

As we came nearer to home he started talking again. 'The best thing for you to do to get rid of this danger would be to marry, then your husband could take care of you and defend you.'

I stopped outside our house and looked at him. 'Will it always be like this if I don't marry?'

'I'm afraid it will. You don't have to rush, just think about it. If you like I'll help you find someone suitable.'

As I went in through our gate I felt faint. I couldn't think which would be the lesser evil. I'd seen the way most Bulgarian husbands treated their wives as unpaid slaves, often beating them just because another man had looked at them. But could I rely on continually being saved at the last moment from the attentions of the police chief? I wanted someone to talk to about it but I was too embarrassed to bring it up with my mother or my grandmother.

Mum started teaching German to a little girl three times a week back in the city. She often used to take her to the zoo, past the British embassy, and would ask if she might go in. More barriers had gone up around the perimeter. The Bulgarian soldiers on guard always said no, very rudely. She tried giving them letters to hand to the secretary, which they would take from her with a snigger. No answer or message ever came back. It was so frustrating to know that there were people inside who surely would have helped us to get home if they had just known that we existed, but if they had looked out their windows at the moment we were passing they would just have seen poorly dressed peasant women. We had sunk out of sight.

One Sunday both my mother and grandmother had to go out and I decided to go back to bed for a rest after locking the door behind them. I was woken from a wonderful dream by a loud banging on the door and window. I lay in bed, shivering with fear, but whoever it was didn't go away and their voices grew louder, shouting for me to open up. Pulling on my mother's cloak, I opened the door and several policemen rushed in, pushing me into the yard. I saw the landlord and his family gathered under the watchful gaze of another policeman.

'What's the matter?' I asked the landlady.

'Shut up or you'll get something,' the policeman shouted.

The landlady blinked as if signalling me to keep quiet. I noticed then that all the neighbours were being rounded up in their yards as well, while others had been pushed out into the street.

'We can't find anyone else in there,' a policeman reported to another man on a horse.

'Where are your family?' a familiar voice asked and I saw the chief coming out of our room.

'They aren't here,' I said, trying not to stutter.

'I asked you where they are,' he shouted.

'They went to church and then the centre of town.'

'When? And with who?'

'By themselves on the bus.'

'We'll see about that. You come with me.'

'Let me dress myself.'

'You're all right as you are,' he said, grabbing me and dragging me to the street, pushing me into the group already gathered there.

We were marched to the yard at the police station and ordered to be silent as we waited to be interrogated. I had no idea what they wanted and then I heard someone whisper, 'partisani' I'd heard the word before but didn't know what it meant. When I was finally taken in for questioning the police chief was there, but he wasn't the one doing the talking. They wanted to know why we were living there, where my mother and grandmother went to church and what other religious meetings they attended. The questions seemed meaningless to me.

'Don't speak to any strangers or go to any meetings whatever,' they told me before letting me go.

As I stumbled out into the street I bumped into Maria's father, who gently asked if I had thought about what he'd said.

'There's a young man who's waiting to see you,' he said. 'Just come and meet him. Later you can tell me what you think.'

'But I'm not even dressed properly,' I protested.

'You look quite decent,' he insisted.

It was Vladimir, the young man who had come up to me at the name day party. We exchanged a few polite words and out of politeness I agreed to meet him again. I didn't know what else to say, I was so inexperienced at talking to boys. We shook hands and Maria's father walked me home. Mum and Granny had returned and were trying to straighten up the mess the police had left. Mum burst into tears when she saw me and even Granny was drying her eyes. They both hugged me. There were bedclothes on the floor, trampled beneath dirty boots, drawers had been pulled out and the contents strewn around the room, letters, photographs, documents, broken dishes and under-wear – everything. Mum's hands were shaking as she tried to sort things out. The landlady had told them the police were looking for partisans.

'What are partisans?' I asked.

'Illegal fighters against the government,' Granny explained.

A few days later, just after Granny had left for work and Mum and I were getting ready to leave, the police arrived again and escorted both of us to the station, where we were taken in front of a young superintendent and the police chief.

'There are some new rules,' the young superintendent told my mother, 'in connection with all foreigners whose position isn't absolutely legal. You will probably have to leave the country as soon as possible.'

'But that's what I've been trying to do for so long,' Mum said.

'So why haven't you?' he asked,

Mum explained how she'd been trying to get to the embassy and how our visas had expired.

'We can't help you get all the way to England,' he said mockingly, 'nor can we give you any visas. That's your problem.'

'Can you advise me what to do?' Mum asked.

'You could legalise your situation here by applying for permanent residence, which means you can't leave the country without special permission, which I can tell you is very difficult to get.'

'Is there anything else we could do?'

'Ha,' he laughed, 'you could get married.'

'Who would take her?' the chief roared with laughter

Chapter Six
A Sort of Courtship

The next day the master at work shouted at me in front of the whole factory, wanting to know why I'd missed a day's work. I tried to explain that I had been with the police but he just went on shouting that I was a liar and lazy with no sense of duty to the country.

'Of course,' he said, 'why should you care? This isn't your fatherland. I really don't know why we have allowed you to work here.'

There was no point saying anything in my defence because I could see the suspicion and hatred in all the eyes around me, so I just walked silently to my place at the machine.

'Just remember that for every day you miss,' he shouted after me, 'you'll be fined three days' pay.'

When we finished the shift I hung back, pretending to tie my laces, not wanting to have to face the others, feeling like an outsider, believing they all saw me as an enemy.

'Come on, girl.' Maria's father had come back to find me. 'It's getting late.'

His kindness meant a lot to me, even though his plans for me were frightening.

The next morning, drinking some tea my mother had made for me and eating a sandwich left over from the previous day, I heard voices outside. I looked out of the window and saw my neighbour, Milena, and Maria and both Maria's parents with Vladimir and the landlady. They called for me to come to the door.

'We're going to the cinema tomorrow,' both girls said, almost simultaneously, 'and we wondered if you and your family would like to come.'

'I'm sorry, Mum's not here,' I said, feeling flustered, 'and my grandmother is away, so I can't give an answer until tomorrow.'

'Listen,' the landlady said, 'we need to get ten people together to get a discount.'

'It's not just that,' Vladimir interrupted. 'It's a good film and it would be a pleasure for us all if you came.'

I still felt embarrassed to be with people who had seen us being marched to the police station like criminals and who had heard the master shouting at me as if I was nothing. I also didn't know how to behave towards Vladimir. He was very nice, but I knew that the others thought I should marry him and the thought terrified me.

'I'm sure your mother will agree,' the landlady urged, 'she likes going to the cinema.'

'OK,' said Vladimir, looking very happy, 'I'll buy the tickets today and we'll meet in front of the cinema tomorrow afternoon.'

'But I haven't got the money,' I protested.

'Don't worry about the money now,' Vladimir said.

When I got home from work that evening I found that my mother knew about the planned trip and although she wasn't keen to be part of such a large group she had agreed. I think she did it for me, aware that I spent too much time at home for someone of my age.

We arrived at the cinema at the last moment as Mum didn't want to be hanging around outside. Vladimir sat himself down next to me and I leaned as close to Mum as I could get as the film started. When I felt his hand trying to slide under my arm I quickly pushed it away. He kept trying and I felt angry, and scared that Mum or someone else would notice. I tried to turn my back on him and was relieved when the film finished. As we came out into the night air I pulled Mum towards home, ignoring the suggestions of the others to go on to a coffee shop.

'May I see you home?' Vladimir asked.

'No thanks, don't bother,' I replied quickly, aware that Mum was shooting me a surprised look.

'Well, maybe another time,' he said, kissing Mum's hand. He went to shake my hand but I just waved as I pulled Mum away.

'He seems quite a nice young man,' Mum commented as we walked.

'When's Granny coming back?' I said, changing the subject.

'I'm not quite sure,' Mum replied, 'but I wish she would hurry up.'

'So do I,' I agreed. Having Granny around the house was always reassuring and there were things I could talk to her about that I would have been embarrassed to bring up with Mum.

The next day was Sunday and we had housework and washing to do. Every chore was a struggle. If you just wanted to wash your hair you had to chop more wood for the fire in order to warm the water in all the pots we had. We also had to bring the water in from outside and carry it out again once it was dirty. Just cleaning the room and ourselves took until the middle of the afternoon. My hair was still wet when the landlady knocked on the door and invited us to her room for tea and biscuits, which she had just baked. She was very proud of her cooking so we couldn't say no and my mother went ahead while I continued drying my hair. A few minutes later Milena and Maria came round, laughing and giggling, and pulled me out.

The landlady had laid the table prettily with a tablecloth she had embroidered herself, serviettes, flowers from the garden and her best coffee cups and Mum was already seated, talking to our hostess's elder sister, while Vladimir was talking to Maria's father, both of them boasting about which of them was the better fisherman. I was ready to turn round and leave but the hostess put a chair for me next to my mother. The coffee and biscuits were passed round.

'What do you think?' the landlady asked me.

'Wonderful,' I said, knowing she liked to be praised.

'When you're married I'll teach you how to make them.'

'Thanks,' I replied, 'but you will have to wait a long time for that to happen.'

'Why?' Vladimir wanted to know. 'Nice girls get married young.'

They all seemed to find this funny.

'I'm not one of them,' I said, without a smile and they all burst out laughing again.

Mum seemed to be as uncomfortable with the direction of the conversation as I was and as soon as we could we made our excuses and left.

'On your way back from work,' Mum said the following morning, 'will you go through the women's market and buy some fresh sheep's cheese?'

I always enjoyed the colour and bustle of the market and that afternoon I lingered among the stalls admiring the fruit, vegetables, eggs, honey, live chickens and other produce that the women were displaying. People who didn't have money would barter with things they'd made, or would swap eggs from their hens for petroleum to light their lamps. One woman was selling butter to get money for her children to visit the dentist. I'd just bought the cheese when I felt someone catch my arm. I turned to see Vladimir smiling at me.

'What are you doing here?' I asked.

'Why, is the marketplace only for females?' he laughed.

We walked home together slowly, talking about this and that. Then we were joined by our landlady's sister, who asked if she could walk with us. We had only gone a few more steps together when we heard shouts and screams coming from round the corner. With a clatter of hooves, soldiers on horseback swept down the street and all the people ran into side streets or yards, wanting to disappear as quickly as possible. Vladimir grabbed both of us and pushed us into the first yard we came to.

'They're rounding somebody up again,' he said quietly. 'Let's see if we can get through to another yard and into a street further along.'

During the five hundred years that they were oppressed by the Turks, the Bulgarians had built a network of small doors in their yards, often hidden from sight, so they could move from yard to yard to reach their relatives, or even their vegetable gardens, without having to show their faces in the street, especially after sunset. Vladimir led us through this maze and we emerged in another street. Just in time, we realised it was lined with policemen and ducked back behind some bushes. A door opened behind us and a man beckoned us into a small room where at least a dozen people were already sitting, talking quietly. My landlady's sister knew some of them and joined in the conversation, still trembling with nerves. A small boy was dispatched to climb a tree and see what was going on. Two hours later he returned to report that the soldiers and police had now gone and we dispersed back to our homes. When Granny returned home that evening Mum dissolved into tears. It seemed she was near the end of her tether.

Although I had told him that I was engaged to be married, the police chief did not give up. Maybe he could see in my eyes that I wasn't telling the truth. The next time I was escorted to his presence he accused me of lying.

'You told me you were engaged to be married, but you aren't,' he yelled. 'You refused to come to my house but you run around with other men. You are a cheat and a liar!'

'I haven't been anywhere except to work and back.'

'You've been seen in the market with a young man.'

'Is it a crime to go to the market? There are so many other people there, some of them are bound to be young men.'

'Don't try to be clever with me. If you don't come with me now you'll be in real trouble.'

'Sorry, my fiancée is waiting for me.' I was trying desperately to keep cool.

'You're lying to me again, you're not engaged and never will be because if you don't want to be my personal friend I've got good reason to get you and your old ones dropped on the other side of the border. I'll leave you there without any identification, so you'll land up in the nearest wartime prison for the rest of your lives!'

He was shouting so loudly and spitting all over my face and I was confused, not knowing what to do or say. I started to cry as loudly as I could, as I had seen my neighbour's daughters do when their parents grumbled at them.

'Anything wrong?' a policeman asked, poking his head round the door. 'Need any help?'

'Get out!' the chief shrieked.

The policeman jumped back out and the chief slapped my face so hard I was sent sprawling off the chair.

'There's a man outside wants to speak to you urgently.' The policeman was back.

'Tell him to wait!' He turned back to me as the policeman left again. 'You, get up and put the chair right.'

I stood up, holding my burning cheek, bracing myself for the next blow when a man came running in, followed by the same policeman.

'I can't wait,' the man shouted, 'your wife has fallen from a ladder and is bleeding all over.'

The police chief cursed and ran out of the office, followed by the man. I took advantage of the mayhem to slip away. As I ran home I bumped into Vladimir.

'What's wrong with you?' he wanted to know. 'Did you hurt yourself?'

He took out his handkerchief and began wiping my face. I tried to stop him but I just started crying. He kept asking me what had happened but I was too embarrassed to tell him. As we walked we bumped into Maria's father.

'Have you two had a fight?' he asked, 'your cheek is swollen.'

'Elena must have had some trouble,' Vladimir told him, 'but she doesn't want to tell me.'

'Have you been called *there* again?' Maria's father asked and I nodded. 'I think it's time you put a stop to this.'

'I know, but I can't decide what to do. Whatever decision I make will give my mother a nervous breakdown.'

'Would you allow me to speak to your mother and grandmother?'

'I don't know, maybe, but some other time.'

'No, now is the best time.' He spoke firmly. 'Your mother too has to make some decisions. I will come round to your house after supper.'

Mum saw my face and guessed what had happened. Her fingers shook as she started applying cold compresses. I said nothing about Maria's father, I couldn't bring myself to talk about the subject, and so she was surprised when he arrived after we'd eaten. They made polite conversation for a few minutes and then he came to the point, explaining why he thought it would be safest for me to marry a Bulgarian citizen.

'But she's so young,' Mum cried, 'She's only sixteen!'

'Not too young according to Bulgarian law.'

'But I have no dowry to give her. Why does she have to become the sacrifice?'

'Don't you understand?' Maria's father sounded desperate. 'All of you could become victims. This man has no human feelings at all. He's worse than a wild animal. And don't worry about a dowry, we will find someone to marry her without that.'

'I don't understand anything,' Mum wailed. 'Why aren't my letters getting through to the embassy? It's against the rules of the whole world.'

Once we were alone again she asked if I had any idea who Maria's father had in mind for me.

'It's only a guess. I think he has Vladimir in mind.'

'Have you two talked about this?'

'Not really. He's asked me to go to the pictures with him, but I've always refused.'

'Would you like to marry him?'

'Not really. I don't know ... maybe that would stop these awful sessions I have to go through at the police station.'

She stroked my cheek. 'My poor little girl,' was all she could say before falling on to the bed in a faint. I ran to the medicine box for the ammonia and held it under her nose to bring her round before helping her into bed and making some fresh tea.

The next day as I left work I pulled a scarf over my head like all the other women, hoping no one would see me, but Vladimir was waiting and caught my arm. I saw Maria and her father hovering in the background. I tried to tell him I was in a hurry to get back to my mother but he insisted on talking to me.

'Look,' he said, 'I'm prepared to help you by marrying you. I've thought about this for a long time and I hope you won't refuse.'

'I can't take this decision alone, I must talk to my mother and grandmother.'

'I'm prepared to talk to your mother right now. Maria and her father can come too.'

'Not Maria, please,' I begged. The more people there were there, the more embarrassed I would be.

So Maria was sent home and the three of us went to look for Mum. Granny was back and I threw my arms around her in relief. Tea was brewed and Maria's father started to talk about the international situation, the impending war and the terrible mess we had got ourselves into.

'I've come to introduce you to this young man who has agreed to marry Elena,' he said, 'which will save you from a lot of unpleasant events and attacks. He is twenty-six years old.'

'Is this the only way we can live in peace?' Granny asked indignantly. 'Must the child pay in this way to protect all of us?'

'But I will treat her nicely,' Vladimir insisted, 'and will care for her as much as I can. I know I don't come from a rich town family, but I do work and we shall manage, even if a little humbly at the beginning.'

'You look a decent young man,' Granny reassured him, 'I have nothing against you personally, but we still haven't lost all hope of returning to our country. If you get married it would then be hard for both of you if Helen decided to go home.'

'I want to go home more than anything in the world,' I said.

There was a short silence. Mum winced as if she had been beaten and Vladimir swallowed hard.

'Well,' Maria's father said eventually, 'it's up to you. We were really trying to be helpful because none of us would like to see you in trouble. If you need anything you can always turn to us.'

'Yes, of course, any time,' Vladimir added before they both left the room.

It looked as if my choices were running out.

Chapter Seven
The Wedding

As I left the factory a few weeks later I sensed an air of agitation among the other workers, everyone discussing, arguing and swearing about something. Some of the men were joking but the women looked frightened and were almost running back to their homes. I couldn't work out what it was all about and then I spotted Vladimir waiting at the gate. His constant pursuit of me was annoying and now the other women would all see him and tease me in the factory.

Before I could tell him off, he grabbed my arm and rushed me to a side lane, hurrying me towards town.

'We must get away from here as quickly as possible,' he said, his face grim. 'I'm taking you to my room for now.'

'But why? I must go home first.'

'Maybe later. We'll see.'

When we reached his house we dodged quickly inside. He locked the door and pulled the curtains. He was frightening me. I had never been in such an intimate situation with a man before, apart from the horrible police chief. I knew I shouldn't be there but I didn't know how to get away.

'Sit down and listen,' he said, pulling up a chair. 'The Germans have entered Bulgaria. There's no telling how our government will react to foreigners like you now. The authorities know you well and this will be a convenient time for them to take their revenge on you, and you know perfectly well who will be first in line for that privilege.'

Now he had really scared me, as I imagined how the police chief might take advantage of this new situation.

'But what about my mother and grandmother?'

'I went to the house this afternoon. Your grandmother has gone to town and your mother is with the landlady at her sister's house.'

'She'll be shaking like a leaf.'

'Shhh,' he put his fingers to his lips and I heard the sound of voices in the yard outside.

'They must be here!' a voice bellowed.

'We know that,' came another, 'just show us which room he lives in.'

I was unable to stop myself from shivering.

'Don't be frightened,' Vladimir whispered, putting his arm around my shoulders and holding me tight as they banged on the door, making it shake on its hinges.

'Open,' someone shouted, 'or we'll break it down and you'll be paying for it even before we arrest you!'

There was no other way out of the room. We had no choice but to admit we were there.

'What do you want?' Vladimir shouted through the closed door.

'Open, and you'll see.'

He slowly turned the key and opened the door a crack. Three policemen barged through, knocking him backwards, his landlady following close behind.

'Ahhh, in my house!' she threw up her arms in horror at the sight of a young girl in her lodger's room and I felt a surge of shame colouring my cheeks.

'See, we've caught them just in time,' one of the policemen joked and the others laughed.

'You have no right,' Vladimir began.

'Of course not,' they jeered. 'And what right has this young lady to be here alone with you?'

'She's my fiancée; we'll soon be married. We just have to consider a few things.'

'Ohhh!' the landlady wailed.

'We'll see about that,' the policeman said, 'but for now you two have to come to the chief and explain "a few things".'

'We haven't done anything wrong,' Vladimir protested.

'Good for you; let's hope you can prove that. Hurry up; we want to get home as early as possible too!'

The policeman winked suggestively and I wished the ground would open up and swallow me. I felt I was being stampeded into a future that wasn't my choosing.

'And in my house,' the landlady spat at me as we were led away. 'Vile foreigners!'

'Well, well, well,' the police chief leered as I was brought into his office. 'How nice to see you again.' He spoke to his men but kept his eyes on me. 'What were they up to today?'

'You know what young people will always do when they find somewhere to hide,' one of them reported and the other two sniggered like schoolboys.

'Out with you immediately,' the chief shouted at his subordinates once they'd delivered their report. 'So you're engaged. When will the wedding be?'

'Very soon,' Vladimir replied bravely. 'As soon as my parents manage to come and my father gets leave from work.'

I was shocked by his ability to lie so convincingly, but didn't contradict him. I was cross with him for getting us into this mess, but if I had to choose between him and the chief there was no contest.

'You'd better hurry before you're mobilised. We're going to need a lot of young, healthy, strong soldiers. What about your family?' he turned to me. 'When will they be ready for the wedding?'

'They want to meet my parents,' Vladimir jumped in before I could answer. 'But that will soon be arranged.'

'I must know by next week,' the chief said. 'Either you two get married by then or I shall have to take other measures. Now we'll go and see what your mother has to say.'

We found my mother still drinking coffee with her landlady. The police chief sat down without invitation.

'We've come to make sure you'll soon be inviting us to a wedding,' he told her.

My mother looked confused and the landlady stepped in quickly. 'We were just discussing that. There won't be many guests. You know how hard times are just now.'

'I haven't saved enough money for a dowry yet,' my mother joined in, having gathered her thoughts.

'Well, you'd better hurry,' the chief said.

'We won't insist on a dowry,' Vladimir assured everyone. 'We'll manage without such customs.'

'What will your parents say to that?' the chief wanted to know.

'They'll agree to whatever I ask them.'

'There's one thing you won't be able to get away with,' the chief smiled unpleasantly. 'I'll want to see a certificate from the doctor confirming that the bride is a virgin!'

'Must that be?' Mum asked, obviously offended at the suggestion.

'See?' he roared delightedly. 'I've got you in a corner this time, haven't I?'

'No, not that,' Mum assured him. 'It's just that it's so humiliating.'

'Oh the great lady!' he mocked. 'But that's what I insist on seeing.'

On that triumphant note he left the room, slamming the door behind him. Vladimir could see how upset Mum was.

'I'll come as soon as you let me know,' he said quietly. 'But time is running out.'

That evening Granny came home with news that the town was full of German soldiers. Mum told her what had happened to us and they talked quietly till dawn before falling asleep. It was my day off and I stayed in bed, not wanting to disturb them. At about nine o'clock I heard a knocking on the window. Pulling back the curtain I saw our landlady. She beckoned me to go out. I dressed quickly, hoping not to wake the others, but Granny waved silently to me from her bed.

'Vladimir's mother will arrive this afternoon,' the land-lady told me once I was outside. I was shocked that they were actually going ahead with this. Mum hadn't given her agreement yet. Everyone was taking decisions without asking my opinion. I couldn't imagine myself a married woman, especially to someone I barely knew, but I didn't know how to stop the bandwagon now that it was rolling. How I longed to be back in England, free of all these worries, riding my bike or lying on the grass in Hyde Park or going camping at the weekends with my father. Why wasn't he trying to find us? We hadn't even heard from Octave in months.

'Well, what was the rush?' Granny asked when I went back in. I told her as she made tea and cut bread for breakfast.

'So what do you think of all this?' she asked eventually when all three of us were sitting down. 'Do you think you could live with Vladimir?'

I hesitated. 'I'm not sure yet. Everybody tells me he's a good person, but he's not like Dad or Octave; no one here is.'

Mum hunted for a handkerchief.

'You're right child,' Granny said calmly, 'everyone has good sides and not so good. We should try to understand and be able to cope with other people. If you don't want to marry him, don't. I shall try to find somewhere else for us to live, maybe in a small village, so we can be rid of that horrible man.'

'Mama,' my mother interrupted, 'you don't know him as we do. He is capable of finding us wherever we go.'

There was a knock on the door. I opened it to find Vladimir and his younger brother on the doorstep. The boy kept looking around him, as if frightened.

'My brother has come with a message from my parents,' Vladimir said when we invited them in. 'They cannot come till Sunday but they agree to us getting married. Just now they can't afford a big celebration, so we won't invite many people.'

'Thank you for the message,' my grandmother said politely. 'But I still haven't heard my granddaughter giving her consent to this marriage.'

'Do you mean you haven't talked this over yet?' He looked astonished. 'Maybe you don't know what happened yesterday.'

'I do,' she replied. 'But I haven't heard what you have to say. Will you take care of my granddaughter, bearing in mind that she has been brought up in a very different manner to you? Will you treat her kindly? Will you do your best to make a nice home for yourselves?' And so many other questions.

'I've said already,' he said, looking uncomfortable beneath her fierce gaze, 'I'll do my best.'

'I hope so, for your own good.' She smiled, as if to soften her harsh words. 'That goes for you, too.' She looked at me and there was a moment's silence.

'So,' she broke the silence, 'if you don't mind, please let us have some time to discuss a few important details and later this afternoon we will tell you our decision.'

'But what shall I tell my parents? My brother must go back with some news today, and the last bus for our village is at seven o'clock.'

'I understand they have agreed. As long as they are not taking part in any financial matters what do they have to worry about?'

Mum looked a little shocked at Granny's abruptness.

'Yes,' Vladimir stuttered slightly. 'You know there is a custom about presents exchanged between the families. They would need to know what they would get so they could return the gifts appropriately.'

'Ahhh, well, nothing from either side. We are not acquainted with Bulgarian customs and we have nothing to give them so we will expect nothing in return. If it is at all possible we will buy something for the young couple to give them a start in life. I haven't time to spend hard-earned money on people I don't even know. That is *our* custom.'

The boys left and Mum and Granny started talking again. Mum described our visits to the police station in more detail, so Granny could understand why marriage to Vladimir might be a preferable alternative.

'Even in the town centre many people are afraid for their lives,' Granny sighed, 'especially now the Germans have arrived.'

Mum broke down into sobs again and I feared for her heart if I didn't do something.

'I suppose they're right,' I said. 'If I do get married maybe we will be safer.'

Mum let out a wail of despair.

'Every girl gets married sooner or later,' Granny tried to calm her. 'And not everyone marries the one they love. That is the law of nature. The rest is luck. The main thing is that the husband and wife respect each other, try to find out one another's likes and dislikes and help and comfort each other in good times and bad. Do you think you and Vladimir could do that?'

She looked at me with eyes full of love and pain. I knew she had given up hope of ever seeing her beloved grandson again, and now she was losing me. We were being forced to deal against our wishes.

'I'll try.' I swallowed hard. 'At least I will be happy to escape any more of these awful interrogations.'

So it was decided that I would be married the following

Sunday. As Mum staggered on her feet Granny made her lie down, gave her some drops and put a cold compress to her forehead. Once she was asleep Granny and I discussed how we could get through the wedding procedures with as little expense as possible. I was aware that she would be borrowing some money and that worried me more than what people might say about the wedding.

'I will buy some cloth,' she said, 'and a young woman I helped to give birth will sew a dress for you. She is the best dressmaker in the area but it still won't be the gown your mother has always dreamed of. Come on, let's go to the shop and see what we can get.' She pulled on her shoes. 'Not quite the nicest shoes for the bride's grandmother to appear in church with,' she joked, 'but they will have to do.'

She and Mum had always been so well dressed and I knew how unpleasant it was for them not to be able to dress decently any more, although they did their best not to mention it. Mum had loved her fashions in England. Octave had sent a photo of his wedding, which looked quite nice, but I knew mine was going to be a real disgrace for the family.

The woman in the shop found a piece of white silk that wasn't too expensive and we took it straight to the dressmaker. She said she would be honoured to make the dress and wouldn't charge us anything.

'I will never forget how you took care of me and my baby,' she told Granny.

The following evening Mum took me back for a fitting. She was terribly disappointed, finding dozens of places where the dress should be taken in or let out. The poor dressmaker couldn't understand her taste but promised to do her best. I was embarrassed by the way Mum found fault with everything.

Our landlady helped Granny with the cooking so we could invite my future parents-in-law back to the house after the ceremony. I was going through the motions, but I still hoped that one day we would be allowed to leave this god-forgotten country.

Mum was still not happy with the dress, but helped me button myself into it and tried to make my hair look decent. Some local girls came, saying it was the custom for them to help me get ready and were disappointed to see they were too late.

'But what about a veil?' one of them exclaimed.

'Yes, you must have one,' the others agreed.

'Well, I haven't,' I said, not in the least bothered. None of it felt like I had ever imagined my wedding day to be. It seemed like just another chore that had to be got out of the way so our lives could run more smoothly. I had nothing against Vladimir, but I certainly wasn't in love with him.

'What kind of bride will you be without a veil?' they all clamoured, and Mum looked embarrassed.

'Maybe that nice little table runner you made for me

would help,' Granny suggested. Mum had crocheted it for Granny before we left England, having done a course in making Brussels lace. Granny hadn't used it; she had put it away until she got back to Vienna. They got it out and gathered and shaped it until one end looked like a flower, which they fixed into my hair with pins, leaving the rest drooping around my shoulders. It seemed rather modern compared to the Bulgarian dress, but the girls thought it was beautiful. I felt very uncomfortable; maybe I had lived for too long among nuns and didn't like being the centre of attention. I would have wished that the whole day was over and done with, had I not been nervous about what would happen once I was married.

There was a small crowd gathered at the gate by the time we emerged from the house, eager to judge if the bride was pretty, which embarrassed me even more.

Our landlady thrust a bunch of flowers she had gathered into my hands. 'Just in case,' she whispered, which I didn't understand. Apparently, I discovered later, the groom's mother was supposed to supply the flowers.

A woman I didn't recognise tried to fix a red flower behind my ear and I tried to stop her.

'But I'm your mother-in-law,' she said, 'and this flower is to make you look pretty.'

'She is pretty,' everyone protested, 'you shouldn't spoil her veil, she doesn't need that!'

'She's still ours, you know,' Granny smiled at the woman. 'Keep the flower and give it to her after the wedding.'

Since my father and brother were not there a local man, known as my 'godfather', was asked to hand me over to my future husband at the entrance to the church. Nikola was a good-hearted man who always found a way to help everyone in the area. He had been a maths teacher at the local school for many years and was well known for being wise about money and finance. Later he became the director of the National Bank of Mezdra.

Vladimir led me to the special wedding altar, a table placed in the middle of the church, bearing a large cross and a bible. We were each given a big candle, tied loosely together with a white ribbon. I was moving in a daze. My godfather balanced crowns on our heads and we walked in procession three times round the table, bowing to the priest at every side as he wafted incense smoke towards us while chanting psalms. It felt almost as if it was happening to someone else and I was just watching from the sidelines. My godfather changed the crowns three times and we both kissed the bible, the cross and the priest's hand. Then he gave us a mouthful of bread and sip of wine. He asked for the rings, but there weren't any because Vladimir had forgotten them. Until that moment my mother had been wiping away the tears, but this made her furious. She pushed to the front of the crowd, pulling off her own wedding ring and putting it on my finger.

Outside the church a crowd waited to congratulate us as we walked out a married couple. People cheered from either side of the street as we walked home, and wished us luck. Mum couldn't be consoled but Granny beamed with pride when she was told her granddaughter was the prettiest bride they had ever seen. They told Vladimir the same.

'But he isn't ugly either,' his mother protested.

I spotted the policeman who always dragged me off to the chief and my heart sank. Not now; not in front of all these people!

'Don't forget to show the proof of virginity to everyone,' he sneered.

'I'm going to punch his face,' Vladimir muttered, but I held on to his arm and my godfather came between them, just as a group of youngsters ran past and pushed the policeman face down into the mud.

When we got back to the house my great-aunt and uncle had arrived. I was so happy to see them and they gave me a nice woollen blanket, a kettle and a beautiful vase as wedding gifts. Borrowed tables and benches had been set up in the yard and the landlady's husband held back the crowd until the relatives were seated. My new mother-in-law was not impressed.

'If it was in my village,' she said, 'everyone would be offered as much food and drink as they wanted.'

'So why didn't you organise it there?' my grandmother snapped. My great-uncle intervened before they came to blows and sat them down with glasses to make toasts.

My mother-in-law insisted I went round every table kissing everyone's hands so they could give me money with which to start our new lives. My great-uncle, seeing the horror on my face, suggested the collection should be done in a more modern way, laying a serviette in the middle of the table for people to leave pennies 'for good luck'.

'If there had been more guests there would be more money,' my mother-in-law muttered.

The celebration went well and as the air cooled the guests left, many of them taking their tables and chairs with them, and the landlady's husband brought out another bottle of his home-made wine and invited us to a last, peaceful drink to wish us all the luck in the world. I knew that we were going to need it.

'Newlyweds usually go on honeymoon,' my great-uncle said. 'But in these dangerous and difficult times it would not be a good idea to go too far.'

'My residence is only around the corner,' Vladimir laughed.

'No, we have decided that you must stay in our flat in the centre until Tuesday. You can stroll around the city and have a cup of coffee in some pleasant coffee shop.'

Vladimir almost shouted with joy. 'Oh thank you, thank you. That would be lovely.'

I felt shivery and didn't say a word. They all noticed but said nothing. What was there left to say? I felt like I hadn't finished my childhood, but suddenly I found myself a married woman and I knew that was going to entail duties I did not yet know anything about. How could I have ended up in such a predicament when less than a year earlier I had been a little convent girl innocently setting out on holiday?

Chapter Eight
A Married Woman

Two weeks later I was preparing something for supper when Vladimir came home from work, looking upset. He threw his bag on to the bed and went out again without saying a word. I heard him talking to his landlord's eldest son but didn't listen to the conversation as I busied myself arranging the table with the few pieces of crockery and cutlery we had. I then sat and waited for him respectfully. If he had something important on his mind, no doubt he would tell me as soon as he was ready. When he came back in he sat down and ate in silence for a while.

'How was your day?' I asked, hoping that might prompt him to confide in me. 'Is the meal all right?'

'You're spending too much on food,' he grunted. 'You should prepare simpler things with cheaper vegetables. My mother managed to feed eight hungry children with a handful of dry beans in a big pot, and her soup tasted wonderful.'

'I'm sorry,' I said, trying to make light of the situation, not wanting to start an argument. 'I'm still learning.'

'Then learn quicker.'

Then he told me we were going to be moving house.

'To something bigger?' I asked, hopefully.

'Don't be stupid,' he snapped. 'We're going to another town. I was told today I must start work on Monday morning in the ammunition factory two hundred kilometres away. I'm not supposed to tell you for fear of eavesdroppers.'

'What about my mother? She'll worry if she doesn't see us and they may start bothering her again if she's on her own.'

He shrugged. 'After a while maybe she'll be able to join us.'

Did this mean I was going to lose touch with my mother and grandmother as I had with my father and brother? I felt like howling, but I knew Vladimir didn't like tears. He'd told me he believed I'd been spoilt by my parents and should start to act like a grown-up.

'How will we transport our belongings?' I asked, trying to concentrate on the practical problems. 'Where will we live? What about my wages, they aren't paid till Wednesday?'

He didn't give me any answers but after dinner we started packing, leaving only the bed and bedclothes. I hardly slept that night and once Vladimir was asleep I let the tears flow, barely daring to breathe for fear of waking him. With everything that happened to me I seemed to be moving further and further from the familiar world I had grown up in, and where I had been so happy as a child.

The next morning we breakfasted on dry bread and tomatoes, all our dishes being packed so we couldn't even make tea. Vladimir reluctantly allowed me to go to my mother for an hour while he arranged our transport. Granny quickly made a bottle of coffee and sandwiches for our journey, but Mum couldn't stop crying and I had to rush back without being able to comfort her. They followed me so they could see us off and Vladimir promised to arrange for them to join us as soon as possible.

'It would be better for us to stay nearer to the capital and the embassies,' Granny said. 'So we can keep trying to get out of the country.'

It was an agonising parting as we were loaded into a lorry with our belongings and set off on a fourteen-hour journey to Kazanlak, our new home. The driver told us he wasn't allowed to have passengers in the cabin, so we had to freeze in the back. We were frequently stopped by German soldiers who wanted to know where we were going and why. We had become refugees within Vladimir's home country. I could understand everything the soldiers said to us perfectly but Vladimir wouldn't allow me to speak to them. Some of them had interpreters with them so they could talk to the locals. Their translations were unbelievably bad, but I said nothing and kept my eyes averted modestly at all times. I didn't want to draw attention to myself or anger my new husband when he was under so much pressure.

We arrived at our destination early in the morning. Vladimir had an address but the driver wouldn't take us there.

'I can't drive through town with a load like this,' he said. 'The Germans have imposed new traffic regulations.'

We found an apparently abandoned home in a side street, with partly collapsed walls round its yard. We unloaded everything and the driver accelerated away. I was left, shivering with our belongings, while Vladimir went to try to find the address. He found it but the landlords refused to unlock it so early, so he came back and we had our last two sandwiches and a cup of cold coffee.

People were waking up, appearing in the street, staring at us. My lips were turning blue with the cold. Vladimir went back to plead with the landlord and returned with a wheelbarrow which we could use to transport our belongings across town, including our bed, table and chairs. Seeing our problem a small boy with a donkey and cart offered to help.

Our landlord and his family were not pleased to see us. Like many others they'd been ordered by the council to empty their guest room to make room for tenants. They were keen to show us just how unhappy they were about the arrangement.

Once we'd got our furniture into the room there was just space for a stove, which we didn't have. There was a cold tap in the yard where I was allowed to wash our dishes and clothes. The only good thing about the whole situation was that we were now a long way away from our old enemy, the police chief.

For a few days we ate only cold food but our landlady, surprised that someone so young was making such an effort to keep things clean and tidy, offered me the use of her 'summer kitchen', which was a shed with two iron rings over a fire. I found chopping wood hard as the logs always seemed to spring back and hit me, covering my head and arms with bruises. I would blow my lungs out trying to get the fire going, my eyes stinging from the smoke while the landlady's children mocked my efforts, making me cry. Cooking over the open fire made our pot black all over.

Vladimir never spoke about his work and I stopped asking him questions. He got to know some of the local people and from time to time would stop to chat with them. But I stayed indoors like an obedient wife. I didn't have enough money to go out shopping. Less than a month after we got there Vladimir told me he'd got me a job at a factory for preserving vegetables and fruit.

'My wages won't be enough to keep us going,' he said.

I didn't reply. I could just imagine how hard it was going to be to work all day and then come home to the cooking and the housework. The only thing he ever did was occasionally chop enough wood to last us a couple of days.

The factory manager didn't seem impressed with the sight of me.

'It'll be hard work,' he warned, 'lifting cages full of jars.'

'I'll do my best,' I promised and a few days later I was washing bottles and jars, soaked to the skin by the ice-cold water. My arms and my back ached unbearably and my fingers were so stiff by the time I got home I could hardly clean and cut the vegetables for our soup. The other women in the factory laughed at me all the time.

'You'll get used to the work by the time you're our age,' they cackled.

I didn't dare to complain to Vladimir too much, knowing he would get angry if I did. The winter snows fell and we continued to work with only a tent for shelter. I began to feel unwell, unable to eat and frequently vomiting, with no strength for the household chores in the evenings.

Hearing me throwing up in the lavatory one morning our landlady told me to go to the doctor.

'I've got no money for that,' I told her. 'I'll soon be better, don't worry.'

I hurried back into our room but she came knocking on the door. Vladimir wasn't pleased but let her in.

'Tomorrow I get my wages,' he said, 'and I'll pay you the rent.'

'It's not that,' she said. 'I think you should take your wife to the doctor.'

'Oh, she's very tough,' he assured her, 'she'll get over it.'

'I don't think you understand,' she persisted. 'I think your family is going to be increasing very soon.'

'We can't afford bigger accommodation,' he said, exasperated. 'Her mother is going to have to wait.'

'You are expecting a baby,' she laughed at the look of astonishment on both our faces. 'Oh dear, oh dear, you young ones.'

My face was burning with shame and she put her arm around me as she talked to Vladimir.

'You must take great care of her and help her with the housework, especially chopping the wood and carrying heavy pails of water.'

I decided to try for a job at a cotton factory, which I thought would be easier. Vladimir wasn't pleased when I told him.

'You're too self-willed,' he said, 'always doing just what you fancy without asking my permission first.'

'I'm asking you now,' I said, surprised by his reaction. I hated it when he talked like that, as if he was one of those old-fashioned husbands who had to rule his wife's every movement.

'Who told you about this factory?'

'A woman I work with.'

'I've told you not to speak to strangers.'

'She isn't a stranger. I work with her.'

'I need to meet her first.'

'Come to the factory tomorrow and you can see her.'

I couldn't understand why he was so upset. He seemed to get irritated at everything I did. The next day he followed me to work but didn't say anything to me. A week later he told me I should have gone to the cotton factory already because the conserve factory was being closed down and taken over by the Germans.

Now that I had his permission I got the new job, working a night shift, running from one reel to another all night long. I was exhausted, but at least I was inside and dry.

I wrote to my mother asking for advice about the baby and Vladimir received a letter from my grandmother ordering him to send me back for the birth so that both I and the baby would be in safe hands. My mother-in-law, being the wife of a railway worker, was able to get free tickets and escorted me. I felt elated at the thought of being back with the two people who loved me most in the world.

I had never seen my mother and grandmother as happy as they were on the day that my first daughter was born. Their praises were without end and I felt like the cleverest woman who had ever lived. She was absolutely gorgeous and we decided to christen her Gloria.

According to the custom in Bulgaria, when a baby is born two important days have to be honoured; the third day after the birth and the fortieth day, the day the baby is christened. On the third day women brought gifts like soap to wash the nappies, socks or home-knitted baby clothes. They brought home-made cakes, biscuits and sweets and the whole afternoon passed with toasts and wishes for a wonderful and happy future. Everyone had to leave by sunset so the doors could be locked to keep all evil spirits out.

My mother-in-law didn't come for the celebrations, much to the disgust of the other women, nor did she come to the christening on the fortieth day. I learned later that although the arrival of children is considered good luck in a family, they prefer the first born to be a boy. The council didn't like the idea of a foreign name, but my godfather, being a highly educated man, at that time still had the respect of most people, so no one dared to oppose him. More presents arrived, and a pile of money.

Vladimir was becoming increasingly upset at my absence and sent messages to his parents asking them to come and bring Gloria and me home. To my secret relief they always seemed to be too busy to make the journey and I was able to get a little more time being spoiled by my mother and grandmother. Little Laurie, as I had taken to calling her, was two months old by the time they finally arrived to fetch me. Having had a good start in life, she was a healthy and happy child.

Vladimir's fifteen-year-old sister, Maslinca, accompanied her mother on the journey. She was a nice girl, although a bit vain, dressed in plain folkloric style. Her greatest dream was to wear town clothes. As soon as she saw me she exclaimed, 'Do you wear these clothes every day?'

'I have no others,' I told her. 'They are the ones I brought with me to Bulgaria.'

My mother-in-law looked in horror at Laurie kicking

around bare-footed. 'The poor child will get crooked legs and a broken backbone,' she exclaimed.

'Of course she won't,' Granny retorted, 'she's a strong, healthy child.'

'I'll show you how to wrap a baby. I've had eleven. I'm a very capable mother.'

'Five of them died before their third year,' Granny reminded her, a little unkindly.

'That was God's will and we can't go against that.'

She proceeded to truss Laurie up like one of the mummies I'd once seen in the British Museum in London. She was as stiff and straight as a log and screaming at the top of her voice. I was crying and begging her to have mercy on my baby but she took no notice.

'Get your coat,' Mum told me, and we hurried to my godparents' house, Laurie's screams ringing in our ears. When we hurried back with them we could hear the screams from the street and a crowd of women were gathered at the gate wondering what was going on. As soon as we walked in my mother-in-law accused me of abandoning my child and leaving her hungry. My grandmother and godparents came to our rescue and unwrapped Laurie, giving her to me to feed as we both continued to sob.

Granny announced that she would not allow me and Laurie to go back to Vladimir if his mother was going to interfere. My mother-in-law put up a few arguments but my godfather finally convinced her that I had been well trained by Granny and Mum and was quite capable of looking after a baby despite my youth.

'It's true we don't know her properly,' my mother-in-law admitted. 'We have so much to do at home, animals to look after, fields to tend. We thought our son would marry a rich girl from our village who would help us with money and with the work.'

'Your son promised us that he would always be kind and take care of my granddaughter,' Granny interrupted.

Eventually everyone calmed down and started to talk reasonably. Those weeks I spent with my mother and grandmother surrounding Laurie's birth were the last to be free of trouble, pain and fear. I would never again be so happy until long after my own children had grown up.

Chapter Nine
Childcare and Other Superstitions

It was dark when I arrived home in Kazanlak with my new baby. There was no one waiting for us at the station. There was too much luggage for us to carry so my mother-in-law stayed with it while Maslinca and I went to the house. As we turned into our street I saw Vladimir talking happily with some other men and our landlady ran to meet us, taking Laurie from my arms.

'Look,' she said to Vladimir, 'look what a pretty little girl you have.'

Vladimir glanced at Laurie. 'Where's Mother?' he asked Maslinca, without even looking at me.

'Why didn't you tell us you were arriving today?' our landlord asked. 'We could have met you with a luggage cart.'

As her husband set off to the station with his cart, the landlady came inside with me, surprised to find our stove wasn't lit. She quickly brought some wood of her own and warmed the room up. I heated up the food Granny and Mum had given me and laid the table, but for the rest of the evening Vladimir spoke only to his mother and sister. I spent most of the time outside, washing nappies and dishes. I guessed they hadn't seen each other for a long time and had a lot to talk about. I was sad that he didn't seem pleased to see me and Laurie, but not surprised. From the day we had married he had gradually grown less and less interested in me as a person, only interested in having a wife to fulfil his needs.

Because the room was small we had to pile the chairs on the table to make room for the mattress on the floor so our guests could lie down. An old soapbox was found to make a cot. While my husband and in-laws went for a drink with the landlord I covered the wood with linen to make it a bit more presentable. I sighed at the thought of the beautiful cot I'd once had in England. But, I scolded myself, there was a war on and I had to be grateful for what I had.

Maslinca wanted to spend some time in the nearest town, so while they were all out over the next few days I tried to catch up on all the washing and cleaning that Vladimir hadn't got round to while I was away, at the same time as cooking and looking after Laurie and chopping the wood. It seemed as if this was going to be the pattern of my life for the foreseeable future. The only good things were that it didn't give me too much time to brood on what had gone wrong, and I did have my precious Laurie with me, on whom I could lavish all the love I had enjoyed myself as a child.

Vladimir became friendly with a neighbour who kept a few doves and told me he'd wanted birds ever since he was a boy.

'My mother would never allow it because of the dirt,' he told me, 'and my father thought they brought bad luck to a household.'

The landlord allocated him a patch in the back garden so he could build a small shelter with scraps of wood. He then bought four doves, which soon multiplied to sixteen. They needed to be fed on maize, which was hard to find in the markets because of the war. For many people, it had replaced bread.

Vladimir seemed to spend all his time with his doves and his new friend and hardly ever looked at his sweet child. As soon as he returned home he would go straight to their pen to play with them, throwing them up in the air and watching them twist as they flew into the sky before obediently coming back down to land. He was always trying to interest other people in his obsession.

'Haven't you got anything more useful to do?' one man said.

'Why don't you play with your little daughter as well?' another asked.

Their remarks vexed him and I said nothing for fear of angering him.

One evening, after spending the whole day with the birds, he told me it was time for me to start work again.

'My wages aren't enough to feed all three of us,' he said. 'You're spending more than I can afford, what with clothes, extra milk and other special foods for the child.'

'But my mother sends me packets of food and my grandmother sews clothes for Laurie,' I said, cautiously. 'Who will take care of her while I'm at work?'

'We'll find a woman to look after her for a few hours. She's a calm child, anyone would agree to get a few *levas* more these days.'

'But I can't just leave her with anyone.' I felt tears of panic rising, my voice catching in my throat at the thought of being separated from my baby. 'She could get ill if she's not looked after properly.'

'You're acting silly again,' he scoffed. 'Hundreds of children are cared for by people other than their parents.'

'Well, if my mother was here ...'

'There's hardly enough room here for us,' he interrupted, 'and we can't afford to have her here.'

A few days later he announced he'd found a woman to care for Laurie.

'Can you take me to see what she's like?' I asked as he prepared breadcrumbs and maize for the birds.

'An ordinary woman like all women,' he dismissed my worries.

'Still I'd like to meet her, see where she lives, what kind of person she is.'

'Can't you see I can't go now, I'm feeding the doves?'

I waited as the food got cold. Laurie needed her evening bath by the time he rushed in.

'Come on then, it's getting late. Let's go.'

When we got there the woman was getting ready for bed and didn't want to invite us in to the small room I could glimpse behind her. 'I have to be up early,' she explained, 'because one of my babies is brought here at six.'

'How many children do you look after?' I asked.

'With yours it will be three.'

'Are they all small? How do you manage to care for them all?'

'Oh, I've been looking after children since I can remember,' she laughed.

'It doesn't look very clean,' I whispered to Vladimir as we walked home.

'It's not so bad,' he said. 'She's the cheapest we can find, so we haven't any choice.'

Our landlady was on holiday for a few days and offered to look after Laurie while I went to look for work. All I could find was a weaving factory, which was an hour's journey time away. I was told to start in two days.

The evening before my first day I prepared enough nappies and food for Laurie for the next day and went to bed with a stone in my heart. I couldn't sleep all night and in the morning I asked Vladimir to take Laurie to the woman for me.

'No,' he insisted. 'It's your responsibility.'

I was blinded with tears as I walked away from the house, preparing to be parted from my baby for the first time ever and unable to wipe the tears away because my hands were so full. The vision of her little hands stretching out towards me, her crying ringing in my ears, were with me all the way to the factory. The machines were horribly loud and fast and there was no time to ask anyone what I should be doing, I just had to get on with it. After ten hours I almost ran all the way back to the woman's house.

Laurie's eyes were red and swollen from crying, her clothes were smelly and covered in stains and she clutched her arms around my neck as I staggered home with everything. Once we got home I prepared her a meal, which she gulped down as if she hadn't eaten all day. I cooked our supper and prepared her more food for the next day before washing her clothes and doing the rest of the housework. By the time I'd finished it was late into the night.

The same happened the following day and as I approached the carer's house in the evening I could hear Laurie screaming in a hoarse voice. My heart started to thump and when I saw her I felt like screaming myself. Her face was smeared with dirt and tears, her nose running and caked. She was lying on their bed while the woman was holding another child with one arm, mixing some soup with her free hand. I didn't even greet her, just wrapped little Laurie up in her blanket, grabbed the bag full of nappies and left.

Once I got home I realised her temperature was high

and her cough was almost suffocating her. I hunted for the medicine my grandmother had given me but there was none left. I discovered Vladimir had given it to his friend in exchange for food for his doves. I begged him to go and ask if there was any left but he refused.

'I will never ask for something back if I have given it,' he told me.

I was so frightened. I knew we couldn't afford to go to a doctor and Laurie didn't seem to be able to breathe. I asked my landlady if she had anything and she found half an aspirin. I decided to give Laurie a warm bath and my landlady noticed there was no wood.

'You will have to chop some wood as quickly as possible,' she told my husband. 'We must get this room warmed up.'

'Yes of course,' he said, obligingly. 'Why didn't you tell me?' he almost shouted at me, letting the woman know that it was all my fault. I didn't answer.

'You should prepare wood and whatever else is necessary as soon as you return from work,' the landlady was telling him. 'You should know that.'

I knew I was going to be in trouble later, but at the moment Laurie was my priority. Once I'd managed to calm her and get her to sleep, I started taking her soiled nappies out of the bag, but they weren't the ones I'd sent, they were just old bits of rag torn into pieces, stained like they had never been properly washed. My landlady was equally appalled and insisted Vladimir did something.

'That woman was always a thief and a cheat,' she said.

Vladimir suggested he ask his sister, Maslinca, to come for a while. I was so relieved when she agreed, but less than a week after she arrived I came home to find Laurie's arm hanging from her shoulder in a strange, twisted position, causing her great pain with every touch. She'd fallen from the bed.

'I know a man who can repair dislocated joints,' my landlady told me.

She gave me directions to his house, saying it was close to a house with a high chimney, although she didn't know the name of the street. The snow was almost knee-high as I wrapped Laurie in a blanket and set off into the unpaved back streets, which were deeply rutted by the wheels of carts. They looked nice and smooth under the snow, but every footstep could result in a twisted ankle. When I did eventually find the house, by asking everyone I came across, the man was out. His wife and children asked us to wait and the moment he came in the man asked Laurie what was wrong with her arm. He took hold of her and examined her shoulder then gave a quick sharp pull on both her arms. Before she had a chance to cry out he held his arms up and told her to do the same.

'Now clap your hands,' he said, and she obeyed.

'That's it,' he smiled, 'but be careful not to fall again.'

They all came out to show me a quicker way home and gave me a piece of home-made sheep's cheese, which he said would be good for a child's bones. Such small acts of kindness stay in the memory for ever.

Maslinca announced that she was going home, but arranged for the landlady's daughter to take over her child-minding duties. I was quite happy about that, although Vladimir was furious she had dared to make arrangements without asking him. The only problem was that if he got home before me the carer would immediately hand Laurie over to him, assuming her services were no longer needed for the day. He would then just lock her in the room while he played with his doves.

As 1940 approached I discovered I was pregnant again. Being in bed with Vladimir was nothing to do with love for either of us, just a matter of satisfying his animal instincts. I had no right to refuse, even if I didn't feel well. It was his right as a husband and my duty as a wife. He was furious at the news.

'It's not mine,' he raged, 'it can't be. I always take care. God knows who your lover is.'

He beat me until Laurie screamed so loudly that our landlord came in and stopped him. I couldn't understand how he could have changed from the young man who had been so keen to help me and save me from the police chief, to someone who now seemed to hate me. I could understand if he didn't love me, but I couldn't understand why he would want to hurt me. I said no more about the matter but I started lifting heavy loads, running fast to and from work and doing anything that I'd heard might cause a woman to have a miscarriage. Nothing worked, not even the continued beatings from my husband, which became more and more regular.

The women at work noticed my condition and suggested I visit the doctor for working women, so that I could get paid leave, at least for a couple of weeks after the child was born. The doctor told me to be more careful and to eat more milk, cheese and eggs, but such foods were difficult to find in the shops and on the black market they were expensive. I only ever bought small quantities of these things for Laurie, and often Vladimir would eat them anyway.

'Where's my milk?' Laurie would ask indignantly now that she could talk.

'I don't know,' her father would shrug, avoiding her accusing stare.

'You drank it, I saw you,' she'd say and he would become angry and throw something at me.

'It's your fault. You should have told me.'

Laurie was turning into a pretty little two-year-old girl.

'You shouldn't dress her so nicely,' my landlady would advise, 'or you should make a dirty mark on her face.'

'Why?'

'Because of the evil eyes.'

I never shared the superstitions of the other women until one day I was out shopping with Laurie and she suddenly stopped talking and began losing her balance and falling over. I thought she was messing about and tried to pull her up by one hand, as I was carrying a heavy bag in the other. Then I saw that her eyes looked dull and she didn't answer me when I spoke to her.

I carried her home and our landlady was in the front garden.

'Oh dear,' she said as soon as she saw Laurie, 'someone has looked at the child with evil eyes.'

Her whole body was burning and she was slipping into unconsciousness. I wanted to carry her to the hospital but the landlady asked if she could try to chase the evil spirits away first. She waved her hands over Laurie's face and murmured some strange words.

'The evil spirits are very strong,' she told me. 'I need help, urgently.'

I was so frightened I would have agreed to anything. We wrapped her in a blanket and took her to a neighbour who was supposed to know about such things. As we entered her garden she was talking to another woman and turned immediately.

'Oh my god, they're bringing an innocent child who's been attacked by evil spirits.'

My landlady unwrapped Laurie. 'Quick,' she said, 'before it's too late.'

The woman touched my child's forehead and said some strange words. Her hands began to tremble. My landlady joined in, both of them carrying out some ritual that was incomprehensible to me, something from the mists of Bulgarian mythology. Soon a weakness seemed to overcome our neighbour and she sank into a nearby chair, exhausted.

'Thank God,' she whispered, 'the child is saved.'

Laurie opened her eyes and smiled. 'What are we doing here, Mummy?' she asked. It was like nothing had happened.

When we got home she said she needed the potty and excreted something green and foul-smelling. My landlady gave me a piece of garlic and made me promise to put it on a ribbon round Laurie's neck to protect her at all times. She was still there when Vladimir came home and I was frightened he would be cross. But when she told him what had happened he picked Laurie up and held her close. She put her arms around his neck.

'You love me, don't you, Daddy?' she said.

'Of course I do,' he replied before putting her down.

That night, before we went to sleep, he told me not to make her look so pretty and not to take her too far from the house for a while.

Two weeks later I took my maternity leave. I was entitled to seventy per cent of my wages for forty days, payable at the end of that period if my new child was still alive. I was very afraid that Vladimir would never to accept the child as being his and that it would be made to suffer all its life.

I gave birth to Henrietta at home, with the help of a local midwife. She told me she had never attended a birth where the mother didn't scream, but I was embarrassed and didn't want all the neighbours to hear what was going on.

'Where's Mummy gone?' I heard Laurie asking the landlord who was looking after her.

'She's gone to buy you a little baby sister.'

Hennie was just as enchanting a baby as Laurie had been, and grew to look exactly like her father. Every time someone told Vladimir that he would glow with pride. The child he had initially denied was his became the apple of his eye and I thanked God for not allowing my efforts to end the pregnancy to succeed. The wound Vladimir had caused in my heart with his false accusation, however, never healed. He had shown that he didn't trust me, that he thought I was a liar and a cheat, when I had never given him any cause to think such a thing.

I didn't go back to work after Hennie's birth. I convinced Vladimir it was going to cost too much to have two children looked after, but really I wanted to do it myself anyway. Everyone kept telling him he was lucky to have a wife who was so good with his children. He agreed when he was with his friends, but always found something to complain about when he came home.

Because we hadn't been to visit Vladimir's home the gossip went around his village that I must be so ugly the family were ashamed for people to see me; I might be a hunchback, or perhaps our children were not quite normal. They began to pity my mother-in law for her bad luck. Irritated, she insisted we visited for the village's patron saint's day. I took the opportunity to go on ahead of Vladimir with the children and visit my mother and grandmother on the way. They doted on the girls and I wished I could stay longer.

Vladimir met us the next day and we travelled twenty minutes by train, but then had to walk three kilometres on rutted earth roads, weighed down with children and luggage. The family all slept on the floor, but they had borrowed a bed specially for the girls and me. When it was time for sleep they rolled out hand-woven lengths of straw, covered with carpets made from the wool of their own sheep. They had one hand-woven blanket to cover the whole family. During the day people used the rolled-up bedding as seating. From time to time they would sprinkle water on the earth floor to keep the dust down. The rest of the furniture comprised home-made tables and benches and three-legged stools for the children.

More and more relatives arrived to stare at us as the day wore on, and the following day, after the church service, the whole village sat at long tables in their yards, breaking bread and drinking *rakia* together, passing the bottles from hand to hand, taking sips as they went. Most of the time I pretended to sip so as not to offend anyone. I didn't really like the taste and I hated drunk people. The bread was so much better than the horrible war bread we got in town. So much food had been brought by visitors that at the end of the day the hostesses were actually left with a surplus. My in-laws taught me to dance their national folk dances and I was impressed by how well my husband moved. Seeing him happy with his family reminded me of what he had seemed like when I first met him, and I wished he could be more like that when he was with just the children and me.

The following day we walked seven miles to visit Vladimir's aunt, who lived in her parents' large house. I was impressed by the way in which the whole family worked together, supporting and helping one another and dividing up both chores and rewards equally and fairly between them. Another of his aunts was a blind fortune teller, who knew who I was the moment I walked into the room, even though no one had told her.

'Poor child,' she said, holding my arm, 'you still have a lot to go through, even worse is to come, but you will overcome all difficulties and then your life path will take a sharp corner, then it will be much easier for you. Your luck may be a little late arriving, but don't give up.'

How right her predictions would prove to be.

Chapter Ten
Going Underground

Back home it was always a struggle to survive on Vladimir's wages and I tried to earn some extra money by sewing and knitting in the evenings, after everyone was asleep and my household chores were done.

The war continued to rage across Europe, but my thoughts were taken up just with surviving from one day to the next. I had no time to think about what might be going on in the wider world. As I worked into the night I could hear British planes buzzing over the town on bombing missions.

Maslinca had married and her new husband, Pencho, was a good friend to both Vladimir and me. Worried by the bombs, Pencho persuaded my husband to find a safe place in a village for Maslinca, me and the children.

'I'll pay the rent,' he assured Vladimir, 'and ensure they have enough food.'

Vladimir didn't like the idea of being left to fend for himself in the evenings but Maslinca turned on the tears, telling him how frightened she was of the bombs and that she needed me with her because she didn't want to be left alone in some strange village, and he was forced to give in. We found a village about twenty kilometres away that could be reached only by horse cart, and Pencho supplied us with enough food to last a fortnight.

The village had a sort of Roman communal bath filled with mineral water that was supposed to heal the sick. Many would make the pilgrimage to the bath during the summer, but it was still winter when we arrived and the place was relatively deserted. We found two rooms. The larger held two single beds and the smaller one had a table and small cupboard. We could cook outside in the yard under a small shelter. Even though I still had to do all the chores, it felt like a holiday because the children were so happy and I didn't have to worry about Vladimir's moods. Everybody liked the girls and took them for walks in the nearby garden. Maslinca changed her clothes three times a day and showed off as much as she could. There were other women who had been evacuated from Sofia and we would meet in the evenings to talk. Sometimes we even danced to a gramophone, although someone had to push the record every now and then to keep it turning round.

Late one afternoon I went to the communal pantry and found a young man hiding inside. I was about to shout out in alarm but he signalled me to be quiet. I turned to run.

'Please,' he whispered, catching my hand. 'I won't hurt you. I only want something to eat.'

My hands were trembling as I gave him a piece of cheese and piece of salami, which was a rare delicacy at the time.

'Can I have some bread?' he asked.

We only had two loaves but I gave him one.

'Please leave now,' I said, 'other people could come at any moment.'

He pushed the food into a sack, adding a few fish conserves, apples and nuts.

'Go now,' he said, 'and don't tell anyone, for the sake of your own life.'

I was scared to death, although I had no idea who he was or why he was being so mysterious. I went inside for a few minutes, pretending to search for matches, before going out again with one of the other women. It was she who discovered that the man had emptied the whole pantry into his sack before going. He must have left in a hurry because he'd dropped some things beside a hole in the fence. The woman started shouting and the landlord came out to quieten her.

'The curfew has already passed,' he warned, 'there will be soldiers and police in the streets. Don't draw their attention to us.'

He took us all into his kitchen and explained that the Germans in the village had been becoming more alert recently because they believed there were partisans operating in the nearby forests.

'They think some of us are helping them with food and clothing and ammunition,' he warned. 'Don't tell anyone about this theft or the authorities might suspect us of supplying the partisans.'

The patrols were becoming more regular, the Bulgarian police and soldiers often being accompanied by Germans. We heard rumours that some local houses had been searched and men had been taken away. I began to worry they would discover I was a foreigner, even though by now my Bulgarian was so good that only an expert would be able to spot my accent.

A few days later Stancho, my eleven-year-old brother-in-law, came to tell me Vladimir was ill and needed me to look after him.

I couldn't face the thought of taking the two children and our luggage all the way to town in a bumpy cart.

'Leave the children,' Maslinca told me. 'Stancho and I will look after them.'

'But Stancho is only a child himself.'

In the end I decided to take Laurie with me so that they only had to worry about Hennie. The journey seemed to last forever and when we finally got home we found Vladimir feeding his doves in the yard.

'Daddy,' Laurie cried, 'we're here.' She ran towards him with outstretched arms, making some of the doves jump away.

'Stay there,' he shouted, 'you'll frighten them.'

I went inside, shocked by the state he'd allowed the

room to get into, with clothes all over the place and every single pot, pan and dish dirty. I couldn't even find a clean spoon. I felt sick. By the time I'd cleaned up, cooked enough food to last him a few days and done the washing it was nearly dawn. I managed to snatch a couple of hours' sleep before Vladimir and Laurie woke up and needed their breakfast. Before returning to work Vladimir ordered me to go back to the village, fetch my things and Hennie and come home as soon as possible. 'Stancho can look after Maslinca,' he said.

In fact, Maslinca returned to the city a week after me, because her husband Pencho had joined the army. The Germans were making things increasingly difficult. I had to apply for a pass in order to come back to the town again and be with Vladimir, and he started to be accused at work of being married to a foreigner from the enemy side. The press and the radio were pumping out anti-foreigner propaganda all the time, which people were accepting without question.

'Do you hear the enemy planes?' I heard one neighbour say to another.

'It's getting pretty dangerous, isn't it?' replied her friend.

'Especially now some of them are living among us, raising their bastards!' said the first, staring hard at the children and me as she spoke.

Their whispers reached the local councillors and we were called to answer questions again, just like with the police chief. The fact that I was married to a Bulgarian was of no interest to them.

'Why are you in Bulgaria?'

'Who is your father?'

'Where is he?'

'Who pays for you to be here?'

'Why have you been heard speaking English to your children?'

'What are your obligations?'

I was advised to stop teaching my children English as it made a bad impression and might raise the suspicions of the Germans. It seemed that, after all, the marriage to Vladimir was not going to help me: all it had done was separate me from my poor mother, so now she had lost both her children and was, like us, being persecuted. She and Granny were told to move out of the room we'd all lived in and were moved to something smaller, not far from Sofia. Granny was still able to earn a little delivering babies and Mum knitted, for next to nothing, and lived in eternal fear of being called in for interrogation again.

When I got home from the police station Vladimir wasn't back. It was his pay day, which meant his colleagues would have persuaded him to go drinking with them and he would be in a bad mood when he got home, ready to use his fist or break something. The news that I'd been questioned, however, seemed to sober him up when he eventually arrived back, making him angry and worried at the same time.

* * *

My inexperience as a housewife showed whenever I went to market. The peasants on the stalls would cheat me and I never was able to bargain like the other women, who could sometimes halve the prices of everything they bought.

In 1942 Vladimir was told he must move to work in another village called Tulovo, which stood at the side of an ancient forest. This forest, with oak trees so huge five people holding hands in a circle could only just embrace their trunks, was a cover for the ammunition factories, hiding them from the enemy planes which occasionally dropped their bombs on the way to or from Sofia. He was promised lodgings and decided that we should all go together as a family.

It was a hot day when we moved and when we found our new house it stood empty behind locked gates as we, and our belongings, once more stood outside. None of our new neighbours seemed able or willing to tell us anything about our landlords. Vladimir disappeared, telling us not to move until he got back. The hours ticked by. The dust was terrible and the children were becoming thirsty. After about six hours I was told by two other evacuated women that they'd just seen Vladimir in the pub with their men.

'We haven't had a drink since we left town,' I told them.

'Give me that bottle,' one of my new friends said, 'I'll find some water.'

She knocked on a nearby door and, on getting no answer, jumped over the fence and started pulling water from the well. A woman immediately came running out of the house, shouting, 'Robbers, thieves, help!'

'Oh, shut up,' my friend said. 'I'm only getting a little water.'

'How dare you trespass in my home?'

'I'm not. I knocked long enough but you didn't answer. There's a baby out there dying for a drop of water. It's a sin to refuse anybody water, or even bread.'

The woman with me was laughing at the scene and other neighbours were coming out of their houses to watch.

'Come on, unlock this damn door, or I'll kick it open.'

The woman from the house stopped shouting and fetched a key, coming over to see if there really was a baby. 'Oh dear,' she said when she saw Hennie lying in the shade of a tree, 'it's true.'

'Do you by any chance know where the landlords of this house are?' I asked politely.

'No, I don't know anything,' she replied, turning away to avoid more questions.

'Yes you do,' my new friends both shouted simultaneously, 'she's your sister, isn't she?'

'She's not my sister, she's my sister-in-law and she won't be back now until it gets dark, so you better go and find another house to stay in.' With that she vanished back into her house.

The two women decided to take charge. Apparently they'd had the same trouble when they'd tried to get into the houses they had been allocated, and had gone to find the mayor to sort things out for them. They went off to do the same for me, and to root Vladimir out of the pub. I would never have had their nerve. In less than ten minutes a large group of people came marching towards us including the mayor, Vladimir, the women's husbands and our landlord, Petco, who was also the chief of the post office. The men all looked deadly solemn, while the women were giggling behind their backs.

The mayor ordered Petco to open the door for us. 'You were told to be here to let these people in,' he said.

'I had to go to the post,' he wheedled.

'Now help them carry their things in!'

When we got into the room we found it full of unwashed clothes, baskets and boxes. My legs began to tremble.

'Couldn't you have cleared this away?' the mayor asked, surveying the chaos. 'You've known about this for two weeks.'

'My wife will soon be back,' he stuttered. 'She'll clean up.'

'You will start cleaning up NOW,' the mayor demanded, pushing him in. The other men waded in to help, throwing everything out into the yard. While everyone else set to with brooms and buckets of water, Vladimir took Hennie off to buy some food, something he'd promised to do six hours earlier. When the landlord's wife came back and started complaining the mayor laid into her as well, demanding that she show me where everything was and made sure we had a regular supply of milk and eggs for the children. That evening we all had supper together in the yard and even the landlords joined us, bringing some homemade *rakia*.

A week later my landlady, Tania, told me I was the best person she'd ever met and christened me 'Countess', because I bathed the children every evening and kept the room cleaner than it had ever been before, and because I couldn't do farm work like killing a chicken. Nor did I eat as much as they all did. She started leaving me in charge of the whole household, including her children, aged seven and eight, when she went into the fields to work. I was allowed to get fresh vegetables from her back yard and take the odd egg or two. From the evening milking she made butter, yoghurt and cheese for all of us. Because I was cooking for all eight of us I could do whatever I chose. The children helped me as much as they could during the day and everyone was grateful to come in to a warm meal. Every Saturday afternoon Vladimir would buy a small lamb from a local shepherd and Tania would bake enough bread for the whole week. On Sundays we would all have a party in the back yard together.

Both Vladimir and I began to relax, feeling we were out of sight of the authorities and doing well, but then I was once more summoned to appear before the town council in Kazanlak, a town about twelve kilometres from Tulovo, and all the old feelings of fear resurfaced. I took Hennie with me on the train and when I got there they told me I had to go to the police station. My feelings of foreboding deepened. The superintendent was wearing military uniform and there were two German officers in the room with him. I didn't let on that I spoke their language, waiting for the Bulgarian to translate everything for me.

'When did you last hear from your father?'

'How much money has he sent you and your mother?'

'When did he send it?'

'Where is your brother?'

'Who else subsidises you?'

I explained I'd heard nothing from either of them for years.

'That's impossible,' they told me. 'It will be much better for you and for your mother if you tell us the whole truth.'

When I went to the toilet with Hennie they turned out my bag and found a snapshot of one of our family parties. They wanted to know who everyone was.

'Why did you marry a Bulgarian?' one of the Germans asked.

'We fell in love.'

'Was that the only reason?' the other German asked sarcastically.

'I can't think of another,' I replied. 'We simply can't live without each other.'

'Ha!' was all he said.

When I finally got back to the village station Laurie and Tania's children were waiting for me and, to my relief, had brought a wheelbarrow with a blanket to put Hennie in.

We returned home with a great deal of laughter to find Tania had prepared a meal.

Every four to six weeks I had to report my whereabouts to the authorities. As the weather grew colder the boundaries around the ammunition factories grew wider and more and more guards arrived in the area. Peasants who owned parts of the forest were not allowed to visit their land, so weren't able to provide enough wood for their own families, let alone supply the markets. Their lives were becoming more miserable than any of them could remember. They had to do everything by hand, with only their horses and cows to help them. Before the war, they told me, some of the richer landlords had owned machines like combine harvesters, which they would rent out, accepting crops as payment. Now everyone who produced food had to hand over a percentage of their production to the state. The amount was calculated in advance so sometimes they were left with nothing.

All the radio stations were blocked apart from Radio Sofia. The Russians were trying to stir up the Bulgarians against the Germans, offering them a 'wonderful' future and Russian radio stations would sometimes manage to get the odd word past the blocks. Everyone would sit silently around their radios in their cellars, listening for these words with all the lights out. A whole sentence could sometimes take as long as half an hour. Vladimir had managed to unblock news programmes from the BBC, which was very dangerous but he wanted to know what the English were saying and I was able to translate for him. Some people who were caught doing such things simply vanished. I was frightened about how he would use the information and sometimes I would say I couldn't understand, which made him furious, but he couldn't shout or hit me too much for fear of being heard.

At nights we could hear the bombing raids on Kazanlak (the Allies never seemed to find out about the munitions factories hidden in the forest near Tulovo), and when Tania asked me if I was managing to sleep at night I assumed that was what she meant. When I said yes, she didn't say any more.

The others in the village tried to persuade Vladimir to let me join them on outings to the baths and on walks, but he always refused. For two years I hardly left the house except to report to the town hall. I never ever got to visit Pavel Bania, the famous baths built above the mineral springs about three kilometres from Tulovo.

In the summer of 1944, two years after we arrived in the village, Tania and Petco were told they were going to be allowed to visit their part of the forest to chop down some trees for winter. Petco had hired a petrol-driven saw for three hours. He asked Vladimir to help him get as much work as possible done in the time. Tania suggested we make it a family outing with the children, who could hunt for raspberries while the men worked. Vladimir wasn't keen on the idea of me going out.

'Oh, come on,' Tania said, 'she's like a prisoner here, working all the time.'

The children joined in the pleading and eventually wore him down. The next morning we loaded up a cart with tools and food and Tania laid a carpet in the back to make the ride more comfortable. The cart had to be pulled by cows as the horses had been requisitioned long before. The men took it in turns to walk beside them. I longed to tell my children about the happy times I'd enjoyed on picnics with the Italians, but I didn't dare breathe a word about my past. It was a wonderful day out.

On the way back we had to walk because the cart was now full of wood, and we met up with a group of women on their way to the mineral baths. They bantered a bit with our men but I didn't take much notice, being more concerned with keeping Hennie from falling into the brambles. Tania touched my elbow and I looked round to see what she was looking at. Vladimir had remained a few steps behind and was walking through the trees, talking to one of the women. There didn't seem anything strange in two people talking. One of the cows stumbled and everyone, including Vladimir, ran to save the cart from falling over.

'Stupid cow,' Tania giggled, 'spoiled everything.'

She was trying to tell me something but I was too preoccupied to realise.

* * *

One night, after we'd been having a meal with Tania and
Petco and their family, everyone went down to the cellar to
listen to the radio while Tania and I washed the dishes.
Kalina, Tania's niece, who was visiting, came running
upstairs, filled with excitement.

'Auntie,' she whispered, 'the Germans are retreating
and probably the Russians will be invading by the end of
the month. We shall have to return home to make new
rakia to meet them.'

'Quiet,' Tania tried to calm her down. 'It's still dangerous to talk like this. You never know what dying animals
will do in their last moments. Just act as if you have no idea
what is happening. There will be plenty of time to celebrate
once they've gone.'

I started shaking uncontrollably and I realised I was
feeling afraid again, this time of the unknown.

'Let's go and listen with them,' Tania whispered.

'I don't know,' I hesitated, 'Vladimir doesn't like me to
be there when the others are listening.'

'Come on, he can't say anything to me.'

She pulled me down the ladder. Everybody was silent,
eager to catch the few words that could be heard during the
pauses in the music. They were all excited and happy but I
felt scared to death. It was a feeling much stronger than
anything I'd felt before. That night I had terrible night-
mares and woke drenched in sweat.

Petco came in to see me in the morning, once Vladimir
had gone to work, and told me the Russians could enter
Bulgaria at any moment.

'Will it get worse?' I asked.

'No one can say for sure.'

Later in the day he sent the children to bring me to the post office. When I got there he was waiting.

'I've heard something on the radio,' he told me once he was sure no one was eavesdropping. 'By the evening the state is going to inform all the foreigners in Bulgaria that they're free to leave the country. I wanted you to know so it won't be a shock. Don't say anything yet.'

I had no idea what I was going to do now, but once I'd sorted the children out I prepared some of our best clothes so we would be ready to leave if the opportunity arose. All the time I was thinking about Mum and Granny, wondering if I could get in touch with them and whether we would be able to escape together. And if we could, where would we go?

That evening we listened to the news and Radio Sofia announced that the president had changed again for the third or fourth time in as many weeks, and then came the news that the Russians had reached the Danube and were expected to enter the country in the next couple of days.

'The Ministry of Internal Affairs herewith informs every foreign citizen living in Bulgaria at this moment that they may leave the country at the southern borders in twenty-four hours, starting from midnight tonight. After twenty-four hours all the borders will be closed and no permission whatever will be given to anyone.'

No one said a word. Petco returned to the post office to await more news and I went back to our room with the children, hoping Vladimir would follow so we could discuss what to do, but he didn't emerge from the cellar until three in the morning, despite me going down there several times and dropping hints. I could hear non-locals taking their leave of friends and relatives all night. If he didn't want to come with me I hoped he would give me some money to take the children.

'Well that's it,' Vladimir said when he eventually arrived.

'Aren't we going to try to get out of the country?' I asked.

'You must be mad!' he said. 'They would kill me without a thought.'

'But they said that the foreigners could leave until tomorrow night.'

'I'm not a foreigner; I'm a soldier in civilian clothes and would be considered a deserter. They would shoot me down. Anyway, I don't want to leave my fatherland.'

'Will you at least help me and the children to go?'

'If you want to go, go now,' he almost shouted, 'but without the children. You will never see them again.'

He stormed out of the room in a rage, leaving me feeling faint. When the curfew lifted at seven o'clock I went to see the local councillor to ask for his help in getting the children out.

'No, no, absolutely no! You cannot take the children.

Their father is Bulgarian, so are they. According to the new law the children belong to the father.'

'What would happen if I did take them?'

'Are you mad, woman? You might get shot as it is. You can't expect any pity from the Germans or the Russians. This is a decisive moment and everyone must help themselves as best they can.'

A young man came running in. 'The cart is ready, sir,' he said, 'hurry!'

They both grabbed their bags, ran out into the street and jumped into the waiting cart.

'They're scared to death,' commented a passing cleaning woman, cackling happily.

On the way home I saw Petco standing in the door of the post office and was about to go over and ask his advice, but he signalled for me to pass by quickly. When I got home I woke the children up and put their breakfast on the table. Taking my mother's wedding ring, the one thing I treasured more than anything else, I went to Tania.

'I need some money to go away,' I whispered.

'You'll be in danger,' she whispered back, 'and I have no money at all.'

'I can give you this ring. It's worth a lot.'

'I'm sure it is, but I have no idea who I would sell it to.'

I knew she would help if she could. I went home, racking my brains for an answer. At that moment Vladimir rushed in, grabbed his overcoat and rushed out.

'We're going to the high road to meet the Russians,

don't you dare leave this room till I return,' he shouted as he went.

It was September 9, 1944. That day the Iron Curtain was drawn, cutting off the east from the west for the next forty-five years and I was trapped on the wrong side in what would soon become known as The Cold War.

Chapter Eleven
Russians in the Kitchen

In 1945 the war in Europe ended, but it made no difference to our lives because we had a new occupying force to deal with. The Russians arrived shaking their fists and shouting in a language hardly anyone in the village understood at the time. The Russians were in high spirits. They were the triumphant conquerors. Their uniforms were ragged and dirty but they didn't seem to care.

'*Nichevo* (it doesn't matter),' they said. 'It's wartime.'

It was a striking contrast to the Germans in their spotless uniforms and shiny boots. The people might not have liked the Germans but at least when they wanted something they asked for it politely and paid for what they took. The Russians simply grabbed whatever they wanted, whether it was a loaf of bread, eggs, chickens or even pigs; not to mention any pretty young girls or women they fancied. Many screams were heard and many fights arose, but the Russians only laughed.

'Everyone is equal,' they'd say. 'Everything belongs to us.'

Even the men who had secretly listened to them on the radio and had sympathised with them before they came were now worried about their daughters and wives.

Twenty-four hours after they arrived we had to pack up and return to Kazanlak, though we had no home to return to. Vladimir was told to report for work the next day or he would be considered a traitor. We had no time to pack properly so we tied up our possessions in sheets and jumped into the lorry that came for us. Vladimir sat in the front to tell the driver where to go; I was in the back with the children and had no idea where we were headed. He directed the driver to the house of a friend of ours. I knew they only had two rooms, one for the brother and his family, the other for the sister and hers. Their seventy-five-year-old father slept on the floor in the kitchen.

Once we'd unloaded all our possessions the friends gave us permission to store everything in their cellar. The men went out to look for somewhere for us to live while I made up beds for the children underground. Having grown used to running freely in the countryside, they now had to get used to sitting still in cramped surroundings. The floor and walls were damp and there was only one small window high up in the wall. The place was full of old barrels that stank of pickled cabbages and last year's wine. Our hosts were poor people too, unable to pay the new taxes that had been imposed on them, but they gave me some eggs for the children and invited us to sit with them in the kitchen. I promised to pay them back as soon as Vladimir returned.

'Why don't you put the lamp on, Mummy?' Hennie asked as I tucked them into their beds.

'There isn't one, sweeties,' I explained.

When the men came back they had to admit there was nowhere for us to go, every spare room had been taken by Russian soldiers. For three months I dragged the kids around town with me, searching in vain for a home, terrified they would grow sick in the cellar as winter set in. Then one day I came across an old woman standing outside a small room and asked her if she knew of anybody with a room to let. She invited me into her little kitchen and told me to make myself a coffee while she searched for some Turkish delight she had somewhere for the girls, telling me her name was Grandma Vesca. Eventually she asked if we would be interested in taking a room attached to her kitchen. She took us up some narrow stairs to a small, clean and sunny room.

'How much is the rent?' I asked.

'Listen, daughter,' she said. 'I'm over ninety. I won't ask for a high rent if you would be willing to help me now and then. My daughter and son-in-law live seventy miles away and I would feel better with someone young to rely on. My sister lives in the other part of the house but she too is growing old. Her daughter lives down the street and comes every evening to see her and does some shopping for me as well, but I know she's engaged and I don't want to be an extra nuisance to her.'

'Of course I'll help you with what I can,' I said, 'but now I must go and tell my husband.'

'Couldn't you move in this evening?' she asked. 'I'm so frightened of the Russians.'

'If we can find a cart, maybe.'

Both the girls begged to move to this new home as quickly as possible.

'I'll lock the door,' Grandma Vesca said, 'knock three times when you come. Please hurry.'

It took ten trips with a small, borrowed cart before everything was moved, with the help of our friends, by which time I'd got the beds ready, the stove fixed, the fire lit and a pot of potatoes boiling. Vladimir went out for *rakia*, cheese and bread and our new landlady came with a bowl of eggs asking if she could join the party, which went on until nine-thirty, when the police curfew hour was nearly due and our friends had to hurry away into the night.

The children and I worked all the next day to make our home nice, hanging out our clothes to get rid of the smell of dampness and sprinkling them with rose water, which we could get free from the nearby factory. When Vladimir came back he looked surprised but, as usual, said nothing.

'Look at this, Daddy,' the children enthused, leading him round the room. 'We did this and Mummy did that ...'

'Good,' he said, patting their heads. Laurie was used to his ways and said nothing.

'Don't you like it?' Hennie demanded. 'Look how nice it is, you don't even look at anything!'

'Of course I do,' he said, picking her up. She was the only one who had any influence over him.

Laurie was six now and wanted to go to school. She could already read and write in Bulgarian and German, although we had to keep that secret, but the teacher at the local school said she must wait another year like other children. Laurie started crying and admitted she could already read. The teacher obviously didn't believe her and gave her a book, which she read without a mistake.

'Who taught you?' he asked, astonished.

'Mummy,' she answered.

'All right,' he said, 'she can come to the first class, but if she finds it too difficult she'll have to wait a year.'

'But I can come with her sometimes, can't I?' Hennie piped up.

'We'll see about that,' he replied, unable to stop himself smiling at the little girl who wasn't yet even four.

We headed home in a good mood, but as we approached I got a funny feeling. So many Russians were going to and fro in our street. Our door was wide open, the kitchen full of soldiers, all laughing and joking at the tops of their voices. There was a big pot on the stove and they were using our pans, frying something, the fat spitting out all over the place. I was furious; the children were struck dumb. Summoning all my courage I crossed the threshold.

'What are you doing in my kitchen?' I demanded.

'Ooohh, nice woman!' one of them said and they all laughed.

'This is mine,' I said, but they just laughed louder.

An officer came in and asked what was going on. I explained it was my home and we had nowhere else to go.

'You have another room upstairs,' he said calmly. 'We had nothing. Now this is ours.'

'But you have taken all my things. Where and with what shall I cook for my children?' I was trembling with rage.

'Oh, don't worry, our cook will give you some borscht from time to time.'

There was more laughter.

'And if you're nice to him, he might steal you a portion of meat!'

Grabbing the children, I rushed upstairs to escape the mockery, weeping tears of humiliation and rage.

Grandma Vesca was sitting in her room, pale and trembling.

'Did they do anything to you?' I asked and she shook her head.

'My sister and I were standing in the yard. They pushed us away, kicked the door open and went in. We were so frightened, my sister went to her rooms and told me to stay in and lock the door. I could hear them shouting and laughing. I didn't dare go out, not even to the toilet.'

'Mummy, I need the toilet,' Hennie said.

'Come on,' I said, 'we'll all go together.'

Taking Grandma Vesca in one hand and Hennie in the other I told Laurie to stay close. We went past the soldiers without catching their eyes. I noticed they'd taken the wood I'd bought only the day before, but there was nothing I could do. When we returned they spotted us and we had to walk a gamut of jeers and suggestive remarks.

They'd been in our bedroom with their dirty boots, opening drawers and cupboards, but didn't seem to have taken anything except a picture of Vladimir in uniform, which had been standing on the windowsill.

I needed to cook and luckily I'd brought the shopping bag upstairs. I began peeling potatoes and Grandma Vesca loaned me a small pot. I went outside to the tiny summer kitchen to cook soup. It was bitterly cold and I had to chop wood and light a fire before balancing the pot precariously on two bricks above the flames. I had no oil or salt or other seasonings.

When Vladimir discovered what had happened he was furious. 'Why did you let all these soldiers in?' he wanted to know. 'Where did you get to know them?'

Hennie wanted her daddy to chase them out, there and then. He went to talk to the soldiers while I fed the family with the soup. He returned the worse for wear, having accepted several vodkas from them. They'd managed to convince him it was their right to occupy whatever premises they found. They were now the official 'occupiers' of the country. They told him that about twenty officers would use the kitchen as their canteen and their cook, Petro, would sleep there. When they left, they assured Vladimir, they would only take what they needed. Vladimir told me to go to the town council the next day to complain. I knew it would do no good but he would have been angry if I didn't at least try. The councillor eventually listened to my case and then waved me away.

'It's wartime for everybody,' he said.

'Ask the cook to tell you when you can do a little cooking,' the Russian superintendent added, 'and to lend you a pot.' Lend him one of my own pots! 'We're not barbarians,' he reminded me, 'we have come to free you from the German barbarians. Be patient, soon everything will be wonderful for everybody.'

Laurie went to school and had to learn Russian from the first day. Even Hennie learned all the songs and recitations, although she didn't understand them. Vladimir got friendly with Petro the cook and they would drink vodka together in the evenings, after all the officers had left. I managed to do some quick cooking in the afternoons, under Petro's watchful eye. Most of the plates were already broken and the pots looked terrible. I mentioned it to Petro.

'*Nichevo*,' he said, 'after the war everybody will be able to walk into any shop and get whatever they need without paying for it.'

'Is that how life is for everyone in Russia?' I asked.

'Well, not yet, but for many people it is. Russia is a great big country. It isn't that easy to satisfy everyone at once.'

Late one evening, while I was cooking in the kitchen, Vladimir was persuaded by another Russian to go out looking for vodka. Almost as soon as they'd left Petro grabbed me and pushed me on to his bed. I shouted but he covered my mouth with his big, dirty hand.

'I won't take long,' he promised, 'Vladimir won't return so soon.'

I managed to twist out of his grip and shouted again.

'Stop, don't make such a noise,' he hissed. 'Somebody might come and we'll both be in trouble.'

'Leave me alone, you have no right,' I was furious.

'All right, all right, in our land no woman ever refuses a man. She's honoured if someone wishes her.'

'Leave me alone and go to hell with your honour.' Grabbing my bag and my pot I made my way upstairs.

'Please don't tell your husband,' he pleaded, following me. 'I might get into trouble.'

Knowing how jealous Vladimir could be, even when he had no cause, I thought he was probably right. I couldn't stop crying as I tried to compose myself. I realised now that he and the other Russian must have planned this together, persuading Vladimir to go out. But I'd never given him any cause to think I would be willing to do that sort of thing, never even smiled at him. I heard Vladimir and the Russian returning much later, singing drunkenly. I peeked out of the curtains just in time to see my husband falling off the horse. It looked to me as if he'd been kicked off, but it was dark and hard to see. On the way into the house Petro intercepted him and persuaded him to take more vodka, one of them holding him tight, the other pouring it down his throat. Ten minutes later the Russians pushed him upstairs and left him unconscious on the landing, laughing mockingly. Once they'd gone down again I pulled him into the room and he vomited.

Only later did Grandma Vesca admit she'd heard everything and I felt very ashamed. She, however, suggested we should get our own back on the Russian with a ten-year-old bottle of *rakia* she'd been saving. Unsure what I was getting myself into, I agreed. She persuaded Vladimir that she wanted Petro to drink with her to mark the death of her son twenty-five years before, but needed him to be there with her. For some reason Vladimir believed this unlikely story and persuaded the Russian as well.

When Petro saw the small glasses she was offering him he laughed. 'We don't drink from thimbles,' he boasted, 'we use proper glasses!'

'These are all I have,' Vesca told him.

'Here, use these,' Petro said, taking two of his own glasses off the shelf.

'No,' she said, 'I shall use a small glass, but you use yours.'

She then doled out the drink, half measures for all of us and a full tumbler for Petro.

'It's strong,' she warned him, knowing he would see that as a challenge to his manhood. True to form he insisted on throwing the *rakia* back in one, leaving himself choking and gasping for air.

'That is strong,' he agreed.

We then left him and Vladimir with the bottle, Vesca

warning my husband to take care. Petro, however, was determined to prove he could handle his drink. Within no time at all he'd passed out on the bed and woke too late to prepare breakfast for the officers. Everyone was furious with him, and he blamed Vladimir. My husband was duly frightened and from then on never went down to drink with Petro again, returning to his old dove-fancying friend for company instead.

When Hennie discovered she had a louse in her clothing I was horrified. I remembered my mother telling me stories of how lice in the First World War were impossible to get rid of.

'I wouldn't let your father in the house with them,' she said, 'until he'd had a bath in the yard, shaved his hair off and I'd burned his underwear. His uniform was disinfected every day of his leave and left in the shed until it was time for him to return to his regiment.'

How was I going to be able to boil or wash anything properly when the Russians took all our wood? They were burning everything they could get by then; fences, floorboards, tables and benches and anything they could steal from people's yards. Vladimir was more philosophical and just laughed when I told him about the lice. 'We used to get them on the first day of school. My mother smeared our hair with petroleum every week. It smelled horrible but we got used to it.'

Over the next few months I waged a personal war on the lice, somehow managing to hide enough wood with a neighbour to boil our underwear every day. I then disinfected anything I couldn't boil. My mother managed to send me various liquids and powders.

When the new Bulgarian councillor and Russian superintendent came to inspect the kitchen one day they saw there were pieces of wood too long for the stove sticking out of the open doors, dropping red hot embers on to the boards. They merely crushed the embers with their boots.

'Where do you cook?' they asked.

'In the shed.'

'Where do you hide the wood?'

'I don't hide the wood, I buy it as I need it, or gather it from the fields, although there isn't much left out there.'

'Our soldiers could help if you were decent to them,' the Russian said.

'I'm not indecent to them,' I insisted. 'I try to survive just like everyone else.'

They exchanged looks but said nothing. The following day Vladimir was summoned to the council after work.

'What do you have against the Russians?' he was asked. 'Why aren't you friendly with them? Why don't you accept any offers from them?'

He tried to explain that he just didn't have any spare time.

'Maybe it's because your wife is a foreigner,' the Russian suggested.

'Not at all,' Vladimir insisted, 'she has enough to do with our two children.'

'Other families have children too, but they like us, ever since we liberated you from the Turks, and now from the Germans, and they find time to enjoy themselves in our company. Apart from that our soldiers need some entertainment, however humble, while they're not at the front. Apparently your wife doesn't seem to like us much.'

Vladimir knew exactly what they were talking about and by the time he returned home he looked downhearted and defeated. They'd told him they wanted to talk to me next.

'You're not Bulgarian, I hear,' the new councillor said to me the next day.

'I am a Bulgarian citizen.'

'You're from foreign parents.'

'So are many people that are living here.'

'Don't be impertinent, you know very well what I mean.' He was getting angry so I fell silent.

'Why doesn't she answer?' the Russian asked. 'We must know what nationality you are.' Still I said nothing.

'Answer him!' shouted the councillor.

I started to go through the whole story again as the questions rained down on me.

'Where are your parents now?'

'My mother is in hospital, she's very ill. I don't even know if I shall see her again.'

'And your father?'

'I don't know. Probably dead.'

I swallowed hard to try to suppress my tears. They kept insisting I must be in touch with my parents. They wouldn't believe me and eventually a policeman was called to drag me away and push me into a dark room. There wasn't even a chair so I squatted on the floor in the corner. They released me a few minutes before the curfew started, warning me to be nicer to the soldiers in the kitchen from now on, and to report back to them every month. I ran through the streets, eager to get back to the children and frightened I would be arrested again for being out after curfew. There were drunken Russian soldiers and policemen everywhere.

Knowing I hadn't been able to cook, Petro came upstairs and shyly presented us with a bowl of borscht. I hadn't eaten all day but the sight of it made me sick. I had a drink of water and went to bed.

For four years I had to report regularly to the Russian headquarters and they asked me the same stupid questions every time. Sometimes they would push me around, occasionally they would give me a few slaps or punches. Always they accused me of being a liar and a danger to society because I didn't want to become friendlier with the 'good-natured and kind' Russian soldiers. They told me I was the one influencing Vladimir not to socialise with them either. At the same time Vladimir was being harassed by his superiors at work, accused of helping a foreigner and betraying the Communist party, which he'd been forced to join. Vladimir was not a particularly courageous man, but he refused to divorce me and send the children to their 'special children's home', where they could be 'educated' the Russian way.

The pressures on our marriage were terrible. We hardly spoke to each other any more. I dreaded the evenings when he would come home, never knowing what mood he would be in. We could afford nothing more than a thin vegetable soup most days, which was never enough to appease the constant hunger pangs we suffered. Sometimes a neighbour would give one of the children a piece of fruit from their garden, which they thought was a great treat. My mother would occasionally send some clothes that she could no longer wear and I would combine the material with other leftovers to make things for the girls. I turned my own coat into two little ones for them. Every night I knitted to make a few extra coppers to buy them pens, pencils and notebooks for school.

Sometimes the children would ask me what I used to do when I was their age, but I was forbidden to tell them anything nice about my home country; that would have been treachery and could have led to the death penalty. So I said nothing about the kind teachers and friends I'd known before Dad left for Canada and I was sent to the convent. I told them nothing of the tennis, basketball and swimming, the roller skates and the bicycles, the picnics, museums and art galleries, the seaside holidays, trips to the theatre and zoo, or the time my father carried me on his shoulders to see King George V and Queen Mary passing for the christening of the future Queen Elizabeth. It was as if I had no past, no life before the endless drudgery, which was all they had ever known. I so wanted to be able to tell them that life didn't always have to be so hard, but I couldn't, not without showing myself to be a traitor to Bulgaria.

The Russian canteen finally abandoned our kitchen after three and a half years of occupation, leaving only one whole plate and one uncracked glass. All the pots were dirty and dented and had lost their handles, but I had no money for new ones. I scrubbed with sand, scratched with knives till my hands were sore and bleeding and still I couldn't get them clean. I whitewashed the walls and the ceiling. The floorboards had been burned away around the stove while others had been pulled up to use as fuel; what was left was speckled with evidence of their knife-throwing games. Grandma Vesca asked her sister to give us a few boards to patch up part of the kitchen and a neighbour mended our stove in exchange for a cardigan I knitted for his daughter.

Chapter Twelve
Mickie

The children did well at school, despite the initial suspicions of anyone with a foreign mother, and once they were established Vladimir told me to find proper work again to help with the finances, because I was spending too much on them.

'They're old enough to look after themselves for a few hours each day,' he insisted.

There was little work available for women at the time and I had to go to the job seekers' office every day in the hope of something temporary coming up. The crowd of women waiting grew bigger each morning and whenever a job came up a man would walk into the crowd, shouting. Before he'd even finished his announcement all the women would be fighting their way to the front with their fists and elbows and I always got pushed aside. Those who were chosen would then be told the job was to dig a few acres of land twelve kilometres away, and would only last a week.

Fights would then break out as other women insisted they needed the work more or had arrived first. For six weeks I went there every day and never came home with anything except bruises on my face.

Eventually I was signed up to clear some bombsites, but when I told Vladimir he was furious. 'You can't work there, where all the men will enjoy making fun of you.'

It felt like I could never please him, whatever I did, but I would constantly forgive him for his unkindness because he was the father of my two beautiful daughters, and my family was all I had in the world.

We were living two hundred and fifty miles from Sofia and my mother's health was getting worse, especially when she heard that Octave had been lost in the war somewhere in Russia. Even though my grandmother was now so old she had to struggle to stay on her feet, she was still helping to deliver babies in order to make a little money on which they both existed.

Then Grandma Vesca's daughter got a job in the local school and needed somewhere for her family to live. Grandma Vesca told us we would have to look for somewhere else. Finding a new home seemed like an impossible task, so many buildings had been destroyed by the bombs, and the Russians had taken the best of those remaining. They had also by now completely taken over the government, and cared nothing for those they referred to as the 'common' people.

Eventually Vladimir found an old lady who wanted some tenants to pay a low rent in exchange for looking after her, washing, cleaning and cooking. The house was nice, bigger, cleaner and more comfortable than Grandma Vesca's, but the old lady was not as pleasant. She was from Croatia and spoke only broken Bulgarian. Her husband had worked on the railways with my father-in-law. The house was also a forty-minute walk from the children's school. Part of the bargain Vladimir struck was that he could keep his beloved doves at the house again. During the day our landlady treated me like a housemaid. Her face would light up as soon as Vladimir came home and she would ask him to play cards with her.

Soon after we moved in a representative of the National Front, responsible for our street, came for a 'friendly chat'. The National Front was an organisation set up by the Russian authorities, who decreed that one person would be responsible for disseminating propaganda to everyone else in their street. Every house had to have someone signed up to the National Front. I always refused to sign, which meant, as a foreigner, that I was constantly under suspicion. She asked me questions about my family, right back to my great grandparents, and decided it would be appropriate for me to do some useful work for the community. Many of the locals were illiterate people of mixed Bulgarian-Rumanian origin, having fled from the great floods before the war and settled on apparently deserted land. My job was to get the ration coupons from the local committee for all the families in our street and to sort them out according to their allowances, place them all in the household books and hand them personally to every family after getting their signature, or thumb-print. I protested that I didn't have much time.

'Well,' she said firmly, 'you'll have to find time. You're lucky I'm not including you in the free labour work, which would mean being out of the home all day long. Everybody is obliged to help building up our new country.'

Vladimir also had to chair the National Front committee in our street, attending meetings every week. I was worried he would find it difficult. He wasn't a very learned person and a mistake could get him in trouble with our communist leaders as well as our neighbours. Now every look or movement either of us made would be closely scrutinised.

When I received news that my great-uncle was gravely ill and wanted to see me and the children one last time, our landlady kindly offered to lend us the money for the rail fares, so Vladimir wasn't able to say anything to stop me. I knew, though, that I was likely to end up in trouble if I didn't hurry home as soon as possible.

The reunion was joyous and when I asked what I could do to help, Granny asked me to do some shopping and, secretly, to get in touch with the priest to ask him to come to see my uncle. It had to be done secretly because the authorities did not approve of religion in any form, and we didn't want to have any more black marks against our family. The priest agreed to come after dark and his blessings seemed to make my uncle feel better. The following morning we had to return home and Granny had prepared what looked like a feast for us to take with us. I was very afraid as we said our goodbyes that I might never see them all again. My mother seemed so poorly, the last of her health and spirits finally draining away.

We heard Vladimir and our landlady laughing over their cards as the girls and I reached the gate of our house.

'Daddy,' Hennie said as she ran up to him, 'why didn't you come to meet us instead of playing cards?'

I quickly took her away, telling her not to be impolite.

'Your big boss is back,' the old lady said, gathering up her cards to go.

'Just a moment,' I said, 'I have your money for you.'

Vladimir was obviously suspicious when I told him my great-uncle and great-aunt had given it to me. All evening he criticised me for everything I'd done, like not getting the first train back and for accepting money. When I gave him an ashtray my mother had sent for him he threw it into the corner of the room with all his might and it shattered into a hundred pieces.

'I don't need anything from her!' he shouted and stormed outside.

I'd been aware of his irritation building as he listened to the children excitedly telling him how wonderful Sofia was and how my mum and great-aunt had promised to save up to buy Laurie a violin when she'd said she wanted to learn to play. I could see his pride had been hurt.

My great-uncle passed away peacefully just four hours after we left. I wished I could have stayed longer to help the three elderly, weak, grieving women with the arrangements. I cried my eyes out as I went about my routine chores, feeling helpless. When Vladimir came in he said nothing; he knew the news already because our landlady had told him, with the pack of cards in her hand.

My great-uncle had left me some money in his will so that we could buy our house for a reasonable price. He suggested we asked the landlady if she was willing to sell, provided we allowed her to stay there for the rest of her life. In his will he had indicated that he wanted the house then to pass from me directly to the children, to give them some security. The old lady was very willing to sell under these conditions and the deal was done. I hoped it would make our lives easier, no longer having to pay rent, but it didn't seem to make much difference; the money would never stretch far enough.

When I told Vladimir I was pregnant again he was furious and demanded to know who my lover was and when I met him. I tried to point out that I never had a moment when I wasn't with him, the children or the landlady but he started to beat me, making so much noise that our landlady came to see what the problem was. He pushed her out and slammed the door but she came straight back in, shouting that she would call the police for treating her indecently because she'd only wanted a cup of coffee. He stormed out and I washed off the blood. My hands still trembling, I made her coffee.

Later, as we ate, the children asked why my face was swollen. I told them I'd had a toothache all day but they obviously didn't believe me and finished their food in silence. They helped me clear away the table and wash up and I went to their room to see how they were doing with their homework. Once I'd tucked them up in bed I returned to the kitchen to find the table and floor covered once more in spilled food. I tidied and washed up again and went to bed. I could hear our landlady, now our tenant, and my husband laughing and joking over their game of cards.

My obligations to the National Front increased. I started dispensing breakfasts to the children of the poorest families, distributing milk and bread spread thickly with peanut butter, all donated by the American Red Cross.

The old lady, though, was growing weaker and when I took her to the doctor he advised her to give up her two packs of cigarettes a day. She just laughed at him and carried on puffing. Most people smoked heavily in those days.

One night, just after midnight, while I was still knitting, I heard a thud from her room and then silence. I was nervous about disturbing her and went to ask Vladimir what he thought I should do. He just grumbled about being woken up and went back to sleep. I tiptoed to her door and listened for a while. Hearing nothing I knocked and asked if she needed anything. At that moment Vladimir appeared behind me, realising something was wrong. I quietly opened the door and saw her lying, face down, next to the bed. Vladimir watched, speechless, as I turned her over and tried to find her pulse. There was no doubt she was dead.

She'd told me previously what clothes she wanted to be dressed in when she went and so we laid her on the bed, lit a candle and changed her. When dawn came the doctor told us she'd had a heart attack. Although her going meant I was relieved of many duties around the house, the place seemed empty without her and it was a long time before I went back into her room.

Rumours began to circulate that this had been a mysterious death and I was called in again by the authorities to be investigated.

'Where did you get the money to buy the house?'

'Can you prove you didn't kill her?'

The neighbours were asked about our relationship and most of them said I was a good person, especially those who brought their children for breakfast every morning.

Vladimir became very silent and distant without his card-playing partner. Even Hennie couldn't persuade him to sit down and have his meals with us. He always ate after we'd left the kitchen, leaving as much mess behind him as he could, as if he wanted to show me who was boss. He grew more resentful as my pregnancy became more obvious. Although I knew it would be hard, I was looking forward to having another baby. My two girls were such a joy to me.

One cold night I realised my time had come and I needed to get to the hospital. I got up and dressed. I had no winter coat. The pains made it difficult to tie my shoelaces but eventually I managed. By the time I reached our gate and was trying to unlock it Vladimir had materialised behind me, still not saying a word. It was slippery under foot and difficult to walk. I kept falling over but he didn't try to help me up, just waited as I struggled back to my feet. As we got nearer to the hospital a passing man asked if I needed any help.

'No thanks,' I said, not wanting to anger Vladimir. 'I'm all right.'

'Who are you, what do you want?' Vladimir demanded.

'Can't you see, the woman could give birth at any moment. She needs someone to help her. If you're the husband shame on you.'

He turned to walk away and Vladimir lifted his fist to strike but slipped and fell. By that time I was ringing the hospital bell and the door was opened by a friend of mine. Vladimir turned on his heel and went home to look after the girls. Less than twenty minutes later our son was born.

The next morning, on his way to work, Vladimir rang the bell to ask whether the baby had arrived.

'You have a son,' my friend shouted from the window.

He turned and walked away without saying a word and five minutes later he came back to ask again what the baby was, as if he couldn't believe his ears. He never came to visit me, but the girls did, and on the fifth day my sister-in-law, Maslinca, came to take me home.

The baby's name was registered as Strashmir, but the girls decided they were going to call him Mickie. Vladimir showed no interest in him at all, despite the girls' efforts to involve him. By this stage Laurie was twelve and Hennie nine and they were able to help me in many ways.

As the weeks went past I was worried that Mickie didn't seem to be growing as he should and took him to see the doctor. She tested my breast milk and said it wasn't good.

'You must have been through some very unpleasant experiences,' she told me. 'You need to find some cow's milk for him.'

I asked all the neighbours if they knew of anyone with a cow that had recently calved and one of them gave me a cup of milk. Mickie was so weak I couldn't persuade him to take even a few diluted drops, but when the girls got home they helped me and he suddenly spluttered into life and started drinking. Maslinca found a woman with a cow. She lived some way away but sold milk at seven each morning and evening.

Everyone who came to see Mickie remarked on how

much he looked like Vladimir, including my mother-in-law. Once she'd spoken Vladimir seemed to sigh with relief, as if she was the only person he was willing to believe. From then on he never doubted that Mickie was his.

Now each morning I had to fit in fetching Mickie's milk before getting the children off to school and opening up the breakfast shop, which always had a hungry queue outside by the time I got there. There was always some new official interrogating me as I tried to mind my own business and get all my chores done.

Mickie thrived on cow's milk and turned into a wonderful child, smiling all the time and hardly ever crying. The girls treated him like a doll, dressing and undressing him and singing him songs.

Vladimir became chairman of the local National Front and was given a radio set that was tuned permanently to the local Communist party broadcasting station. In between the news bulletins they played music and Mickie would happily sit listening as I got on with my chores. He created the most joyful atmosphere in the house, even managing to make Vladimir smile.

When Hennie persuaded their father to take them to the local visiting fair Vladimir suggested Mickie went too, startling all of us. As soon as Mickie was dressed and ready Laurie said, 'Mummy, aren't you coming as well, now that we're taking Mickie with us?'

I would have loved to. I hadn't been to any kind of entertainment for years.

'No,' Vladimir said hurriedly, 'she'll have to clean up while we're away.'

I waved them off with a smile then went indoors and sat down to cry. Was I too ugly to be seen with? Did he really hate me so much? I couldn't understand why he treated me the way he did, and if ever I tried to ask what I had done wrong he just ignored me, or grew angry and hit me.

Although we seldom made love, I found I was pregnant again a year later and dreaded telling Vladimir. I chose a moment when the girls were in their room, hoping he would be too ashamed to beat me with them in the house. He was just as furious as before.

'How can you abandon your children to go out meeting your lover?' he wanted to know. He was certain once again that he wasn't the father. Nothing could convince him I was innocent and he threw every insult he could think of at me. There was no reasoning with him.

I had stopped working when Mickie was born, so I could look after him. As soon as he was a year old, Vladimir told me I must go back again.

'Who'll take care of Mickie?' I asked.

'The government are providing crèches for children up to three, to help working mothers,' he said. 'There are only two in the town but as he's our third child he'll most likely get a place.'

'It won't be easy for me to keep the house going,' I warned, 'after working for ten hours.'

'That's your problem. I've been going to work every day for years now, no one takes pity on me.'

'When you come home all you do is enjoy yourself with your doves,' I said.

He punched me hard.

'That's none of your business.'

As I pulled myself up and went to wash the blood from my face his friend, the dove-mate, rushed in, saying, 'Did you hear?' He stopped as he saw me. 'What have you done?' He turned to Vladimir. 'How could you, in her condition?'

Vladimir pushed him out into the garden. 'Come and see my two new chicks, they're a wonderful pair.'

'No. I would never have believed you could be so brutal,' the man said. 'You're worse than my father. I'm going and I'm never coming back again.'

Losing his friend made him even more furious, kicking over everything that came in his way.

'Hey, what's wrong with you?' our neighbour laughed from over the fence. 'Have you met a witch?'

'Worse,' my husband answered, continuing to feed his doves.

Vladimir arranged a job for me through his National Front friends at a factory for making cotton reels. It was three miles away and operated a three-shift system. I was to start on the night shift, working six days a week. The work was hard and dangerous; accidents were happening all the time and many of the workers lost fingers or hands. For a fortnight I worked at the factory during the night and looked after Mickie during the day, never getting more than two hours' sleep.

They told me there was a place at the crèche where I should drop him off on my way to work on a Monday morning, and he could stay all week. He was only a year old and the girls and I never wanted to be parted from him for even a moment. He was such a joyful child. But what choice did I have if Vladimir insisted?

The staff at the crèche wouldn't allow me in to see where he would be staying.

'At the end of the week you can take him home to bathe him and change his clothes,' the woman on the gate told me.

'Won't he have a bath at least once a day?' I asked.

'You must be crazy!' she laughed, showing a row of rotten teeth. 'Be satisfied that we'll take care of him and feed him while you're at work.'

With a heavy heart I passed him over and watched as she carried him away, his hand stretched out to me, his little face distorted with sobs. I too cried all the way through my shift.

'You'll soon get used to it,' the older women assured me. 'We've all been through that.'

At home the girls cried too, but their father didn't say a word. The week seemed to last a year. The next Saturday I was on the day shift.

'We'll meet you, Mummy, when you come out of work,' the girls said, 'and bring Mickie home with you.'

My shift seemed to last forever, but eventually the bell rang and I rushed out. The girls were already at the gates of the crèche as they promised. We pressed the bell and waited. After what seemed like an age one of the carers came out, looking irritated by the interruption.

'You can't take him home this week,' she told us. 'He has measles. He's under quarantine.'

'For how long?' I asked, horrified.

'I can't tell you exactly,' she said. 'At least another fifteen days.'

With that she turned away.

'Is he all right?' I shouted after her. 'Tell us about him.'

'Of course,' she called back as she disappeared through the door. 'We take good care of all of them, like our own children.'

We cried almost all the way home. Vladimir said nothing that evening and I later discovered he'd been told about Mickie the day before but hadn't wanted to tell us.

Every day I went to the gates to ask how my little boy was. Usually they just shouted down to me from the top window 'He's all right', then vanished, slamming the window behind them. On the thirty-sixth day a woman carried him out to me. He said nothing when he saw me, just put his little arms round my neck and squeezed with all his might, which wasn't much. The woman handed me a bag of clothes.

All the way home I talked to him, but Mickie didn't seem to notice. When I put him on the floor at home he fell over. Thinking I'd dropped him I apologised and lifted him, but he sank to the ground again with a moan. He was too weak to stand on his own two feet. He was deathly pale, but I assumed that was because of the measles. Crawling into a corner he played silently with his home-made wooden train.

When his sisters came home they rushed to see him and for the first time since arriving he smiled, seeming to trust them. But still he said nothing. I decided he must be scared after all he'd been through. When Vladimir came home Mickie crawled further into his corner, trembling and shaking his hands and his head. He didn't want anyone to touch him and we could hardly persuade him to eat, just a few spoons of soup. When the girls helped me undress him for his bath we discovered he was just skin and bones.

He seemed to enjoy the bath, smiling when the girls poured water over him or washed his tiny fingers and toes. I lifted him out and left his sisters to put his pyjamas on, even though it was early for bedtime. When we unpacked his bag we discovered that half the clothes weren't his and half of them were so filthy and ragged I had to throw them away. If I'd had any alternative I would have thrown them all away.

The next morning he cried when the girls left for school and crawled back into his corner. Since he only seemed to feel safe there I brought him some breakfast, but all he wanted was to hold a piece of dry bread in his hand, sucking on it from time to time.

My next-door neighbour, Ivanca, came to call with her five-year-old daughter.

'They give them bits of dry bread to keep them quiet in those places,' Ivanca explained. 'Most of them they tie to chairs all day.'

'But he's so weak,' I said.

She shrugged, 'He would be after so long in there.'

I could hardly bear to think that I had done such a thing to my own baby. I didn't care how angry Vladimir became with me, Mickie was never going back to that place.

Chapter Thirteen
Family Disgrace

I had to work for one more week in order to qualify for help from the state when the next baby was born, but I told Vladimir that was all I was prepared to do. He could see I was adamant. The girls were so keen to have me and Mickie back home they agreed to look after their little brother while I did six more nightshifts, and Ivanca agreed to pop in from time to time and check that everything was OK. Vladimir always liked to look the good parent in the girls' eyes, so he gave in.

That week I literally ran home at the end of every shift, terrified of what I would find, but each day Mickie grew a little stronger and I was able to get a couple of hours' sleep in the afternoons while my little carers remained on duty, before I headed back to the factory for the next shift.

When my mother heard I was having another baby she actually managed to make the journey to see me. I was nervous about how Vladimir would react, but he controlled

his temper, and the girls were thrilled to see their grandmother. As soon as I stopped work I had to go back to my
duties for the National Front and I was working with the
ration coupons when my birth pains started. It seemed that
this child was in a hurry. Laurie came home from school
just in time to take over the distribution of the coupons and
I set off on the long walk to the maternity hospital, which
had recently been moved further from our house. My
mother came with me and Vladimir didn't even ask where
we were going.

Half way there I realised I couldn't walk another step
and Mum flagged down a passing phaeton. Because I
wasn't screaming the nurses didn't think there was any
urgency and went on gossiping amongst themselves instead
of calling the midwife. When the midwife did come she was
horrified to see how far on I was and that the baby needed
turning round. She was a good midwife and succeeded in
saving my third little girl.

'I'm going to call her Rosa, after you,' I told Mum.

'That's wonderful,' she said, 'I would really like to see
her christened in church.'

'I suppose I might be able to manage that,' I replied,
doubtfully. The state didn't approve of religious christenings
and I was worried about getting into any more trouble.

When we got her home we put Rosa in Mickie's cot.
He was going to have to sleep with one of his big sisters
from now on. A few minutes later he came into the kitchen

to look for us and uttered his first words since coming home from the crèche.

'Baby ...' he said, pointing to the other room, 'crying.'

Now that I had four children I was allowed by law to take four portions of the breakfasts that I doled out to other families every morning. We needed that additional food badly.

Once again my mother-in-law told Vladimir that the new baby looked like him.

'All your children look like you,' she said, 'they're all beautiful like you are. I'm proud of them.'

Thankfully, he believed her.

Vladimir's youngest brother Josef was doing his military service and the first the family knew that something had gone wrong was when the authorities came looking for him. Josef had vanished. My mother-in-law was interrogated and a week later I was told I was not needed for the distribution of ration coupons any more. They could give no reason, just told me that another woman would take over. I also had 'no right' to the free breakfasts for my children any more. I remained silent, knowing that arguing always got people into more trouble.

Vladimir was silent most of the time anyway, but he started to mention that people at his work were being sacked or sent to less well-paid jobs in remote towns. Sometimes he would say that he'd heard there was going to be a clearance among the members of the Communist party. I was surprised he wanted to discuss such matters with me.

Both Vladimir's parents died within a few months of each other. His father died first of throat cancer and then his mother became ill. The daughters who lived with her decided it would be a waste of money to send her to hospital, so they kept her at home. We couldn't afford to go and visit her when she was ill.

One evening Vladimir returned from work too upset to eat. He went to bed early and when I asked if he was unwell he just grunted at me from beneath the blankets to leave him alone. I heard him going out during the night and he didn't come back for a long time. Eventually he told me he was going to leave the ammunition factory and look for other work. I was surprised, knowing he quite liked his job.

'I'm fed up with the attitude my superiors have towards me,' was all he said.

'It's difficult to find work nowadays,' I reminded him, 'particularly as you haven't mastered any other profession.'

'It's time for you to take over the duty of earning bread for the family,' he snapped, 'including me.'

In the end I found out from the wife of George, one of Vladimir's colleagues, that they had both been sacked. Vladimir's crimes had been to be married to a foreigner and to have a brother who had disappeared from the army. The two men went searching for work every day and sometimes they would get something for a day or two, but the jobs never paid as much as they'd earned as foremen. Eventually Vladimir suggested we sell the house and move to Sofia.

'With friends and relatives to help,' he said, 'maybe it will be easier to find work.'

'The house actually belongs to the children,' I reminded him, frightened of losing the one bit of security we had. 'You go to Sofia and find work and a place to live and then we'll join you. We'll find some decent people to rent the house from us and we can use the money to pay the rent in Sofia.'

We argued for some time. He accused me of wanting to make our lives as miserable as possible and insisted that selling the house was now the only thing that would save us.

'How could you even think I'm such a horrible person?' I wanted to know. 'You've beaten me almost to death, treated me so badly, and still I've stuck with you. As for the children I would readily give my life for them, you know that!'

'Do you think I wouldn't, you stupid woman? I love them more than you do.'

'I hope so,' I replied, trying to keep calm.

'If we don't sell the house we'll die of hunger.'

'What would we have done if the kids hadn't inherited the house?' I wanted to know.

'But they have and the best thing we can do is to take the papers and see how to proceed with the sale tomorrow.'

'What about the kids, aren't you going to ask them first?'

'They're too young to understand. One day they'll be thankful to own a house in Sofia.'

'Alright, you go and find work in Sofia, a house to buy, and we'll follow.'

'How can I go without money?' he demanded.

'I don't know. You've never told me how much you earn or what you do with your money. Whatever you've given me, penny by penny, couldn't be anything near the whole of your wages. You must have saved up, at least enough for the journey to Sofia.'

Infuriated, he picked up a piece of wood and began beating me, making me shout with surprise and pain. The girls woke up and came running in, throwing themselves between us, begging him to stop. Hurling the stick to one side he strode off and they helped me to get up and wash off the blood, their cheeks streaked with tears. I couldn't lift my arm and thought that my shoulder had been dislocated. Laurie made a sling, as she'd been taught at school.

'Don't move your arm until it gets better,' she warned me. I wished I could.

They helped me to the bedroom where we found Mickie quietly crying.

'It's all right,' I tried to reassure him. 'I'll soon be better.'

'But why?' he asked, still sobbing.

'Do you want to come in to my bed?' Hennie asked. She knew just how to comfort Mickie, and he let her carry him away.

A few weeks later Vladimir told me that every

employer in town had been instructed not to engage him. The situation was getting worse every day. We now only had two chickens left, so soon we wouldn't even have eggs. I had no option but to give in and allow him to sell the house so we could move to Sofia. We went to see a solicitor, an elderly gentleman who one of the girls' teachers had recommended.

'I think you would be making a great mistake if you try to sell the house,' he warned. 'It's in trust to the children and only the mother can execute the sale on their behalf. The mother can then only draw half of the sum from the bank and not for six months at the earliest.'

When we got home Vladimir disappeared, returning to announce he'd found someone who would agree to give him half the price of the house in advance if they could move in straight away. The price was very low. The family came to see the house that afternoon. They were nice people and there was nothing I could do to stop him going ahead. A week later we moved into one room to make space for the new owners, our furniture packed like it was in a warehouse. We had only one bed between us.

We sent the two older girls to my mother and grandmother and Vladimir promised to find us a house in Sofia. I'd heard so many of his promises I didn't hold out much hope. Saying goodbye to the girls broke my heart, although I tried to keep up their hopes that we would soon all be together again. Mickie cried his eyes out. I knew Vladimir was planning to go without leaving me any of the money from the sale, so I waited until other people were there to say goodbye and asked him to leave something to buy food for the three of us. Wanting them to think he was a good husband and father, he left me enough for a week.

'Oh, come on,' the wife laughed, 'these two little children need much more, at least now you have money to give them.'

Grudgingly he handed over enough for another week.

'After all,' I said, 'it is their money.'

He picked up his cases, gave me a threatening look and walked out without even kissing the children.

Once more we were reliant on the kindness of others. The new owners of our home would bring us food when they were cooking. The wife would sometimes look after Rosie while Mickie and I stood in the queues for rations. She also paid me to knit pullovers and jackets for them. With Vladimir away, at least I wasn't living in fear of being hit all the time and both the children were healthy. Then a terrible influenza broke out in the area. Medication was rare and a lot of people were dying. At one time our landlord's whole family was sick and I was trying to nurse all of them at once, changing compresses, rubbing them with natural remedies and cooking soups. Then my neighbour, Ivanca, and her daughter fell ill and I had to nurse them too. They were all just starting to recover when the three of us were struck down. I hardly had the strength to stand up to tend the children and I was terrified they would slip away. Ivanca and my landlady became our carers; we all survived by looking after one another.

For three months I heard nothing from Vladimir, although I got a lot of letters from Mum and the girls, who were having a wonderful time together.

It was impossible to keep an eye on the children all the time and one day Mickie, and the little girl he'd been playing with, disappeared. He'd only been wearing his knickers at the time. The little girl's grandmother and I searched everywhere with increasing panic and eventually the whole street was involved. After several hours a man appeared at the end of the road holding the two three-year-olds' hands. Both of them were black from head to toe. He'd found them standing on the railway platform watching the trains. The station porter had told him they'd been there for hours; they had even been for a ride on one of the locomotives.

'Why did you run away, Mickie?' I asked, once I'd got him into the bath.

'I didn't run away,' he said, 'I only went to the station.'

'But why?'

'I wanted to see if my big sisters were coming back.'

'How did you find your way there?'

'By the sound of the whistle.'

'I've never heard such a clever little boy,' said my land-lord, who'd been listening from the door.

'How would you have come back?' I asked Mickie.

'The same way. I noticed all the houses and shops.'

'But why did you take Kitza with you?'

'She's my friend. I asked her and she came.'

Our landlord invited us to supper and lifted his glass in a toast. 'This is for the health of that wonderful little boy,' he boomed. 'I'm sure he will become a great man and I hope one day to have such wonderful grandchildren myself.'

I was so proud of all my children; at moments like that they made all the struggles and suffering seem worthwhile.

A few days later I received an official invitation to go to the town council. I had no idea what they wanted but a familiar feeling of dread filled my stomach. I took both the little children with me at the appointed time.

'Where's your husband?' was the councillor's first question.

'He's gone to look for some work.'

'But where?'

'I don't know. Wherever he finds some.'

'Well,' he sneered, 'you've got yourself into a fine mess, haven't you?'

I said nothing.

'That brother-in-law of yours played the role of patriot so cleverly while he was in the gymnasium here, but he turned out to be a filthy traitor!'

'Why a traitor?' I asked. 'I thought he was killed during a shooting in the barracks.' In fact my brother-in-law had escaped and run away to Turkey.

'Who told you that?'

'I think my mother-in-law did.'

'Ahh, and what did your husband say?' His tone was so threatening Rosie started crying and Mickie pressed himself close to me.

'Why have you brought those bastards with you?' he shouted, making them both cry louder.

'I can't leave them at home alone,' I said quietly. 'They aren't bastards.'

He began accusing me of things I couldn't even imagine. Were we never going to be free of this?

Chapter Fourteen
Like the Gypsies

By the time Vladimir had been gone seven months I'd sold everything I could, even things I had cherished. The children were growing out of their clothes and shoes. Rosie was starting to stand alone and soon would be running around with her brother.

Late one evening I heard someone trying to open the gate, which the landlord had fixed with a strong lock. When I heard the landlord challenging the stranger I went back to bed, sure he would deal with it. A few minutes later there was a knocking on our door.

'Don't be afraid,' a voice shouted, 'it's only your long-lost husband.'

Mickie and I jumped up and opened the door and there was Vladimir in new clothes and brand new shoes, all his belongings in one small case.

'Where are my sisters?' Mickie asked as he clung to his father.

Not recognising him, Rosie hung on to me.

'This is our Daddy,' Mickie told her importantly.

'Daddy?' she said and after a few seconds' thought lifted her arms up.

He told us he had found a nice house and as soon as the deeds were handed over we would leave. I told him I'd been called in front of the councillor a few times and he had scared and threatened me.

'He won't see you from now on, nobody will harm you any more,' Vladimir assured me.

The next day we went to see the solicitor and I discovered that Vladimir had spent all the money he'd received so far and still owed money to the vendor of the house we were buying. We didn't even have enough money to hire transport to move us to the city. The new owners of our old house agreed to let us stay a few more days, but it couldn't be any longer than that because their sons were coming to live with them. Changes in the taxation laws were also going to eat into the rest of the money when it finally came. All this, Vladimir informed me, was my fault. We spent our last two days and nights in our neighbour Ivanca's kitchen, dozing on chairs while the children squashed on to the bench, our belongings standing in the yard outside.

The goods train delivered us to Sofia at dawn and we were unloaded on to the platform while Vladimir went in search of another cart to take us to the new house. I sat on the platform, cuddling the little ones, covered with a blanket. A soldier, delivering something to the station, agreed to take as much of our heavy stuff as he could fit into his lorry. It was three hours before Vladimir came back with a donkey cart for me, the children and the last of our belongings, by which time it was raining. The gypsy driver loaded as much as his cart could take and we carried the rest. Vladimir was carrying more than any donkey could have managed and I had Rosie on my back, Mickie in one hand and a bag in the other as we trudged towards our new home.

For two hours we walked, with Rosie slipping off my shoulders and Mickie constantly stumbling on the stony road. Every few yards Vladimir had to shout to the driver to stop in order to pick up things that were falling off the cart. By the time we arrived we were wet to the skin, exhausted, cold and hungry.

The house that Vladimir had talked of so glowingly was actually only a part of a house. It was one normal-sized room and a smaller one. It was built of stone and the floor was earth. There was a corridor that led to the other part of the house, and we had the rights to half of it, although we were going to have to build the dividing wall ourselves. It was less than half the size of the house we'd sold.

Over the following week we whitewashed the walls, found some second-hand linoleum to cover the floors and squeezed as much furniture in as we could. The girls came home and Mickie was overjoyed to see them. We were a complete family once more. Vladimir found work in a factory a long way from the house. The work was harder than before, but at least the wages were similar to what he had been earning. The best thing about it was that the authorities weren't bothering us and we were being left to get on with our lives.

Now we were often eating the 'gypsy pie', consisting of bread and oil, which had so shocked me when I first came to Bulgaria sixteen years earlier.

Sometimes Vladimir's family would invite him out to the country to get some vegetables, apples or eggs. He usually declined, being too tired from work, and when he did go he took the children only so they could help him carry.

By now many other people were arriving in the capital in search of work, doubling the population. Everyone was splitting up their houses to make more room but sometimes they didn't bother to register and got into trouble, even going to prison and never returning. New laws were imposed and passports were introduced. One law was about citizenship, and decreed that everyone had to live in the place where he or she was born, unless they were specialists or very necessary for certain industries, mostly working for Russia. Everyone was being scrutinised, back as far as seven generations. Some people found ways round the law because they had relatives in positions of power or were rich enough to buy their citizenship. Corruption sprouted everywhere. We were among those who had no rights at all, even though Vladimir had been born in Sofia and had finished school there.

I had just sent the older girls off to school one morning and was still feeding the younger ones when someone banged on the door. When I opened it two militiamen pushed their way in, looking around the room.

'Where's your husband?' one of them demanded.

The children clung to me and silent tears ran down Rosie's face.

'He's at work. What's this all about?'

'You have to leave the town within twenty-four hours,' he shouted. 'That's what it's all about.'

'Why? What have we done?'

'You'd like to live in the capital, wouldn't you?' he sneered.

'This is our house, we have four children ...'

'That has no significance at all,' he said as he walked out. 'By this time tomorrow you must have left altogether.'

I was stunned. I couldn't even cry. I just sat down as I heard them march away, hugging the children to me. A few moments later a light tap on the window made me jump. It was one of the inmates of the neighbouring 'Home for Elderly Invalids'. She had seen the visitors and wanted to know what they wanted. I didn't know her well and wasn't sure how much to tell her.

'They wanted to know where my husband was,' I told her.

'They're horrible,' she spat. 'They're killers, all of them. They can do anything and they don't care a damn. A person's life is nothing to them! You must be very careful. Before they came we were given three meals a day, now we only get tea and bread for breakfast and something for supper. That's it! They say we shouldn't eat too much in case we get fat, which would be bad for our health. So many of us have died since they arrived. I hate them, but I have nowhere to go. God help me and all of us.'

She finished by making the forbidden sign of the cross. Someone called her name from outside and she hurried away.

The rest of the day passed in a dream as I tried to work out what to do. When the girls arrived home from school I heard them giggling as they came into the garden. They were so good at getting over unpleasant events and finding the fun in life. Mickie immediately told them what had happened. I tried to make it sound less frightening but they knew how serious it was. When Vladimir arrived home his face was pale and his hands were trembling.

'You're home early today, Daddy,' Hennie said, laying a plate in front of him.

'Yes,' he almost whispered.

'Eat, while it's still warm.' I told him, putting off the moment when I would have to hear whatever news he was carrying.

He managed only a few spoonfuls of soup before breaking down into sobs, burying his face in his hands. The girls jumped up and cuddled him and the little ones joined in. It was a while before we were all sufficiently recovered to start piecing things together. He'd been told the same as me and had been sacked from his work. Vladimir was devastated and the girls bewildered. The little ones were wondering what was going on and I was trying to work out how we were going to start picking up the threads of our life. Then there was a knock at the door.

One of the girls' teachers had decided to pay us an unannounced visit to see how they were getting on in their new school. 'You have wonderful children,' he told us, 'congratulations. I wish that at least half the class were like them.'

For a moment the girls forgot their troubles and smiled. It didn't cross their minds that they might never see him again. Thinking that a teacher might have some answers for us, Vladimir eventually told him what was happening to us.

'It's not legal to be given such short notice,' he said, amazed, 'especially with four underage children. You should go to the headquarters of the militia to appeal, especially as you were born and brought up in Sofia.'

'Maybe you could go to your cousin,' I suggested, 'he's in a high position in the Ministry of Defence.'

'Wonderful idea,' the teacher exclaimed. 'Come on, I'm going down to the centre myself, let's go together and on the way I'll explain a few ways you could defend yourselves.'

'Don't you think it's rather late?' Vladimir asked.

'Not at all,' the teacher laughed. 'We'll find somebody to help you.'

Reluctantly Vladimir agreed to go, although he thought it was absolutely useless. He came back late, not having been able to see anyone.

The next morning it was raining, adding to our gloom as I sent the girls off to school as usual.

'Will you be back by this afternoon?' I asked Vladimir as he left. I didn't like the idea of being on my own if the militiamen came back as promised.

'We'll see,' he muttered. 'I have a lot of things to arrange.'

During the morning I noticed the woman we had bought the house from coming to our gate several times and trying to look through our window. Later the old woman from the home came to see me.

'I heard that the chief of the local militia is her cousin,' she said when I told her about our landlady. 'They grew up together under the roof of their grandparents. She has used him to help her in her dubious deals ever since he was given this post.'

I wasn't good company that morning and after a while she left, wishing me good luck. By late afternoon, when the militia returned, the girls still hadn't come home because they were rehearsing for their end-of-term concert.

were already broken. The girls had cried quietly as we worked. I'd tried not to, but there was an uncomfortable lump in my throat, which made it hard to talk.

'What's happened here?' he asked, looking around bemused.

'Father, couldn't you have done anything?' Laurie asked. 'Our teacher said he had sent you to somebody who could help.'

'Oh, stop that nonsense,' Vladimir snapped. 'He can't help us.'

'What are we going to do now?' Hennie asked as she helped me to wrap the little ones up in a blanket to protect them from the drizzle that was falling steadily.

'Why didn't you ask them for an allowance or something?' he asked me. 'Or a receipt with a stamp from the council?'

'Perhaps if you'd been here they might have given you something,' I suggested.

'Yes, Father,' Laurie piped up, 'where were you all this time?'

'That's my business!' he snapped and for a moment I thought he was going to hit her.

'Are we going to sleep here?' Mickie asked. 'It's cold.'

'I'm hungry,' Rosie sobbed.

'I think we could all do with a bite,' I said, 'nobody's eaten yet.'

'Do you think I have?' Vladimir demanded angrily.

'We saved some soup,' the girls said, 'let's just sit on the doorstep and eat it.'

They marched down the garden with heavy steps, bringing the mud with them. Our landlady emerged with a wide grin on her face and greeted her cousin, their leader. They all laughed loudly together and then came to the door. They didn't bother knocking.

'Come out all of you!' their leader shouted.

I felt as cold as a corpse as he looked in and saw just me and the two little children.

'Where are the rest hiding? I told you, you must leave this house or I'll chase you out and lock the door; then you won't be able to take anything with you.'

I could hear the landlady chuckling with the other three militiamen.

'I'm waiting for my husband to return,' I said.

'Where's he gone?' he roared.

'To work.'

'You're lying. I heard yesterday he was fired, for good. So where is he?'

'I don't know,' I said, and it was the truth.

'What about the kids, where are they hiding?'

'They're at school.'

I noticed that a number of the inmates from the invalid home had gathered at the fence, craning their necks to see what was going on. The old woman I'd spoken to was at the front.

'Well, you'll have to start getting your things out, and hurry, I can't wait all day.'

He sat down in a chair and folded his arms.

'No,' I said, 'I'm not going to move anywhere. This is our house. We have nowhere else to go. We can't stay on the street with four children. I'm sure my husband will be able to prove that we have the right to live here.'

'You and rights?' he bellowed. 'You'll make me die laughing!'

The landlady and the other militiamen joined in his merriment.

'I hope you all burst,' a voice shouted from the crowd outside.

'Who said that?' He jumped up and ran out towards them. They all drew silently back.

'Aren't you ashamed of yourself?' the old woman shouted. 'How can you be so cruel to tiny children?'

He lurched towards her, trembling with rage, but a warden caught her and pulled her back out of his reach.

'Don't take any notice of her,' the warden said, putting a finger to her temple. 'She's not right up here.'

'Then make her shut her damn mouth before I get too nervous.'

The other militiamen were still laughing at the scene as if they were watching a play.

'What are you sniggering at?' He turned on them. 'Get going and throw their rags out of here!'

I was sitting on the bed with Rosie on my lap and Mickie leaning on my back. I didn't move as they threw a couple of chairs out.

'Not here,' the woman shouted, 'this is my part of the garden!'

'Over there,' her cousin ordered the men.

At that moment the girls came through the gate.

'Look what these bad people are doing,' Mickie said and started crying.

'Sshhh,' Laurie picked him up to stop him talking. I could hear the mutterings of the crowd from the home growing louder as their warden tried to push them back inside.

'Poor woman.'

'Such nice children.'

'How can they be so merciless?'

'Whatever will they do now?'

'Monsters!'

'Shame on you!'

'May God send you to hell!'

'The plague will attack you and you will die!'

Other passers-by were stopping to see what was going on and joining in the abuse. The chief grew tired of it and disappeared into his cousin's kitchen for coffee, leaving his men to finish the job. Once everything was in the garden they fixed a large padlock to the door, locked it, gave it a couple of tugs to ensure it was secure and then marched off, laughing.

By the time Vladimir arrived we had tied most of our clothes, towels and bed linen into bundles and pushed our plates, cups and other breakables in between. Many things

'Like the gypsies do?' Mickie asked.

The girls sat on the doorstep, each with a little one on their lap, and I put the bowl on a chair in front of them and gave them a spoon each. I then sat on a piece of wood beside them, holding an umbrella over their heads with one hand and some bread with the other. Vladimir paced around like an angry lion as he ate. Then I took my turn.

'We could get a cart and take these things to your village,' I suggested. 'We could use your parents' old rooms, may they rest in peace.'

'Nonsense,' he snapped. 'What would we do there with no money, nowhere to work and no school for the kids?'

'At least we'll be out of the rain,' Hennie said. 'And our uncles promised to help us if we needed it, didn't they?'

'They can hardly feed their own families, how could they help us?'

At that moment Vladimir's cousin, Ivan, who lived at the other end of Sofia, came in through the gate. He offered to help and asked where we were going to go.

'We'll have to go to my mother-in-law in Mezdra,' Vladimir said. I was stunned.

'How can we all fit into one room?' I asked. 'They can't feed us either. They don't produce any vegetables or eggs like your brothers do.'

'At least there's a school and some possibility of work.'

'The room isn't very big,' the girls said, 'but they wouldn't turn us out.'

'Send the girls there by train now,' Ivan suggested.

'Elena and the little ones can stay with my wife while you and I pack everything up and send it off after them.'

'I don't have that much money,' Vladimir muttered.

'Oh dear, well I'll ask my brother-in-law to lend you some for the fares, but you'll have to pay it back as soon as possible.'

Despite Vladimir's reluctance to borrow money or allow me to go anywhere without him, he wasn't able to come up with a better plan. The girls went off on the train, assuring me they would be all right. Ivan found a cart and I helped them load it as the light faded and the rain grew heavier. Ivan's wife was a kind woman and lit the stove to warm the little ones. Her two boys played with them while we cooked vegetable soup and opened our hearts to one another.

The two men returned at dawn, wet and hungry, and we agreed to get a couple of hours' sleep and travel on the afternoon train. I felt ashamed that we were going to have to be a burden to my increasingly frail mother, instead of being a help to her.

Chapter Fifteen
Head of the Household

By the time we got to Mezdra my mother had found a cheap room just round the corner where she and the girls could sleep. The rest of us would stay with my grandmother in their one room and kitchen. When we were told that our belongings had arrived at the station my grandmother took us to a neighbour who agreed to lend us a cart, but not the donkey to pull it. So another night was given over to loading, pulling and pushing to and fro. By the time we returned the cart to its owner at sunrise, I was covered in cuts and bruises from where I'd stumbled on the uneven stones.

The smaller things my grandmother had taken inside, the heavy items were piled up outside and she stood guard over them all night. The following evening she cooked the sort of meal that we hadn't had for ages. Both she and my mother seemed happy to have us there, but it still felt like we'd invaded their lives. That night Vladimir went with my mother and the girls to make more room for the rest of us to lie down.

After I had put the little ones to bed my grandmother showed me where the food cupboard was, containing the flour, cooking fat, sugar and vegetables. She explained which pots and pans she used for what and where she usually went shopping. Then she gave me a bunch of keys.

'From now on,' she said, 'you will be the main manager of the household.'

I went to bed, exhausted, with Rosie next to me and Mickie at the foot of the bed. I must just have dropped off when I heard someone clanking around among the pots and pans in the kitchen. I looked across the room and noticed Granny's bed was empty. Worried, I went through to the kitchen and found her trying to get out a basin.

'What is it?' I asked.

'Cold water,' was all she could say.

I took her back to bed and fetched the water for her. She wanted a cold compress for her heart. I did as she asked.

'Go and call George,' she said quietly. 'Tell him to bring his syringe.'

George was my godparents' son. He'd studied medicine and had reached a level that was higher than a nurse, but not quite a doctor. He was called an assistant doctor and was allowed to take certain decisions if there wasn't a doctor nearby. I ran across the road and tapped on the window, conveying her message.

'Go back to her quickly,' he said, 'I'm coming.'

Two minutes later he arrived and I held Granny so she could sit up in bed. She pointed to a prescription pinned to a calendar on the wall. George scanned it quickly and then looked back at her.

'Pull up her sleeve, quick.'

I did my best, with trembling fingers, as he filled his syringe and injected it into her arm.

'My heart,' she said in her native German, 'my heart, it will kill me.'

'George, please, what can we do?' I asked, terrified.

'We shall just have to wait a little and see.'

Her head fell heavily on to my shoulder and we laid her down.

'I'll stay with her,' he said. 'I think maybe you should fetch your mother and the landlady. Hurry.'

I ran, panic-stricken, to Mum's room, but the street gate was locked. I shouted for her but there was no answer. I pulled a stone up from the street and banged on the iron gate as I shouted. Eventually the landlady's widowed sister opened her window and asked who I was and what I wanted. I told her and asked her to wake my mother.

I ran back and found George standing beside my grandmother's bed. She was lying flat and her hands were crossed on her chest.

'What happened?'

'I'm sorry,' he said, 'there was nothing more to be done. Her time had come and she knew it. Yesterday she told me what the doctor had told her. It was quick and she didn't suffer.'

I dropped into a chair, completely crushed, as people started to hurry in, first Mum with George's mother, who was Granny's best friend and neighbour, then Granny's landlady. No one could believe it. Granny had always seemed so strong and never complained about her health. Mum sat on the bed, speechless, and laid her head on Granny's hands. She was too shocked to cry. George's mother, Nikolinka, stood next to her, silently wiping her eyes and the landlady dropped to her knees next to the bed, sobbing.

'I think she must be dressed and prepared for the burial,' George broke the silence, 'before she goes too stiff. I'll inform the doctor so he can sign the death certificate.'

In the wardrobe, Mum found a package of clothes which Granny had prepared specially for her burial. As she opened it a savings book fell out with a letter in Granny's handwriting saying, 'This is to pay for my burial'.

Mum broke down. 'What will we do without her?' she wailed.

By this time George's father, Nikola, had arrived. He took the book from Mum's hands as she sobbed inconsolably.

'If you take this to the bank I don't think they'll give you the money,' he said. 'Would you mind if I arranged this?'

She was happy to let him take charge. Granny had helped so many people over the years, old and young, and had never bothered to ask how much they could pay her. Everybody was happy to pay what they could and to attend the burial. Laurie and Hennie took care of the little ones, even though they, too, were crying all the time.

Even without Granny, life had to go on and the rest of us had to continue with the struggle to survive. Over the coming days Mum sold almost all of her jewellery and whatever else she could get a price for, and often George's mother brought us big bowls of food to keep us going. George provided Mum with medication and our landlady gave us a big jugs of sheep's and goat's milk. I carried on knitting to earn as much as possible. I could see that Mum's health was not good, although she was doing her best to cover it up.

When Vladimir applied for a job in the electrical department of the railway company, which was responsible for all the lighting at the stations and along the track, he was told he must get permission from the local Communist party secretary, and was summoned to see him. Vladimir was terrified that they would investigate his whole life, including the incident over his brother, who had still not been found. He came back hours later saying he had been to the office but never got a chance to meet the secretary. The following morning a militiaman banged on the door and walked straight in.

'Why didn't you come to the secretary yesterday?' he shouted at Vladimir angrily. 'You always complain about not being given work anywhere! Now they invite you specially and the comrade secretary waits for you and you're too lazy to come. You should be ashamed of yourself!'

I noticed that one or two passers-by had stopped outside the window, attracted by the shouting.

'I did go there,' Vladimir stuttered, 'but I couldn't find which room to go in.'

'Well, now you'll come with me and I'll show you.'

Once they had gone Nikolinka, George's mother, tapped on the window and told me that her husband had been to see the chief of the electrical department the day before and he had promised to talk to the secretary and convince him to engage Vladimir. That was the way everything was done, by people putting in a good word for others. If you didn't have contacts you didn't have a chance.

Vladimir returned at lunchtime.

'After the "interview" with the party secretary,' he said, 'where they made me feel lower than the ground I was standing on, I was sent to the chief of the electro-department. They explained what my duties were and gave me some working clothes. The trousers were too long and the top was too tight. I was entitled to shoes too, but they didn't have any to fit me.'

He gave me the clothes and I cut some of the material from the trousers and inserted it into the jacket to try to make both fit better. His work was mostly going to be outside in all weathers, but at least there was now the hope of a monthly salary.

A month later he was sent to a small station about forty

miles away. There he was allocated a room in which to sleep during the week, returning home only at weekends. The room was two metres long and one and half metres wide and contained a sofa and a chair. But he said he didn't trust me alone and would come home every night, returning on the train at three in the morning. His mad jealousy cost us money for train tickets, sleepless nights and a lot of inconvenience, but at least we all got a few peaceful hours during the day.

After six months Vladimir was ordered back to the main station near to us, his duties being to maintain the crossing lights and the barriers of the railway tracks for the whole region, twenty-four hours a day.

At two o'clock one morning, two of his colleagues called to take him to repair the crossing lights on the line that passed through the town. It was half-past seven when a man from the small local hospital came to tell me that Vladimir had been taken there. He wasn't able to tell me what had happened, just that I had to hurry. I rushed out, asking Mum to look after the little ones.

I could hear him moaning as I approached the hospital, begging to be helped. I found him lying on the floor on a thin, worn-out blanket just inside the entrance. Two cleaning women were standing over him.

'We're waiting for the ambulance to come from Vratza,' they told me.

'But why have you left him here in the draught?' I asked. 'Why not inside in the warm?'

'They said they were coming and we should be ready for them.'

A doctor heard me shouting and came over. 'It's useless to carry him in again,' he said. 'His pains increase with every movement. Don't worry too much. We did what we could but our hospital is very small and we haven't the necessary equipment. So we're sending him to Vratza. They'll come any moment now.'

I bent over Vladimir, trying to find out what had happened.

'It hurts all over my body,' he moaned. 'I fell from the traffic lights post.'

Eventually the ambulance arrived and the driver told me to lift Vladimir in. I begged the two women to help me. With the help of a male nurse we each took one corner of the blanket and lifted. Once he was comfortable I went to get in too.

'You can't come with us,' the driver told me. 'We have to pick someone else up in another village. There's not enough room.'

As they drove off I heard one of the women say to her friend, 'Poor woman, with four young children.'

I went into the hospital to see if I could discover anything more. They told me he'd been brought in by two tractor drivers, and that he hadn't been able to walk. Apparently he had no visible wounds, just bruising.

As I plodded home I thought about everything that had happened to us since we'd married. Vladimir was certainly not the same man who had first courted me, and his jealousy had nearly driven me mad, especially as I'd never even looked at another man. And then there was the violence. But I knew he'd had a violent upbringing, beaten by his father and brothers, and during his military service, and life had been hard for him over the years, just as it had been for me. He was the father of my four beloved children and that gave us a bond that nothing could break. My main worry now was how would we manage if he couldn't work.

Nikolinka suggested I go to see Vladimir's chief and ask for a free return ticket to Vratza so I could visit him. The chief looked a little embarrassed when I got to his office.

'I wish him the very best,' he said, 'and hope he'll soon be back at work with us again. We do like him.' He gave me a ticket for the next day.

When I arrived at the hospital early the following morning the registrar wouldn't let me in to see him. 'Only Sundays and Thursdays,' she told me.

I didn't go away, just hung around, trying to work out which ward he would be on. A patient was waiting for his wife to bring him something and approached me, asking who it was I wanted to see.

'His name's Vladimir,' I said quietly as the registrar was still watching. 'He was brought here yesterday with great pains.'

'Maybe he's the one in the single room. I'll go and see. If I find out I'll come and tell you. If my wife comes tell her I'll be back.'

He returned just as his wife showed up and told me how I could reach the ward, with a bit of luck. The three of us sat on some chairs by the entrance and waited for a moment when the registrar was distracted by the telephone. Eventually my chance came and I slipped in. I could hear Vladimir moaning with the pain from the corridor and went into the room, shocked by how filthy it was. He was covered up, right over his mouth.

'Why didn't you come earlier?' he grumbled. 'I'm dying here and you don't care.'

'I couldn't get here before and if they see me now they'll chuck me out.'

'The pain is so bad.'

'What happened?'

'I was repairing the lights at the level crossing, my colleagues told me the power was turned off and it was safe for me to work. As soon as I started I felt a tickling, then trembling and I let go of the wires and fell.'

'Why didn't your colleagues help you?'

'I don't know, they ran away. I called out to them but they'd vanished.' I could see he was close to crying.

'Where does it hurt the most?'

'My whole body hurts, but mostly my left leg.'

I uncovered his legs and found an illuminated light bulb, wrapped in newspaper and placed next to them. I couldn't imagine what it was for and was worried that the heat would set light to the paper. I decided not to say anything so as not to scare him. At that moment a cleaner came in.

'What are you doing here?' she asked angrily.

'I came to see my husband.'

'Only on Sunday and Thursday, between two and four o'clock. Now get out before the doctor comes.'

'Don't you think this is dangerous?' I asked, pointing to the light bulb.

'That's none of your business,' she snapped. 'I come to change the newspaper from time to time.'

When I got back I went to see Vladimir's boss again and asked why his fellow workers had deserted him. 'They told me they were scared,' he said. 'After a while they went back to help him but he wasn't there any more.'

'They must have gone back a long time later because the tractor didn't pick him up till half past five. I want you to arrange for him to be sent to the Central Transport Hospital for Railway Workers. He's hardly getting any care where he is now.'

'I'll see what can be done,' he promised, 'although I'm not very strong in the medical department of our ministry.'

'If you hear of some work that I could do, would you please say a good word for me? You know I have a big family to care for and Vladimir won't be able to work for a long time.'

'I will bear that in mind.' He was trying to sound hopeful.

I went back and forth to Vratza as much as I could in the coming weeks, and about a month after Vladimir got there, Nikolinka decided to come with me, bringing biscuits and a box of Turkish delight, which she knew he loved. The registrar stopped us as we went in.

'Your husband isn't here any more,' she announced. 'They sent him to the Central Hospital for Railway Workers.'

At that moment a doctor I'd seen before came past. 'Have you come to take your husband to Sofia?' he asked.

'I didn't even know he would be sent there,' I said.

'We can't do anything for him here, the hospital in Sofia is bigger and better equipped. You should take him as soon as possible.'

I looked at the registrar. 'You told me he'd already been sent.' She looked at the doctor, trying to justify herself. 'That's what I heard.'

'Why didn't anyone tell me till now? If I hadn't come today how would I have known that I must take him to Sofia myself?'

Nikolinka explained our financial situation to the doctor and asked if it wouldn't be possible to take him by ambulance.

'We have only two ambulances now and they can not leave our region. It's up to you to find a way to transport him.'

Nikolinka said we would have to go home and try to organise something. 'Could we see him for a few minutes?'

'Of course,' the doctor said. 'But the sooner you can get him to Sofia the better his chances.'

When we got to Vladimir we told him something was

going to be done for him in Sofia. 'I can't move at all,' he kept saying, 'how will I get there?'

When we got home we went with Nikola, my godfather, to the local railway surgery. 'You're responsible for him,' Nikola insisted, 'he's a railway worker.'

Eventually the doctor and Vladimir's chief engineer arranged for a worker to come with me to Vratza to help get him on the train to Sofia. The ambulance from the Central Hospital would then meet us at the station.

It was a terrible struggle but the worker and I managed to get Vladimir on to the train. Vladimir kept moaning, 'I'm dying, I'll never get there.'

As the train drew into Sofia I looked out of the window, hoping to see the ambulance assistant waiting. There was no one. The worker got off and disappeared as soon as the train stopped, his job finished. The conductor came round checking the wagons and told me we must get out because the train was ready to go to the depot. He knew about Vladimir's disability and after a while offered to help me get him off the train. We laid him on the bare platform and I went in search of the ambulance assistant. I found him waiting at the entrance to the station, grumbling because it had taken me so long to find him.

'Where's the patient?' he asked.

'Lying on the platform.'

'Well, hurry up and bring him here.'

'But he can't move,' I protested, unable to hold back the tears any longer.

'Shame on you,' a passer-by scolded the man. 'Can't you see the woman needs help?'

'It's none of your business,' he snapped back. 'No one pays me for carrying patients.'

'Come on then,' the passer-by said, 'get the stretcher out and I'll help. Not for money but out of humanity, of which you seem to have very little.'

The three of us went back to the platform and lifted Vladimir on to the stretcher, carrying him across three railway lines to the parked ambulance. The assistant pushed the stretcher in and curtly told me there was no room for me to travel inside the vehicle. I ran after it as fast as I could, terrified I would lose sight of it since I had no idea where the hospital was.

When we finally arrived the admissions staff grumbled at me because I hadn't given them the papers from the hospital in Vratza. I handed them over meekly.

'Now you can go,' they said. 'We'll take over from here.'

'Couldn't I help getting him undressed?' I asked.

'That's our business,' they said, carrying him away.

I begged the porter to open the gate for me but he just shouted I must be stupid if I didn't understand that no visitors were allowed, whatever the situation. I was left standing in the street without a penny to pay for my return ticket, over a hundred kilometres from home and at my wits' end.

As I stood there a man came by who recognised me. 'What are you doing here?' he asked.

'Come on, let's see what we can do,' he said when I'd finished my story. I followed him as if in a dream, as he bought me a ticket and we got on the train to Mezdra together. I didn't know how to thank him and promised to return the money the next day.

'You needn't bother too much,' he said. 'Your grandmother has helped my wife so often. She even saved our child's life. I'm glad I can return at least a little for the good deeds she's done me.'

Even after her death, I thought, Granny is still helping me.

Chapter Sixteen

Amputation

I didn't dare tell the children the whole truth of what had happened to Vladimir. They would have been so angry and full of hatred they might well have said something and got the family into trouble. I just told them Daddy was going to need a lot of looking after when he got home.

'I'm sure he will,' I heard my mother mutter in the background.

The following day I went back to Vladimir's boss and told him what had happened. I could see he was embarrassed, even though it wasn't his fault. Later I discovered he too was on the Communist party's blacklist, although at that time they still needed him for his expertise. Then I went to the local railway surgery and told them the whole story. The head doctor assured me he would find out who was responsible and would make sure they were punished.

'I don't think punishment would make anything better for my husband now,' I said.

He promised to keep in touch with his colleagues at the Central Hospital and to keep me informed. On the way home George caught up with me. 'Did you know the woman who cooks for the patients in our surgery is leaving at the end of the week? Why don't you apply for the job?'

'I don't think the party would allow me,' I said, 'and I've never worked as a cook.'

'Oh it isn't difficult,' he assured me. 'Most of them are on a diet anyway, similar to how you cook at home. I'll ask the nurse to give you some advice.'

When I got home I told Mum about the offer and asked if she would be able to help with the kids. 'I'm not very strong, you know,' she said, 'but I would hope I could look after them for a few hours.'

With my stomach full of butterflies I set out to apply. The party secretary kept me waiting for ages before being admitted.

'Who told you about this job?' he shouted as soon as I walked in.

'I heard it from a woman,' I said, 'I don't know her name.'

'Jobs like these are given first of all to OUR people,' he continued to yell. 'What happened to that husband of yours? Where is he now?'

'In hospital, in a critical state,' I whispered.

'He'll have to get better and start working again.'

'I don't think he'll ever be able to work again, that's what the doctor said. I have four children and my mother isn't in the best of health either.'

'That's your problem. I have other important things to do.'

'When may I come and get some information about the job?'

'You can't. Now get out of here! Quick!'

George told me later that the job had gone to the wife of the party secretary of the local railway workers.

'He got his job because he claimed to have proved himself during the German occupation by giving food to the partisans,' George explained. 'Actually everyone knows what really happened. He was looking after his father's sheep in the pasture when some partisans came up and asked him for something. He was so frightened at the sight of their guns he gave them a bag containing a piece of bread, a piece of cheese and an onion. When he told his parents they were as terrified as him and forbade him to say a word to anyone. From then on only the father grazed the sheep. After the war our friend went into town for a job and had the luck to bump into the partisan to whom he'd given his lunch bag. Because he was illiterate he didn't get the job, but he told his father about the meeting. When his father talked about it in the pub that night he learned that if you knew a partisan you could get some benefits. The next day the father went to see the ex-partisans and told them the story and how the Germans had threatened them and how they'd stayed silent. "Then my son risked his life to save the partisans from starvation," the father said, "and now he can't even get a job." So they gave him a director's post, but, not having any education, he made a mess and they had to cover up for him. They tried to give him an education but he was too stupid and idle, so they ended up making him a Communist party chief.'

This man's wife, it seemed, was just as badly educated, and now she'd been given the cook's job. I was deeply disappointed, being the only person in the family who could work at the moment. A few days later, however, George told me that the official's wife had been unable to cope and the job was once again vacant. Mustering my courage, I went back to the party secretary.

'Hmm,' he grunted as I came in. 'You again. I've been thinking about your family and we've decided to close our eyes to certain facts and events in your lives. Above all we're taking pity on your children. We ARE human, you know. So you can take over the job you wanted.

'But beware, the slightest mistake and you will never ever get another job again. Do you understand?' he roared.

I felt stiff, speechless and scared and hardly managed to whisper, 'Yes.'

My new duties meant starting at five-thirty in the morning, so I would have to leave home at five. Having managed to get Mickie and Rosie enrolled into two different nursery schools, I was going to have to find people to take them there in the mornings and pick them up again in the afternoons; I couldn't rely on Mum, she was becoming too weak. I made uniforms for them both from clothes the older girls had outgrown.

As I walked into the ward to see Vladimir the follow-ing Sunday he burst into tears. They'd amputated his left leg just below the knee. He was still in great pain and from time to time he tried to grab hold of the missing part of the leg.

'What am I going to do now?' he moaned. 'How am I going to live without my leg?' I couldn't think of any words to comfort him, I felt so sorry for him.

'You'll get used to it,' the patient opposite piped up. 'At least you can work with both your hands. I've lost my arm.'

'But how will I walk?'

'With crutches. I've been using them for the past five years. I go to work as well.'

'But I'm so ill and I have four children.'

'I have three and my wife died last year,' said a man in a corner bed.

I had a feeling they were teasing him and I knew how sensitive he was about being laughed at. I didn't tell him I was going to start work the next day, afraid it would spark off one of his jealous tirades.

'It's time for me to go,' I said. 'It's getting dark already.'

'You're always in such a hurry to leave me all alone here.'

'But the children ...'

'I know, they're always more important than I am.'

'I'll try to come again next week.'

'Bring me a box of wafers,' he said, 'a big box.'

'All right,' I said, thinking I could buy two litres of milk with that money.

On my way out I asked the nurse why they'd taken off his leg.

'The doctors discovered he had a thrombosis and would have died if they hadn't acted quickly,' she explained.

'How long before he can come out?'

'It depends how long it takes the wound to heal. His heart is worrying the doctor as well.'

I'd just turned thirty-four and I felt like I had the weight of the whole world on my shoulders.

I was nervous about the job as I turned up the first morning, fearful I wouldn't get everything done on time and that my every move would be watched. There were fifteen beds in the surgery and in the past the cleaners had helped the cook to hand the food round to the patients, but I was told the rules had changed and I must do all that myself. The whole day was exhausting but when I got home at eight I found Mum and the girls had cooked a meal and laid the table. I felt like crying but put on a brave face. Their good news was that Mickie's teacher had allowed Rosie to stay with the older children, so they could both be in the same school.

The next Sunday I sent the older girls to see their father, with a bag of wafers as he'd requested, but he told them he wanted Turkish delight. The girls only had enough money for their tickets and a couple of cheap buns but they went to the small kiosk in the corner of the entrance and asked how much Turkish delight would be. They had enough money for five small pieces if they went without their food. They gave four of them to their father and saved one to share between Mickie and Rosie.

When I told Vladimir the following week that I'd started work he was angry I hadn't asked him first, then he started worrying about who would look after him when he came home.

'You'll just have to stay in bed till someone comes,' I told him.

As I was leaving the nurse told me Vladimir had developed a heart disease, which was complicating his condition.

'Don't ask for him to be sent home too soon,' she advised. 'It wouldn't be good for him, or you. He needs to be under continual medical observation. He's become very nervous and vulnerable.'

At the nursery they were worried about how weak Mickie was and wanted to feed him up a bit, but Rosie told me when they pressed food on him he vomited it up.

At the surgery my workmates did whatever they could to make my job heavier and more unpleasant, especially the cleaners, but George told me the patients had been saying the food was much better. At the weekly report meetings none of the senior staff said a good thing about me if there was a superior member of the Communist party present.

They just didn't mention me. I discovered that the information from these meetings was passed on to higher people, and I began to understand how the system worked. I watched as cleaners offered their superiors a few eggs or some fruit from their gardens, or some home-made wine or *rakia*. I had nothing to offer in the way of bribes, so I became invisible.

I saw so little of the children that the last thing I wanted to do on Sundays was head off in the rain to Sofia to listen to Vladimir complaining, but it was my duty. He was only forty-four and it felt to him as if his life had ended. He'd been ambitious once, but he was lazy and had wasted too much time with his doves. He was a skilful painter and people always wanted to commission him, but he never bothered. The nurse stopped me in the corridor.

'Your husband's wounds are healing and I heard the doctors saying he could be discharged, although his heart condition is still unsteady. You could take him home for a while if you'd like.' I must have hesitated. 'I know your situation is rather difficult, but a change of environment might do him good. Perhaps for a few weeks. I'm sure he'll have to come back soon. He needs continuous supervision and treatment.'

'Are you saying I should take him home today?' I asked. 'You see I haven't enough money with me for his fare.'

'That's all right, we won't tell him now and during this week I'll ask our male nurse to teach him to walk with crutches.'

'Thanks,' I said, 'that would be fine.'

Nothing I did was right for Vladimir that day. 'I want to go home,' he shouted, making all the heads turn.

'What are you shouting about?' the nurse asked as she came in to take their temperatures. 'We're looking after you like a baby, you should be happy here.'

He covered his head with a blanket and refused to talk and the nurse made a sign with her hand that I shouldn't worry. As I was leaving he uncovered his head and told me to bring his best clothes next week, as though he had any.

'I will,' I assured him and left. I felt so sorry for him it brought tears to my eyes. I could imagine just how deep his despair must be. He might have been unkind to me over the years, but his life hadn't been easy either.

Chapter Seventeen
The Kindness of Others

The following week I was allowed to bring Vladimir home, even though he couldn't manage to move on the crutches they'd given him, feeling all the time that he would fall. He grumbled and cursed all the way back to Mezdra. When he got home the children threw themselves at him joyfully and my mother offered him a cigarette. George came round and said to call him if Vladimir started to feel unwell. Vladimir didn't seem to welcome any of their good wishes, just wanting to be left alone. After supper Mum took the girls to her room as they still had some homework to do and, as usual, I prepared the clothes for the little ones for the next morning.

'Why are you doing all that?' Vladimir wanted to know. 'You can do that tomorrow.'

'I have to go to work early,' I explained. 'The girls will come and take the little ones to kindergarten.'

'Who's going to stay with me?'

'Mum will come as soon as she gets up.'

'When will you come back?'

'As soon as I finish work.'

'I want to know the exact time.' He was becoming upset.

'About two o'clock, I hope.'

The answer didn't satisfy him and he continued muttering until he fell asleep. In the morning the girls made tea and sandwiches and left them beside his bed. But he didn't touch them, telling my mother he would wait until I got home. He refused to share the soup that Mum warmed for the girls at lunch time.

When I arrived home at a quarter past two I was met at the door with a torrent of accusations about how I was out enjoying myself while he was waiting for me at home. Mum and I were both terrified by the power of his anger. I tried to explain all the things I had to do before going back to make the patients' suppers but he didn't believe me, calling me a liar and accusing me of not caring about him. The fact that I kept peeling potatoes and cutting up onions while he was ranting at me just proved to him how little I cared. I was more afraid of being late for work than I was of my husband's accusations, so I just had to keep going.

I rushed through my work as quickly as I could and just as I was about to leave one of the doctors asked me to translate a sentence for him.

'I'm sorry,' I said, 'but I'm not supposed to speak a word of English, otherwise I might lose my job, or any job, and that would mean we would die of hunger. Unless I get authorised permission I don't dare to do that.'

I rushed home, terrified of what sort of scenes would greet me. The children managed to cajole their father to join us at the table for a meal my mother had cooked, which he ate in silence. He wanted everyone to know how weak he was. Afterwards I had to wash him, bringing water in from the well outside and then carrying the heavy pails back out to empty them. How I would have loved to have running water in the house.

When everything was finished and the kids asleep, Vladimir went on and on about his miseries and I sat listening, without saying a word. 'You're not listening to me,' he said.

'I am,' I assured him, 'I just didn't want to interrupt.'

'Come and sit on the bed.'

As I got close he grabbed me and punched me with his fist, using all his strength and pent-up anger. I fell against the table, knocking it over and causing so much noise the kids woke up and saw my blood.

'Shut up!' he roared as they started crying, frightening them more, until Rosie was screaming. I tried to comfort them but their cries brought in the landlord and his wife.

'Now look here,' the landlord said, 'I didn't want you here in the first place. I let you live here because of your good grandmother, but if you think you can shout and wake all the other tenants in the middle of the night you'll have to move out. As it is you haven't paid me for the last four months! I'm only putting up with you for the sake of the children.'

'Look what you've done to your poor wife,' his wife berated Vladimir. 'She works like a slave from morning to night to keep you all alive. If you beat her who's going to feed you?'

One of their other tenants, a little the worse for drink, had now joined them. 'You should be ashamed of yourself,' he said. 'You must be mad.'

I could see they were making Vladimir even more furious, but he said nothing. I apologised to the landlords and promised it wouldn't happen again, although I wasn't confident. The little ones tried to help me wash the blood off as their sisters had done so many times before. My face was swollen and my left eye almost closed. Blood was still running from my nose. Vladimir fell asleep as I was putting them back to bed, so I lay down beside them for a couple of hours before getting up for work. My face was still swollen and blue beneath the eyes and I felt so ashamed.

The head doctor gave permission for the cleaners to take the food round the patients for me, but in exchange I had to wash the whole staircase that evening, which made the cleaners chuckle with malicious pleasure.

A few days later some medication was stolen at the surgery and we all fell under suspicion. We were called before the local members of the railway Communist party, like in a courtroom, and told that we would each be investigated. The meeting went on and on, with the same things being repeated over and over again.

When they finally asked if there were any questions a

silence fell on the room and we could all hear a banging downstairs. One of the male nurses went down to see what was happening and returned to announce it was my husband.

'What?' I couldn't believe my ears. 'How did he get here?'

All the cleaners came down with me, anxious to see this man, and we found him banging on the windowsill with his crutch. 'Come on,' he shouted, 'haven't you got a home, children, an invalid to take care of?'

I felt so ashamed and saw the party secretary smiling sarcastically as she left the kitchen.

'He must be altogether mad!' the other women decided.

All the way home he shouted and cursed at me, causing everyone in the street to turn and stare, witnessing my humiliation.

Despite all our hardships, the children managed to achieve wonderful things. At school the girls were part of a team for artistic athletics, and had been chosen to attend competitions. They ended up as national champions and their school was announced as having the best team in the country. As a reward they went to a summer seminar for trainers, high up in the mountains near a tourist complex, and returned as the youngest trainers in Bulgaria. I was so proud of them.

Vladimir's temper became worse and he hit Mickie hard for no reason at all, causing terrible bruising and frightening all the children with the ferocity of the attack. Mickie started wetting himself every night and the pain from the bruises just didn't seem to fade. Apart from treatment with ultra-violet rays and medication at the surgery, I tried everything any woman recommended; compresses with leaves of walnut trees, cotton wool pieces soaked in melted goat's fat, a cream containing rabbit's fat, a lotion of nettle roots. Nothing worked. The doctors said it might take a year for him to mend.

It seemed so unfair; he was such a good-hearted child. If he were given a sweet during the day he would bring it home to divide up between everyone.

Vladimir's health seemed to be deteriorating almost daily but the doctors told me there was nothing more they could do. They fitted him with a prosthesis, which he believed would make him feel free and independent again. I felt sorry for him as we left the hospital because I was sure it would be harder than he was anticipating and I knew he was not a fighter. When we reached the train he found that he couldn't get on without help and became enraged with frustration.

Every evening we would go for a twenty-minute walk in the street for practice and he would order me to walk behind him so I could catch him if he fell. The streetlights were out by then because the council had decreed that no 'normal' people would be roaming the streets after ten at night, so we had to negotiate the bumps and potholes in the dark.

His physical problems did nothing to distract Vladimir

from his jealousies and paranoia. Without telling me, he started following me back from work to see who I was with. He would always arrive home a few minutes after me and refuse to tell me where he'd been.

The hospital commissioned him to make some signs on glass and it seemed he might be able to earn some money at last. Then one evening I came home to find him lying across the bed, having difficulty breathing. George came and gave him an injection to ease the breathing and the next morning the doctor said he must go to the surgery. George found a cousin who owned a car, a rare luxury in those days, and Vladimir was admitted to the emergency room. The next day I was told that I must take him to Sofia for special treatment, which meant another nightmare train journey with him complaining all the time.

'Oh, stop moaning,' another passenger told him. 'I lost my left arm during the war. Soon after I returned home my wife died of tuberculosis, leaving five children to be raised. I haven't stopped working for a day. There's no one to look after the kids or me and now I'm going to visit my eldest daughter who's also got tuberculosis. You should consider yourself lucky.'

Others joined in the conversation and Vladimir fell silent until we got off. 'Stupid people!' he muttered once they were out of earshot.

The stays in hospital became more frequent and each time he came home he seemed to be sicker and our daily walks became shorter. He found it difficult even to sit up for long. His confidence went and he could hardly stand to have more than two or three people around. Everything annoyed him. The children had to be quiet all the time. Sometimes they would forget and burst out laughing as they played and he would explode. Nothing seemed to please him. Life became hard for all of us, especially Vladimir himself.

Eight months after the accident we still weren't receiving any of the sick money we were entitled to, even though I'd been before several committees to decide if we were eligible. Vladimir had particular difficulty getting to one of these, and one of the committee experts turned to us with a look that could freeze blood.

'Well,' he asked. 'What are you waiting for?'

'For my leg to grow,' Vladimir replied. It was the first joke I'd heard him make for as long as I could remember and I wanted to laugh, but I knew what the consequences would be if I did.

'Trying to make fun of us, you stupid fool? If you don't take your words back you might not get any help at all.'

In the end, after begging and running to every authorised institute for signatures and stamps, I managed to get the equivalent of thirty-five per cent of his average wages. Many years later I discovered he should have been entitled to eighty-five per cent, but we were being punished for our family history.

One day, after Vladimir had been confined to bed for some time, Laurie came home from school with her class teacher, who was also the head trainer for athletics; a good-looking, highly intelligent woman. As we had a cup of tea she heaped praise on Laurie. I could see how proud it was making Vladimir.

'The whole school committee has chosen Laurie to be sent to study in the Academy of Sports,' she said, 'specialising in artistic gymnastics. She will receive a grant and have all her accommodation paid for. We'll try to do the same for Hennie when she reaches that age.'

I couldn't believe what I was hearing. I was so happy. There would never have been any way I could have afforded to send her to such a place.

'No,' Vladimir announced. 'I've been feeding her and paying for her schooling till now. It's her duty to work and care for me!'

Laurie turned pale and had to sit down. All three of us stared at him in amazement. The teacher tried to explain what a wonderful opportunity it was and how Laurie would be able to earn far more in the long run, but he was deaf to her arguments.

'No!' he shouted again. 'She is my daughter and you cannot manipulate her against my decision. I do not agree and that is my last word.'

Laurie was struggling to hold the tears back as she showed her teacher out.

'Don't worry too much,' the teacher whispered as she went, 'I'm sure we'll find a way. Just leave it to me.'

I was so angry I could hardly contain myself and banged around in the kitchen until I was ready to go to work. Laurie was being offered a chance for a better life than the one we had been forced to live, and her father was willing to ruin her chances. I couldn't understand how he could say such things and live with his conscience. I stayed angry all day.

When it was time to leave work one of my colleagues told me they'd seen Vladimir waiting for me, behind a tree outside. I ran home, diving into a shop on the way to buy some cigarettes and seeing him hurrying past on his crutches. Then I went to my mother's room to collect her and take her home with me. Hennie and the little ones did all the talking at supper; Laurie, Mum and I hardly said a word.

A few days later the doctor asked Vladimir to paint some more signs but he refused, saying he wasn't well enough.

'I'm sorry about that,' the doctor said. 'Having seen you hurrying along the street the other day I thought you were feeling better. No one does these signs as well as you and I even managed to raise your prices.'

A few days later Vladimir started to feel very unwell and two carriers were sent to the house to take him to the hospital. When he came home the next time he seemed to have lost interest in everything except sitting in the doorway watching the world go by. Then one day he fell off his

chair and couldn't get back up. This time he was hospi-
talised for six weeks, which gave Laurie's teacher time to go
through all the necessary arrangements for Laurie to be
admitted to the Academy for Sports. At least some good
had come of poor Vladimir's decline.

Once she had been accepted, he could do nothing to
stop her going and her excitement knew no bounds. Life at
the academy proved to be tough for her. Having no extra
money meant she had to do without a lot of things, and
didn't always get as much to eat as the others. At the time
she didn't tell us that she had fainted a couple of times from
hunger. The little money I was able to give her wasn't
nearly enough. There was one other girl as poor as she was,
and the two of them had to stay in the hostel together
when the others went out enjoying themselves. Laurie even
had the few clothes she did own stolen from a washing line.

Despite everything, she ended up being chosen for the
national team and told us she might be going to Russia for
at least six months to receive special training for the forth-
coming Olympic games. I knew the Russians looked after
their athletes and made sure they had enough to eat, and
she would also get to see a bit of the world. She might even
end up as a trainer in the best teams. It all seemed too good
to be true. I couldn't believe that something wasn't going
to come along to ruin it for her.

Hennie was asked to paint some slogans for the coming
celebrations of the 'liberation' of Bulgaria by the Russians.
Her work filled our tiny room and I tried to get Vladimir

involved, but he refused, so we left him alone. The better Hennie did it, the more the school gave her and often we would be up until after midnight, cutting and painting and she still had to do her homework before going to bed. Then one evening her father suddenly got up without a word and started measuring and painting the letters straight on to the strips of cloth, without having to draw them first as we'd had to do. He was finished in no time and Hennie was so grateful she threw her arms around him, kissing and cuddling him. He began to cry. God only knows what was going on in his poor mind. He even went to the school to help her put the decorations up, and she was given some money as a reward for her efforts.

'I'll give a few *lev* to Mickie and Rosie,' she said, 'and we'll give the rest to Laurie, shall we Mum?'

'You do just as you please, darling,' I said, hugging her. 'You've worked so hard and slept so little.'

'I bought these for you, Dad,' she said, giving him a packet of cigarettes. He cried as he took them. I went into the kitchen to wipe my own tears away before anyone saw them.

A year after the accident Vladimir's sick pay ran out and he had to apply for a disability pension, which meant another round of institutes, hospitals and committees. Each time he was mistreated and humiliated and made to suffer and wait. There seemed to be no end to the cruelty of the system. Our debts were growing to the landlords of both our rooms. Some days we had nothing to eat at all, but the children never complained.

A week before Lent everyone in Bulgaria has a meat feast, but that year we didn't have a single piece of food. When Hennie returned from school the first thing she did was open the cupboard to get some bread, as she was hungry. There was no bread, and I felt my heart was being ripped out. She said nothing.

'Aren't we going to have supper soon?' Mickie asked.

Hennie must have seen my expression or change of colour because she picked him up and started throwing him in the air.

'Didn't you eat in kindergarten?' she asked.

'Of course we did,' Rosie said.

'Well, for once we won't have supper,' Hennie teased.

'I was only asking,' Mickie murmured.

Hennie played with them both, making them laugh until they got tired. I felt like I was going to lose consciousness. There was a knock at the door and our landlord's son was there.

'I've been hunting recently,' he said, 'and I was lucky enough to catch more pheasants than we need, so I've brought you a few. We've just baked them so eat them while they're still warm. This is a small bottle of home-made wine to wash them down.'

I was too stunned to speak but Hennie came to my rescue.

'Oh, thank you so much. We love pheasants.'

I burst into tears and as he left I noticed he was having to use a handkerchief as well. Just as the children were about to fetch my mother, Nikolinka tapped at the window with a whole loaf of bread, still warm from the oven, a bowl of *sarmi* (cabbage leaves stuffed with mince and rice) and a plateful of hot cheese pies. Moments like that restored my faith in the kindness of my fellow men.

While Vladimir was in hospital three of his brothers came to visit him. One of the nurses told me about the visit.

'They were convincing him to sign something. I told them he wasn't well enough to understand what he was signing and that it wouldn't be legal.'

'When was that?' I asked, with an unpleasant sense of foreboding creeping over me.

'Two days ago. Didn't he tell you?'

The nurse and I went to see him together. He was surprised to see me and the nurse started measuring his blood pressure.

'You didn't tell me your brothers had visited you,' I said. 'Funny all three of them coming together. Did they bring you something?'

'Only some cigarettes,' he said, slightly stuttering.

'Cigarettes?' The nurse was shocked. 'You're not supposed to smoke, that's very bad for you. I shall take them away.' She opened the drawers but found nothing. 'Where have you hidden them? Give them to me.'

Vladimir was looking embarrassed. 'I don't know where they put them.'

The nurse turned to the other patients. 'Do any of you know where they are?'

'We haven't seen any cigarettes,' one of them said.

'They didn't bring him anything at all,' another added, 'they were only showing him some letters or papers.'

'It was something about our land in our village. I don't know exactly what it was about.' Vladimir didn't look well.

'Did you sign anything?' I asked.

'No, I don't know, I can't remember. Oh, leave me alone.'

The other patients nodded, silently telling me that he did.

'It's all right,' I said, seeing he was getting confused and embarrassed, 'don't worry.'

I vaguely remembered his parents telling us that Vladimir was entitled to an acre of their land on which to build a house, but he had never had the money to do so. Two of his brothers had built their own houses and the third lived in the house built by the grandfather, for which Vladimir was supposed to have been compensated. I was pretty sure the papers would have been something to do with that.

I managed to save enough money to buy myself another ticket to Sofia a few Sundays later. The little ones could still travel free and Nikolinka gave us some money for helping her shift some coal, so we were able to buy a ticket for Hennie as well. We decided to leave early and pick up Laurie from her academy so the whole family could be together for once. It was freezing cold in the unheated railway carriage and the children played games with the steam coming from their mouths.

When we got to the hospital the porter told us that children weren't allowed inside and would have to wait out in the cold. Laurie and I went straight to the head doctor who said that as Vladimir couldn't leave his bed, they could come in.

When he saw his children Vladimir cried all the time. The little ones had a song they wanted to sing to him but were afraid they would be turned out into the freezing street. The other patients asked the nurse to allow them to sing. They danced and sang and Mickie even told a few jokes and riddles. The other patients gave them sweets, biscuits, nuts and apples. One even gave them a five *leva* note.

When we got back out into the street we gave half the food to Laurie. She didn't want to take it but we insisted, knowing she could eat it for breakfast and it would last her a week. Mickie and Rosie whispered together for a while, and then gave her their five *leva* note.

'I can't take it,' Laurie said, 'it was given to you.'

'Mum will give us some if we need it,' they replied. 'These are for you to come home for Christmas.'

Laurie came to the station to see us off, and waved until our train disappeared from sight. I was so proud of them all.

Chapter Eighteen
The Deathbed Scene

Only a few days later a message came from the hospital saying I should go back to see Vladimir. I couldn't understand it, but did as they said and arrived at breakfast time the following morning. As usual, the grumpy porter didn't want to let me in.

'It's too early,' he shouted, 'how many times do I have to tell you?'

But when I insisted that he called the doctors and asked, he immediately lifted the barrier. Vladimir was in a terrible state, complaining he needed the window open for air but refusing to allow the nurse to give him oxygen, believing she wanted to kill him. The other patients bravely wrapped themselves up against the cold and the nurse allowed the window to be opened for a few moments. He clung to my hand and wouldn't even let me go to the toilet. When he eventually dozed off and I escaped the ward for a few minutes, the nurse caught me on the way back and told me to prepare myself for the worst. I asked her if I had time to go and get Laurie, but she advised me not to put the child through such an ordeal and I realised she was right.

When I got back to his bedside Vladimir was awake and upset about my long absence.

'Where were you? You left me all alone and they wanted to take me away,' he cried.

'Ask him who wants to take him away,' one of the other patients whispered.

Vladimir turned to the wall and seemed to calm down for a few moments, then he began pushing against the wall.

'Go away, all of you! I won't come with you. You hate me and you always have.'

'Who's calling you?' I asked.

'My old ones, my cousins, all of them from our village. They keep pulling me.' His voice was trembling with fear. 'And I don't want to go just now.' Then suddenly he turned back and spoke in his normal voice. 'Why have you closed the window again? I need air.' I opened the window a little. 'No, wide open, I said!' I looked at the others. They nodded their agreement. Vladimir caught my hand and began crying. 'I've been bad to you. I never believed you. I've done much harm to you time after time. I should have let you go then. There was still time, and I had the money for the fare. You might have had a better life. But I was jealous and selfish. I didn't want anyone else to look at you.'

He covered his face with the blanket and squeezed my hand tighter and tighter. Tears were running down my face and the lump in my throat was suffocating me. He turned back to the wall. I felt so sorry for him. He must have been carrying his guilt all those years, unable to find the strength to be a better husband and father.

'Go!' he shouted at the wall. 'I told you I won't come with you now. My wife is here and I stay with her. My children are waiting for me!'

After a while he turned back.

'Where are the children? How are they? You must look after them. Do you hear me? I didn't do enough for them, but you must.'

'Of course I will,' I said quietly. 'I always have.'

'I know, but I cared more for my doves than I did for them. My mother was right when she told me that doves in the house bring bad luck.'

'Don't worry,' I tried to comfort him, 'the kids will be all right, you'll see.'

He turned back to the wall and dozed off. His grip was hurting my hand but I couldn't get free. With my other hand I closed the window. It was getting so cold. One of the carers brought me some soup and a cup of yoghurt, which I had to eat with my left hand while he clung on to my right. I could hardly swallow anything but the warmth of the soup felt good. Some of the patients made signs to me to drink straight from the plate. I tried but without success. None of us slept much that night as Vladimir argued with his parents, siblings, long-forgotten uncles and cousins, even schoolmates.

When he was quiet the other patients talked about how the souls of the deceased came to lead the way to the world beyond for their next of kin, supporting them on their journey, making sure the evil spirits didn't snatch them and draw them down to the underworld. To help them leave this world without fear, someone should hold their hand.

The night was long. My back ached from the uncomfortable position and my hand was blue from the force of his grip. Every so often the nurses tried to persuade him to take some oxygen, but he refused. When they suggested I might lie down for a while on the sofa in the corridor he roared 'No!' at them, and no one said anything more.

In the morning the doctor gave him an injection to ease his pain and he fell asleep, giving me a chance to freshen up and have a cup of warm tea. The doctor noticed my blue hand and shook his head.

'I wonder where you take all that strength from,' he said. He didn't know that I had very little strength left. I worried about Mum and the children, but I knew I couldn't leave Vladimir on his own.

When Vladimir woke he seemed better and I wondered if the crisis had passed. I called his brother, Mladen, who lived in Sofia, and asked him to come to the hospital. Vladimir didn't seem very glad when I told him. As the day wore on he returned to his delirious state, gripping my hand, begging for air and talking to the wall. A doctor came and gave him another injection, but I wasn't sure why he was doing it. One of the other patients came to talk to

Vladimir and told him he should ask my forgiveness for everything he'd done to me, but Vladimir just cried and said he wasn't able to do so.

'I can't beg you to forgive me,' he sobbed later, 'I can't, it makes me feel humiliated, I can't.'

'But I have forgiven you long ago,' I assured him.

He squeezed my hand so hard I almost shouted with pain. Then I felt his grip grow weaker. He sighed heavily and let go. It was ten minutes to midnight. After a short while, like in a dream, I heard the doctor saying, 'There's nothing more we could do. My condolences.'

I could have stayed in the hospital till the morning, sitting on a chair in the waiting room but I preferred to go out. There was no point going home as I would have to come straight back in the morning, so I went to stay with Vladimir's cousin, Ivan. Someone at the hospital said she would contact Vladimir's old boss for help but I still had to get a coffin, arrange the transport and a dozen other bureaucratic jobs. Two railway men arrived the next morning to help. My last task was to help dress my husband for his coffin.

I shivered as I entered the dark, damp morgue. The smell made me feel sick. The man whose job it was to dress the bodies after autopsy looked as if he, too, had just risen from the grave. My fingers were stiff and frozen but I did my best to be helpful as we dressed Vladimir. All the time we worked the man cursed me for being scared, spoilt, ungrateful, lazy and good-for-nothing. I didn't argue with him. I just wanted to get out of there as quickly as possible. I was used to being shouted at.

I bumped into my brother-in-law standing at the hospital gates, waiting to see what he could do to help.

'Could you come to the burial,' I asked, 'and inform your brothers and sisters as well?'

'I'll see what I can do,' he grunted.

Plucking up my courage I went on. 'Could you lend me a few coppers to help me out with the burial?'

'I'm sorry,' he said. 'Just now I can't.'

I went to fetch Laurie from her college. By the time we reached the station I saw my two helpers. We already had our tickets and they were going to be loading Vladimir on to a later train. All I had to do was find someone who would transport the coffin from the local station to our home. The only way would be in one of the horse-drawn carts that waited for business outside the station. But the carters refused to carry a dead person. Eventually I found one who took pity, although he said the doctor had instructed him not to lift anything heavy, so other men had to be found to help with lifting the coffin.

It was bitterly cold, the men stamping their feet to keep them from freezing as they waited for the train to arrive. The carter covered his horse with a blanket. It was almost midnight when the wagon was transferred to the railway line nearest to the street where we were waiting. With a lot of shouting, pushing and pulling, the coffin was loaded on to the cart.

Once it was inside our room, there was hardly any room to move. Now I had to get permission for the grave from the council, and find someone to dig it out in the frozen earth.

The burial couldn't be until four in the afternoon because the gravediggers couldn't dig any quicker. I knew there would be a lot of gossip about what the deceased was wearing and whether the sheets inside the coffin were new, but by then I didn't care any more. His work colleagues had made a red five-beam wooden star, which was later placed on the grave. That was all that was allowed, by the strict orders of the Communist party. Nor were we allowed to stop at the church for a funeral mass.

The procession had to travel up a hill and the horse pulling the burial cart slipped and skidded, threatening to throw out the coffin. More men were summoned to help push.

'He doesn't want to go,' someone behind me whispered.

After the funeral my brother-in-law suggested he adopted Rosie, as she was young enough to adapt to village life, which would lighten my load. They all started talking about what to do with my children as if I wasn't there. They seemed to think I wouldn't be able to cope without Vladimir, but he had always made my life harder, not easier.

I ignored them and concentrated my attentions on Mum and the children. Mum was at her wits' end at the thought of all the hardships the family was going to be facing now there wasn't a man in the family.

The next day I was entitled to a day off and I had to go to the graveyard to light a candle, sprinkle a little water and leave a few bites of bread on the grave, as well as to hand out something to anyone else who might be there at the time. According to the traditional religion, banned by the Communists, the soul of the deceased continued to wander around for forty days and expected to be fed by his or her dear ones. Something was supposed to be left every day.

'What's that for?' Mickie asked, obviously concerned at the sight of wasted food.

'That's for your father,' I tried to explain, hardly able to keep the doubts from my voice.

'When will he come to eat it?' he asked.

'He'll come later,' Rosie assured him. 'Just now he's too shy to come out.'

A kind neighbour came to see how we were doing a few days later, bringing food and some toys for the children.

'I noticed at the children's New Year party in the kindergarten,' she said, 'your poor little ones didn't get anything from Father Frost (Father Christmas). I saw how disappointed they were, although so brave. They said no word! You should have seen them, sitting in a corner, holding hands and just watching how all the other children were enjoying their new presents.'

I sat down, unable to stop the tears.

'But,' my neighbour went on, 'the parents and teachers filled up two paper bags with sweets, nuts, apples, whatever we found, and asked Father Frost to hand them over to your sweet ones. They were so pleased, thanking him with shining eyes. I told them they could open the bags and see what was in them, but they both said they wanted to take them home because they wanted to share everything with their big sisters, their mum and their granny. Well, that was a lesson for us adults to learn.'

'I was so engaged with the arrangement of my husband's funeral,' I tried to explain, 'I forgot. I feel so guilty, poor things.'

In fact I hadn't realised that the parents were supposed to give Father Frost the presents beforehand. The woman was kind and often came back with toys or clothes that her own children had outgrown.

There were many forms to be filled in if I wanted to receive an inheritance pension for my children. I tried to get free meals for at least one of them. Any widow with four father-less children was supposed by law to get free meals for two of them. But the rule wouldn't work for my children, I was told, because they were half foreign.

Mum's health was getting worse but I had so little time to care for her. Eventually she had to go into hospital.

An election was on its way and everyone had to vote. Some were forced to do so, with police and soldiers virtually pressing guns into their backs. The very ill were excused and the head doctor arranged for Mum not to be moved because her heart was weak. But while the doctor was away voting himself, the party secretary ordered the staff to force her to go. They took her by car but she fell on the steps and lost consciousness. She was taken to the main hospital in Vratza.

I was getting ready to go and visit her when a telegram arrived, announcing that she was dead and that I was to collect the corpse as soon as possible. I couldn't bear the thought that after all we had been through together she had been alone at the end. How different her life would have been if only she had decided not to follow Granny to Bulgaria all those years before.

Chapter Nineteen
A Widow's Lot

I had to organise a coffin for my mother and get it down the deep, cold, awkward stairs into the morgue, with the help of a kind patient. Two frightened-looking men were waiting among the corpses because they'd been told I would help them with the dressing of their niece. I did so and they waited while I dressed my mother, with tears streaming down my face, and then they helped me carry the coffin out to the horse and cart I'd hired. I so wished I could have had one last chance to say goodbye to her, and tell her how much I loved her. I wished I could have been holding her hand, like I had been able to hold Vladimir's.

I had intended to look after my mother so well in the last years of her life, now that I didn't have Vladimir to worry about, but the chance had gone. I was all alone with the responsibility of the children.

The cart's driver was grumbling about the cold. It was ten degrees below zero and the snow was so deep the poor horse became stuck several times and we had to climb down and dig the wheels out. By the time we got home, three and a half hours later, I was too stiff and frozen to be able to get off the cart. Laurie and the landlady helped me down and half carried me inside.

The earth was so hard the gravediggers weren't able to dig a big enough hole for the coffin and it had to lie crooked. Now Granny, Vladimir and Mum were all lying together in a row, with not even a decent gravestone by which to remember them.

'Age?'
'Thirty-six.'
'Married?'
'Widow.'
'Children?'
'Four.'
'Parents?'
'None.'
'Siblings?'
'None.'
'House?'
'None.'
'Land?'
'None.'
'Nationality?'
'Bulgarian subject.'

'I said, what nationality are you!' the councillor's secretary shouted at the top of his voice.

'By husband, Bulgarian. By father, English. By mother half-English, half-Austrian,' I answered quietly.

'You are in a real mess,' the clerk said contemptuously. 'I don't think you'll be granted any pension at all.'

I'd been through this interrogation so many times, but there was no other path for me to follow. I had debts I was never going to be able to pay off. By the time I moved out of my mother's room the rent hadn't been paid for a whole year; the other room we were all living in was the same. There was nothing left to sell apart from my grandmother's iron bed, on which I was sleeping with Mickie and Rosie, and the bunks which the girls slept on. A neighbour was bringing us milk three times a week and a lump of home-made goat's cheese once a month, even though I could no longer pay her anything. She suggested that when Laurie and Hennie got married I could give her the iron bed. I didn't want to promise that and asked her to stop bringing the food but she just laughed.

'Don't worry,' she said, 'pretty girls like yours don't become old maids. I'm sure I won't have to wait very long.'

A new doctor joined the practice. She was a powerful character and she found out about a lodging room for railway workers that was coming free. It was one room with a kitchen that had running water. Although the toilet was shared with another family that was inside too, and had a flush. If I wanted it I had to move immediately, before someone else got in there. I couldn't believe my luck. My landlady's son-in-law offered to help and we spent the whole night heaving our possessions across town, with an exhausted Hennie helping to push the cart. Although it was a lot better than places we'd lived before, I was still going to have to paint it as soon as I was able, and put tin patches on all the rat holes. The problem with the running water was that it wouldn't stop running when it was meant to.

When I got home from work the following lunchtime I found seven men standing in the room deciding whether to let us stay or throw us out immediately in favour of an engine driver who wanted it. To my relief, the doctor arrived at that moment and laid into them for even thinking about putting a poor widow with four children out on to the street and they backed down before the force of her tongue.

Another neighbour, called Dimiter, volunteered to fix the stove and help the children bring our coal from the old room while I went back to work. By the time I got home again that evening the fire was burning and he and his daughter were helping Hennie fix the beds.

A year after Vladimir's death the children were granted the minimum pension. It wasn't enough to even pay for the milk they needed. Laurie decided she would have to leave the sports academy, giving up her chance to travel to Russia, to help out with the money. I tried to dissuade her but she was adamant. She found that every decent job she went for, the party secretary wouldn't give his consent because he wanted the job for one of his relatives. In the end she found work in the conserve factory, separating out beans from the stones and earth.

I started taking in more sewing, charging less than most other dressmakers just to get the work, sometimes just accepting some milk or bread or other food in payment. A professional dressmaker who lived nearby found out and went to the militia station. One of the officers was a very special friend of hers and I was summoned to the station the next day.

'I've received evidence that you've been working illegally,' the chief accused me. 'You're earning a lot with your sewing machine and not paying any taxes. That's illegal!'

'Every woman sews or darns for her family,' I replied. 'With a sewing machine it looks nicer.'

'You're sewing illegally for other people, taking the bread out of the mouths of poor professional dressmakers. I shall order that your sewing machine be taken away.'

'But my wages aren't enough to buy new clothes for my children, so I have to alter and reshape old ones.'

'But you do sew for other people as well, I can prove it!'

'Maybe I do, but as a present or in return for a favour.'

'I see,' he dragged the word out with a leer. 'So how will you return favours after I deprive you of your sewing machine?'

'I shall have to find another way to earn a few coppers,' I said, barely holding down the rage that was boiling inside me. 'So if you accidentally see me at some late hour, in some unusual place, with some person who would not like to be publicly accused of indecent activities, don't be surprised! If you try to take measures against me, be sure I shall drag that person through every possible bit of dirt, so that everybody will spit in his face with pleasure, and I shall make sure it gets public proclamation, explaining who forced me to do it.'

'Get your dirty self out of here!' he bellowed, pointing a grimy finger at me. 'But remember, I haven't finished with you yet.'

In the coming years we were all forced to attend political education lessons, as well as Russian language courses. I hated the former because they were so certain theirs was the only right way to arrange things, but the latter were not too hard since we spoke so many languages already. Laurie and Hennie were becoming pretty young women and Laurie was able to go out in the evenings when she'd finished work at the conserve factory, and even started doing some amateur acting. Then she announced that a young train driver, Bojidar, had proposed to her and she was thinking of accepting. I was so frightened she was going to fall into the same trap as I had done. A young man who was charming and considerate before the wedding might change a great deal after it.

'I know what you mean,' she assured me with a hug. 'You were always so patient with Dad, you know how much I witnessed and how many times I was scared that he might kill you or Granny in a moment of anger. Do you think I've forgotten?'

At that moment Hennie rushed in and dropped her school bag, rushing straight out to fetch the little ones. We noticed that the strap was broken yet again. A few days later I was passing the school on a train and I looked out to see if I could see her in the yard. There was my tomboy daughter holding a boy by the coat and beating him on the back of the head with all her might with the schoolbag. So that was how it kept getting broken.

At the age of twenty-one, Laurie decided to marry Bojidar and looked very pretty on her wedding day. She went to live with her in-laws. I hoped for the best.

Hennie applied to the State Academy of Theatrical Arts and was accepted, but came up against the same problem of being a foreigner.

'Your father has been dead for a long time,' she was informed (it had been four years), 'so his origin doesn't count any more. You therefore have no right to attend any university.'

Hennie fell into a deep depression, saying she had no reason to live any more and I feared for her safety. The only job she was able to get was working on building sites but the manual labour seemed to restore her spirits. When she came home on visits she talked so animatedly about the lifting equipment that she operated that the little ones both wanted to go and work with her as soon as they were able. Hennie's high spirits dived again when she was robbed of six weeks' wages and she plunged back into depression.

But no one could have all bad luck and, through

friends, she managed to get a job in a travelling theatre group on half wages. It was a chance to get into the business without a university degree and she grabbed it.

Because of an outbreak of flu, our little hospital was very busy. We had twice as many patients now as we had beds, so mattresses had to be squeezed in wherever there were a few spare inches, even in the corridors. Not only did I have to cook twice as much food, I also had to put in at least one night a week voluntary time as a 'patient carer'. Then Mickie caught the flu and almost died. The doctors at the hospital knew my position and said they didn't think it was safe for him to come home while his heart was still weak. They offered to keep him, but I knew I wouldn't be able to afford to come and see him every day. I remembered what had happened when I'd put him into the crèche, and was terrified he might have a similar experience, but what choice did I have?

Even once Mickie had regained enough strength to come home, he still wasn't able to carry his own books up the hill to school and other boys had to be found every day to help him. I was told he would probably never be able to do heavy manual work. Mickie's teachers had told me he was talented musically but I had been so busy rushing around trying to keep the family warm and fed that I'd never had time to find out more. When I heard there was going to be a concert at the school I managed to find the time to go, although I was nervous that if I didn't leave promptly I would be late for work and again get into trouble.

I hated the fact that I always had to be working or rushing home to do chores, never able to take the time to give my children the attention I so much wanted to give them. They had all been so good about it, never complaining and always trying to help in any way they could. Perhaps every mother wishes she could do more for her children than she does.

When I heard Mickie singing and playing the accordion with another girl I couldn't stop myself from crying. The crowd was cheering and shouting for more after each song and I stood transfixed, even though I was so frightened of being late to work. How could I not have known that my child was so extraordinarily talented that he could affect a crowd like this?

That evening we had a long talk in the family about what we could do without, in order to save enough money to buy Mickie a cheap accordion. When I heard that the Transport Group for Art Matters had decided to open a musical course for the children of railway workers it sounded like exactly what Mickie needed. He started taking piano lessons and became the only pupil to be given a key to the hall at school where the piano was kept so that he could practise in the evenings. He would often stay in there for more than five hours at a time.

To help me with the finances, Mickie, with Rosie's help, started making bathing trunks for his friends at school. They did it in secret to begin with and I kept wondering why I found different threads in my sewing machine from the ones I'd been using the night before.

So many people were kind to us in those years, giving us food when we most needed it, or helping out with tasks I couldn't manage myself, although sometimes men would suggest that if I didn't have money I could pay for their services in a different way. I was always outraged they would think such a thing. I was surprised how often I overheard someone saying something like 'Don't worry about her, she's young and pretty, I'm sure she earns quite a lot in an easy way'. Such words always hurt me and made me cry when I was alone in bed at night.

Despite only being forty years old, I became a grandmother when Laurie gave birth to Ina in 1959. She was a lovely child and when Laurie had to go away for a while Ina came to stay with us, and was looked after perfectly by Mickie and Rosie while I was at work. I was always so proud of the way my family cared for one another.

When Mickie was eleven the doctor told me it would do him good to go to the Mineral Bath Hospital for Heart Diseases. He warned me it would be hard to get a place, so I decided to go there myself and try my luck. The doctor at the hospital listened carefully to everything I had to say.

'I would be very grateful,' I ended, 'if you would be so kind as to allow him a place here.'

He looked at me for a few moments. 'Of course I'll give him a place, and I'm glad I can do so. I have often wondered how to thank your grandmother for saving my life when I was still a young student.'

Yet again, Granny's good work had come to my rescue.

Mickie stayed at the sanatorium for two and a half months, spending three hours a day in their schoolroom, even learning how to knit fishing nets. Although he remained a delicate child, his strength grew to the extent that he was eventually able to swim across the Danube with his schoolmates.

Laurie's second child, Harry, was born just two years after Ina, and Laurie began to work part-time as a hairdresser. While Laurie was settling into family life, Hennie's acting career started to take off and she began working in the best theatres in the country. By the time she was ten, Rosie had taken over many of the routine household tasks like shopping and washing.

Although the years were passing I never wavered in my ambition to return to my homeland one day. I always knew that England was where I belonged and, however long it took, I was still determined to get back there.

Chapter Twenty
The Years Pass

When I was ordered to present myself to the chief director of the newly built Chemical Combinate in 1966, I was too frightened to go, fearing a trap and more interrogations like the many I'd been through. I suppose I hoped that if I ignored the summons they would forget about me. I should have known better. The next day two militiamen arrived at the house and escorted me there in their jeep.

To my amazement, it turned out not to be a trap. They wanted me to be one of their interpreters and they were even willing to offer me a flat in a newly built block to go with the job.

The head doctor at the local surgery was not impressed when I went to ask for permission to do a two-day trial in the new job.

'So,' she sneered, 'you're not grateful that we took pity on you when you and all your children were dying of hunger. We allowed you to work here, although other women needed to work as well, we gave you a wonderful flat with running water, now you want to leave us all of a sudden, without giving us any notice.'

'I was asked to go because there is an urgent need for interpreters,' I said. 'I suppose I will have to tell them I can't accept their offer.'

'No, no, you just go. I only want to remind you that after you lose your nice cheap flat, and your job here, and as soon as they don't need you any more at the Combinate, then you will be on the street, unemployed and hungry! But now go, you must be there by eleven o'clock.'

I realised she'd been told to make sure I arrived by eleven. She had deliberately kept me waiting in order to make me late. If I hadn't gone to her for permission she would have reported that I was disobeying her again, and she couldn't quite resist the chance of telling me how much she hated me once more.

When I arrived twenty minutes late at the Combinate no one told me off, in fact they greeted my arrival with cheers. They addressed me as 'Madam Helen' and everyone was kind and understanding. They all helped me with the technical terms and my English started to return as if I'd never stopped speaking it. It was as if I'd passed into a different world.

Three days later the chief of Central Transport Hospital handed me my documents for my fifteen years of work with them. 'We're very sorry you're leaving,' he told me. 'We've never had such an intelligent, loyal and hard-working person in our whole system. We all wish you the best of luck in your work. You deserve to be treated as a human being which, I'm ashamed to say, I know you haven't always been in our system. That's just between us, at least for the next two years, until I retire.' He laughed and squeezed my hand. Why, I wondered, did all the nice and kind people feel they had to be quiet while the bullies were allowed to make all our lives such misery?

Everyone at the Combinate was so self-confident, the way they moved, smoked, drank coffee and sought out the company of foreigners, even though they couldn't speak the languages. Many of them could use typewriters and telexes with ease, while I was writing out everything by hand. Everyone seemed so young, well dressed and elegant. I was conscious that I didn't have the right clothes to fit in. One day important people from the ministry arrived. I was called in to sit next to the minister and the head of the French team. An argument broke out and a German specialist interrupted. Without thinking I translated what he'd said. His interpreter shot me an accusing look and I apologised.

When the dispute had calmed down and coffee was being handed round, the minister and the French specialist simultaneously offered me cigarettes. I politely refused, which surprised them both. Plates of biscuits were placed in front of me and everyone invited me to try them. My hands trembled as I reached out to take one. I wasn't used to such treatment from people in authority.

When the conference was over and I was slipping away to get home to the children, having already missed my bus, they caught me and insisted I joined them for a meal. I couldn't believe how much food there was; although I was so busy translating, I hardly had time to eat any of it. At the end of the meal they parcelled up what was left for me to give the children. My boss drove me home in his car. I was embarrassed to think he would see how humble my home was.

'You needn't worry,' he assured me. 'Most of us have travelled the world and seen much poverty. In England many people complain about everyday things which people in Bulgaria would call luxuries. I'm not the sort of person who respects people because of their standards of living, I respect them for their character, behaviour, attitude to others and abilities.'

He came into the flat and introduced himself to Mickie and Rosie, who watched wide-eyed as he took out the roast beef, potatoes, peas, asparagus, olives, fresh tomatoes, cucumbers and green salad, while I made a cup of tea. Then came two big boxes of yoghurt, a big packet of butter, a lump of Cheddar, ham and two dried sausages, plus a whole loaf of white bread and a box filled with pastries. As he left he promised the kids that one day he would take them for a ride in his car.

I was still being paid the lowest wages possible, even less than the women who pretended to clean, but the directors arranged for me to get extra money for working late hours. It wasn't long, however, before I was made aware that they 'knew all about me'. I was told that it was believed by the authorities that I was 'so clever they could not find out who my connections were, who sponsored me, and in what currency I was paid'.

Because the conditions at the Combinate were so primitive by international standards, other interpreters didn't stay long, so there was always work for me. When Mickie left school my boss persuaded him to join too. It might not have been the career of his choice, but at least he would be earning money until we could find a way to pay for him to go to the musical academy. He worked there for two years, saving enough money to buy himself a second-hand piano. I could tell his health wasn't good, but he never complained until one night shift when he broke down with stomach pains. It turned out he had a perforated ulcer. The doctors said the fumes at the Chemical Combinate were not good for his health and it would be better for him if he could go back to his love of music.

He stayed in hospital for a month, during which time I contacted an old school friend of his, who had become a coordinator of the young groups of musicians who were sent around the country to play in restaurants. Mickie was given a place in one of these groups and although it meant taking a cut in wages, it was the kind of work he loved. Within three months, however, he was recognised as the best pianist among all the young groups in the country. I was so proud of all my children.

Each month, after getting his wages, Mickie would buy something useful for the flat, like an electric iron, an electric stove, a washing machine and a boiler that gave us hot water.

Rosie and I spent a lot of time alone now, as she was working hard to get into university. She wanted to become an actress like her sister. The more she looked forward to it, the more I feared she, too, would be refused entry. Hennie, meanwhile, had become well known in the country and had married a fellow actor, who I'm afraid I didn't find very charming. Soon she was expecting her first child and living in Burgas.

Rosie ended up getting the highest marks in her whole class and the professors at the university said she should be offered a place, even saving a room for her at the hostel and as the fourth child of the family she was entitled to go free, but for some reason her acceptance was delayed, and arrived too late. The professors advised her to try again the following year; they were all very surprised by the problem. I wasn't, and it hurt to see poor Rosie trying to hide her disappointment.

Rosie went to Burgas to be with Hennie to prepare for the baby, and Mickie travelled to Yugoslavia to work for three months. Suddenly I was living all alone for the first time in my life. When I needed the space for my family I'd had nothing; now I was on my own I had all the space I could possibly need. I felt so lonely and sad. My family had been all I had ever had in life and now they were growing up and making lives for themselves.

Of course there were compensations, like when Laurie would leave her little ones with me when I didn't have to work.

When Hennie's baby was due I travelled the five hundred kilometres to Burgas to help. It was the first time I'd seen the sea since I'd watched the white cliffs of Dover disappearing behind us on our trip from England to Vienna to look for Granny thirty-four years earlier. I was thrilled to find that, even after so many years, I had not forgotten how to swim. Hennie gave birth to a son, Ivan, a few days later. Soon afterwards Rosie got her first professional acting job.

The English specialists were all leaving the Combinate and I missed them. The Germans were so serious and stern, and the Italians loud, and often rude. I had to learn all the technical terms again in Italian. The latest director didn't like me and I knew that when the Italians went, I would have to go too. Eventually, now over fifty years old, I packed up my dictionaries and left. The pension I was awarded was just enough to survive on and I gave English lessons to young children to supplement it. The work was illegal, but thankfully no one gave me away.

Hennie was offered the part of Louise in *Treachery and Love*, a really important part, and she asked me to look after Ivan because her mother-in-law was away. Even though I didn't get on with Vasil, her husband, and although I found Ivan a difficult child, I agreed because I knew it would be a big break for her. After the first performance the audience roared their approval. Ivan and I took flowers to her dressing room and an elderly actor came in and fell on his knees, kissing her hand. 'You are a goddess,' he said, with tears in his eyes. A famous Danish playwright told her he'd never seen such a wonderful Louise in forty years. She was so embarrassed and I was so proud.

Rosie's career was also doing well. She had often worked as Hennie's understudy, even though there was ten years between them. Now she was starting to play in the big state theatres and soon met the man destined to be her husband. Meanwhile Mickie continued his travels and met Karina, his future wife, in East Germany.

Hennie and Rosie's old school friends would often visit me, bringing coffee and cakes, and we would chat for hours. They would see me as someone to ask for advice about bringing up children or marriage problems, a bit like people had once viewed my grandmother. I liked it when I felt I was being useful to them.

When Mickie's son, Alan, was born I applied for a visa to go to East Germany. It took four months to arrange but I got there. East Germany was the best-run country of the Eastern bloc and coming back to Bulgaria each time was depressing. After one long stay with Mickie and his family I came back to find the authorities had dug a deep ditch along the length of our street, the earth piled so high it reached the crowns of the lovely lime trees, threatening to kill them. Every two hundred metres or so a few rough planks were thrown over the ditches to make bridges, which threatened to break under everyone who used them.

The earth was spreading over the whole street, being brought into the houses on people's feet or the wind; everything was covered in mud, no matter how often you cleaned. Often a child fell into the ditches, as well as drunks, who stayed there until some early-morning worker found them. There were many other streets in the same state, staying like that for months as if no one was responsible for the mess. How I longed to see clean streets, well-tended trees, smiling people and happy children like in other countries. Life in Bulgaria just seemed to get grimmer and harder with every passing year.

I found that if I brought presents from East Germany for the visas lady, I would be issued my next one more quickly. I hated lowering myself to giving bribes, but if I didn't I would hardly ever be able to get to see Mickie and his family.

Rosie's husband, returning to Sofia after three months working in Norway, announced he was leaving her. The news shocked Rosie so much she had some sort of attack and remained unconscious in hospital for nine days. When she woke the doctors told us she was still haemorrhaging slightly, which was leaving her weak. When she came out of hospital a fortnight later she could no longer afford the flat she'd shared with her husband, even though she managed to get a job as a stage manager. She was allowed to leave her belongings in the cellar of the theatre with the scenery and costumes, and she would sometimes sleep among them, on a sofa. At other times she would sleep on the railway station, trying to look as if she was waiting for a delayed train, and once she slept in the theatre's garden. Whenever their husbands were away on business, her friends would invite her to stay with them. If she had two free days in a row she could come home to wash her clothes and get a decent night's sleep.

Although I'd been told I would be allowed to stay in my flat, in 1982 the authorities, as always, changed their minds, and I was forced at the age of sixty-three to move into the cheapest room I could find. Because my new landlords were away during the week I was their caretaker as well, which meant I could use their tiny shower. The water and toilet, however, were once more outside. I was back to slipping and sliding through snow in the middle of the night, freezing to death as I washed up outside and brought in wood and coal. It was hard to go back at my age.

Mickie and Karina had a second child, a daughter, Alina, and I happily packed my bag and went back to help, so Karina could return to her teaching work.

As well as worrying about Rosie being homeless, I was also uneasy about Laurie's marriage. Like Vladimir, her husband was very jealous, and seemed to have been brainwashed by the Communist authorities. I knew he'd often beaten her for nothing. She wanted to leave him but for the sake of the children she endured the marriage patiently.

Apart from anything she had nowhere to go until Rosie got a room again.

Rosie eventually found an abandoned basement, the windows broken, the taps stolen and even parts of the floor pulled out. Wires stuck out of holes in the wall where sockets had once been and a horde of stray dogs and cats had to be evicted, leaving behind piles of dried droppings and the bones of pigeons the cats had caught and feasted on. There were even some skeletons of other dogs and cats scattered around.

Once we'd managed to clean it up with the help of friends, I planned to move in with her, so that she would have some furniture. Laurie also joined us, as her children, now grown up, were no longer at home to protect her from the beatings. The three of us slept together on a large single bed at a friend's house while we worked in the basement whenever we could.

Laurie got a job in a big steel factory, producing steel slabs. It was hot, heavy work, but at least it gave us an income. During the days we shovelled the foul-smelling dirt into bags, with towels tied round our faces so we didn't faint. In the evenings, under the cover of darkness, we would carry the bags to a place where all the shops dumped their rubbish, knowing that if we were caught we would be fined, or even imprisoned, since we had no money to pay the fines. Laurie's son, Harry, joined us in our efforts. We would pour water over the floor to try to soak and soften the dirt, and worked as quietly as we could, knowing the neighbours were members of the Communist party and could be a danger to us. They couldn't believe there was anyone left who wasn't a member of the party, but they didn't find out about us for a long time. After twenty days of backbreaking work the place was finally habitable.

A few weeks after we moved in we decided we should go to the council to legalise our stay in the basement, so as not to get into trouble.

'What?' the chairman shouted indignantly. 'You've dared to accommodate yourselves without my permission? Do you know that some people have been waiting twenty years for accommodation? You must leave this place immediately.'

We tried to explain that Laurie worked in the steel industry, which gave its workers the promise of accommodation, as they were necessary to production, but he was in too much of a rage to listen. We went home and waited to be thrown out.

Living there was difficult, because there was often someone in the room trying to sleep after a night shift and, because our windows were at street level, there was a lot of noise. I was usually the first up each morning, boiling water for tea and coffee, making sure everyone was up in time for work. I did a lot of the washing and cooking. Sometimes I had to get up early in order to queue a few hours for foods which were hard to get like milk, yoghurt or bread. All too often I would reach the front of a long queue only to discover they'd just run out of whatever it was I needed.

One night, when my great-granddaughter, Ina's daughter, was ill and needed yoghurt I had to queue three consecutive times between hal past two and eight o'clock in the morning before getting a carton. Meat was too expensive for us; we had it only once a week, or less.

I remembered the way the Russians had boasted about how wonderful the world would be under Communism after the war. It had turned into a nightmare for everyone who wasn't in a position of authority. Everyone was unhappy with the state of life, but most of us were afraid to speak up after decades of oppression and bullying.

Still, the authorities didn't find the time to come round and throw us out of the flat. Although I lived in a constant state of fear, there was a lot of unrest growing among the younger people. They were beginning to get information about life in the west and were no longer convinced that Communism was the best system under which to live. Their disenchantment was growing daily, although no one dared to protest openly. Everyone wanted to keep a low profile and stay out of sight of the authorities.

Mickie and Karina moved to a beautiful flat in Berlin, opposite the famous Berlin Wall that separated us from the west. Being on the seventh floor we could see over to the free world. I still believed that one day I would be able to get back across that wall. I had no idea how I would do it, but the dream kept me going.

* * *

Back in Bulgaria, Rosie made some indiscreet comments without realising a television crew was filming her, putting herself in danger. Mickie told her to come to Berlin as quickly as possible, which she did. We were living in increasingly dangerous times as the Communist party began to realise it was losing its grip on the population. After so many decades of stagnation things were suddenly changing fast, but I feared it might be too late to make any difference to me.

Chapter Twenty-One
Re-kindling the Dream

Laurie needed a break from work and when Mickie invited her to stay in Berlin she asked me to go with her. We took Yana, her little granddaughter.

Two days after we arrived we heard that the Berlin Wall was going to be taken down. It was May 1989, over half a century since I'd set out from England to visit my grandmother. It didn't seem possible that all the barriers that had stopped us from getting home for half a century could just disappear overnight.

We put all the children to bed after lunch so they would be able to stay up late to watch the historic moment. At about ten that evening we all set out for the Brandenburg Gate. The mood of the crowd matched the excitement I was feeling inside. The surrounding square was full of people and others had climbed on to the wall itself in order to see both sides of Germany. Snacks and drinks were being sold in the streets and young people were dancing to their own songs. Balloons were being prepared for release the moment the clocks struck midnight. It was like a carnival was in progress.

Finding the crowds too claustrophobic, I discovered a place on the steps of a small building where I would have a good view, leaving the others to roam around. A young couple arrived beside me with a ten-day-old baby in a carrier bag under the father's overcoat. A family with four children, and another about to be born any moment, told me they'd come all the way from Chicago for this. There were different languages being spoken all around me. Everyone was talking to strangers as if they were friends.

Speeches were made from the top of the Brandenburg Gate, the speakers clinging to the marble angels. Shouts and cheering could be heard coming from the other side. The crowd began counting down the last thirty seconds. I joined in. It felt so wonderful to be allowed to shout at the top of my voice after so many years of whispering.

'Three, two, one ...' There was a moment's silence and then the first strokes were heard. The roar that went up was deafening. The cheering turned to singing and there were people from both sides clinging to one another on top of the wall. Neat, tidy German housewives were producing bottles of champagne and glasses from their handbags. Corks were popping and fireworks were going off. On our side it was the usual official displays, but from the west we could see the most beautiful sights soaring up into the skies, such colours and patterns, such mighty explosions.

A huge crane swung over the arch. There was an American singer hanging in a cage, singing about a new free life for everyone in the world. Someone tapped me on the arm and when I turned I was handed a glass of sparkling champagne.

'*Zum Wohl*,' the pretty young mother said as she clinked my glass with hers.

I saw my grandchildren coming running out of the crowd. 'Granny, Granny, did you see the fireworks? They've made a hole either side of the gate! Just enough for a person to get through. Come and see.'

We all squeezed through the narrow slits that had been bored through the thick masonry of the wall and walked around the park on the other side like everyone else. Women were offering the children from the east chocolates, oranges and cookies, even western money.

The next day there was a marathon with runners from both sides of the wall. Many of the runners got 'lost' and never returned to the eastern bloc. We just walked around the west looking at the graffiti and watching people hacking souvenirs out of the wall. Yana and Alina found someone who was chipping pieces with a hammer and asked in German and Bulgarian if they could collect some of the small pieces. He answered them in pure Bulgarian, inviting them to take whatever they wanted.

In the following days we crossed over every afternoon and wandered around until late in the evening, although we had no western money so we couldn't buy any of the wonderful things we saw. Laurie wanted a slice of sizzling hot doner kebab and little Yana just wanted an attractive drink with a long coloured straw and a slice of orange on the rim of the glass. It took so little to please them after living in the east all their lives.

Back in Bulgaria, the fall of the wall did not make things any easier in the following years. Everyone tried to make money in any way they could, but things were harder than they had ever been in the past, with just a few people at the top becoming very rich very quickly from the changes.

One day in 1996, Rosie came home and told me that a friend of hers had applied to go to England as a tourist. 'Why don't you try to get in touch with the British Embassy?' she suggested.

'I'm still so scared to go anywhere near there,' I confessed. 'You know what happened before.'

'But Mum,' she insisted, 'times have changed a bit because of the international laws that the present Bulgarian government is obliged to obey.'

'But you know they always manage to get round these requirements and do whatever they want.'

'Maybe,' Rosie said, 'but still you could try. We all know you've never stopped yearning to go home to your native land. Until recently you were still hoping you might find out what happened to your father and his family. Even though you don't mention it any more, I know you still have the addresses of your uncles.'

'You're probably right,' I said quietly, all the happy memories of my early years in England flooding back. 'I'm getting old, child. After all I've gone through I don't even dare to think I might go home again. Home? Where to? Everything is lost forever. Even if some good fairy came and told me I was free to go at last I haven't got enough money to take a tram to market, let alone travel to London.'

'But Mum,' Rosie was refusing to let go, 'maybe you would feel a bit comforted if at least you could be recognised as a British citizen again.'

At that moment Laurie rang the doorbell and handed me a bunch of flowers.

'These are from my boss,' she said. 'I told her I was coming to see you and she sent them because she thinks you're such a nice person.'

I was touched and while I searched for a vase Rosie told Laurie what we had been talking about.

'Yes, Mum,' Laurie joined in, 'why don't you try? So many people nowadays are managing to get visas for England and some of them haven't even returned.'

'I know,' I was weakening in my resolve, 'but I'm so afraid to go to the embassy. I feel old and vulnerable now. I don't dare to think that I shall live to see better times.'

'We know how downhearted you are,' Laurie said, 'but not many people who have been treated like you have survived. Try, just one more time.'

I gave in, because I knew they were right and that the dream of returning had never left me, however frightened

I might be. I dialled the embassy number that Rosie got from her friend. A stern Bulgarian voice asked what section I wanted to be put through to.

'I would like to speak to a consul or vice-consul, please,' I said, aware that my voice was shaking.

'What about?' the voice demanded. 'Do you want a visa?'

'Not exactly. I simply want to have a few words with a member of the embassy.'

'Have you a British passport?'

'No, not now, but I did have one a long time ago.'

'Oh, how long ago?'

'Just over sixty years.'

'Oh. Well, wait a moment.'

A few minutes later she was back on the line.

'Go to the embassy tomorrow morning at eleven o'clock and tell the porter that you have an appointment with Miss Morell.'

'Thank you,' was all I could say. My heart was beating so loudly and I must have turned pale because Rosie brought me a glass of water and told me to sit down. She looked as worried and excited as I felt. I told her what the woman had said.

'Mum, that's wonderful!'

'I don't know if it's good or bad.'

'Of course it's not bad. You must gather whatever things you have left that would prove you lived in London.'

'There's not much left. They took so much away, destroyed so many things ...' Thinking about the past upset me and made me angry and full of hatred for the people who'd treated us so badly for so many years. I always tried not to show my feelings, fearful they would lead to something worse.

'There is the copy of my father's birth certificate. It doesn't look at its best, but maybe they will acknowledge it.'

'Of course they must,' Rosie insisted. 'Do you know where it is? You've never shown it to us.' She seemed a little offended.

'I couldn't,' I said, 'you were too small to understand how dangerous it would be to mention such a thing. But I do know where it is.'

'Where?' she was becoming impatient.

'It's hidden in the bible.'

'But they always used to shake the books out when they searched.'

'I know, and I was always at my wits' end when they picked up the bible, praying to God they wouldn't see anything. They never did. They were always so busy mocking us, pointing to their heads with their fingers to show that they thought me mad to believe in anything other than the good "father" Stalin.'

Rosie found the bible and I went straight to the pages, which I knew by heart, and carefully unstuck them, tearing one of the corners as my hands shook. Inside was the birth certificate. I handed it to Rosie to read.

'Who is Albert Edward Piu Pius Dear, railway engineer?' she asked.

'That's my grandfather, who took part in the building of the Orient Express to Istanbul.'

'Wow!' was all she could find to say.

Chapter Twenty-Two
A Guardian Angel

At exactly eleven o'clock I was led to the office of Miss Susan Morell, the vice-consul of the British Embassy in Sofia. I found it hard to believe that I had actually been able to walk straight into the embassy after all the years of trying. How could it have been so impossible to get near the door, and yet now I was being invited in? I was so shaken I couldn't even take in my surroundings as we made our way through the corridors. Miss Morell was a tall, good-looking, well-built young woman, who welcomed me with a broad smile.

'Please,' she said, 'sit down and tell me what's troubling you. Would you like the help of an interpreter?'

'I haven't spoken English for many years,' I confessed, 'I have forgotten so much.'

Her Bulgarian secretary sat down with us immediately. Miss Morell seemed very eager to hear my story and I began rather unsteadily. I'd never been in such a nice office before, the furniture shining as if only just polished. Beautiful pictures hung on the walls and the flowers in the two big vases were wonderfully arranged. At first I felt as if I didn't fit in in my shabby clothes, and then I remembered our house in London and I started to feel almost at home. I'd just got as far as explaining how Granny came to be living in Vienna and why Mum had decided to visit her before setting sail for Canada, when she interrupted me.

'This is getting interesting,' she said. 'Mimi, would you make us a nice cup of tea? I think we all need it.'

Mimi jumped to her feet and was back in no time with a tray of tea and biscuits. The tea was the best I'd had since working with the English specialists as an interpreter, but I hardly had time to touch the biscuits as I continued with my story, trying not to make it too long. When I got to the part about how we'd been pushed away from the embassy, not even allowed to get too near to the main entrance, Miss Morell and Mimi were horrified.

'Unbelievable!' they both exclaimed together.

'I didn't give up hope for a long time,' I said, 'and kept trying to get to some English member of staff, but the last time I came here I had almost got to the main gate when two civilians caught hold of me tightly on either arm and dragged me to the militia station. They tied me to a chair and repeated the same questions they'd asked me hundreds of times before: who was I working for? Who paid me? How did I get the money? Every time I said I didn't know I would receive a blow to the head and I would fall over, still tied to the chair. They would pick me up and start again. I must have fainted at one point and when I woke up I was soaked, blood running down my face, which was all swollen, my eyes half-closed, my ears burning with pain. They told me that next time I dared to go near the embassy I would be shot on the spot and my children would belong to them. "We shall do with them whatever we wish, and they will kiss our hands," they said, and then threw me out into the street.'

'Oh my God,' Miss Morell exclaimed. 'Which year was that?'

'Around 1967 or 1968,' I said, 'when my youngest child was finishing school.'

'That was the worst time,' Mimi confirmed.

It was almost time for the lunch break when someone cautiously entered the room, needing an urgent signature.

'That isn't even half the story,' I said. 'Maybe I could come another time and tell you the rest.'

'You should write a book,' Mimi exclaimed.

'I insist you do,' Miss Morell agreed. 'Now please, show me what you have brought with you.'

From my bag I produced the few things I'd been able to hold on to through the years, including my father's birth certificate. They were all damaged, but still recognisable. There were a few school certificates and a few snapshots taken in well-known places around London.

'I shall send everything to London,' Miss Morell said, 'and inform you of their answer as soon as it arrives.'

With that she gathered everything up and left the room while Mimi reminded me of the biscuits and poured me another cup of tea. A few minutes later she returned.

'There you are,' she said, giving the things back to me in a big envelope, 'take care of them. Well, that was a nice change from our usual routine, which is not always so pleasant.'

'I'm sorry to have taken up so much of your time,' I said, standing up.

'Not at all,' she said, shaking my hand again with the same broad smile.

Mimi saw me out and I returned home with slow, unsteady steps. Rosie wasn't there and I was just putting the big envelope inside my old school case, where I kept all my documents, when she came rushing in.

'What happened, Mum?'

'I don't really know. Miss Morell said she would send these things to London and then she gave them back to me.'

'She must have faxed them,' Rosie explained.

'But she was only gone for five minutes.'

At that moment Yana, my great-granddaughter popped in on her way home from school and I tried to remember every detail of the morning for them.

'After all these years,' I finished, 'I'd forgotten what it felt like to be treated as a normal person, as an equal.'

I hadn't much hope that anything would come of the visit, but still I found it hard to sleep that night with all the memories that had been stirred up.

It had just passed eight o'clock the next morning and I was washing up the teacups while Rosie rushed off to see someone who needed an urgent translation. The telephone rang and I'd hardly got the receiver to my ear when I heard an excited voice say, 'Please come to the embassy at nine o'clock. Come in through the side door.'

'Yes, all right,' I stuttered and the line went dead.

I felt a surge of panic, unable to imagine what was going on as I dressed myself as decently as I could. For the first time in a long time I noticed how worn out my shoes were, even though I'd cleaned them so carefully.

'From the hat to the shoes,' my teacher in England had always told us. It was a good thing she couldn't see me now.

I must have run nearly all the way, and felt a pang of guilt when I saw the queue of people waiting for visas, and went looking for the side door. 'Over here,' I heard Mimi's voice say, and she almost pulled me in. The door closed and locked automatically behind us. She escorted me back to Miss Morell's office.

'Please sit down.' Miss Morell's face was shining all over. 'I've just received the answer from London.' My knees went soft and I sank into the chair. 'You have never, ever, stopped being a British citizen. So, welcome back!'

They both hugged me as I tried to take in the news. There was a giant lump in my throat and it was some seconds before I could say. 'I can hardly believe it. Thank God! At last!'

'Well it's true. Every one of us here in the embassy is so glad for you.'

'Will I get a British passport?'

'Of course. Now our consul would also like to hear your story. Would you mind telling it to him some day?'

'I would be happy to, just tell me when.'

'I'm sorry,' Mimi excused herself, 'I'm going to have to leave you for a couple of minutes. They need me in another room.'

When she'd gone Miss Morell pushed a ten pound note into my hand. 'Have something nice to eat with your children,' she said and I was unable to stop the tears coming to my eyes. As I walked out it seemed as if every member of staff had heard my story and they were all smiling as if rejoicing with me as I passed. As they opened the doors for me and helped me over the steps I felt like a queen. I'd never been treated so courteously. I also felt a bit embarrassed. This time Miss Morell herself showed me back out through the side door.

'From now on you'll be a frequent and welcome visitor,' she told me. The concierge had already ordered a taxi to take me home – me in a taxi! I couldn't take it all in and I was scared to feel too happy in case my hopes were dashed by some new disaster. Experience has made it hard for me to ever let myself go, or to enjoy myself with all my heart, because I'm always expecting something terrible to happen. It was as if some wicked spell was hanging over me and my children.

Rosie returned home from an unpleasant day of translating between a Bulgarian small businessman and a German representative. At least they'd paid her and she'd bought a few things from the corner shop.

'It's not much, Mum, but still better than nothing,' she said. 'What happened at the embassy?'

'Well, Miss Morell ...'

'Someone's knocking at the window,' Rosie interrupted.

'Oh, that's Mimi.' I rushed to the door. 'Please come in. Don't be shocked, our rooms are very humble.'

'It looks lovely in here,' Mimi said. 'So nice and clean.'

'Well, that's about all we can do,' I said, worried about what this sudden visit might mean.

'I've just come to give you a few hints regarding your meeting with the consul tomorrow.' She seemed slightly embarrassed.

'Tomorrow?' I asked, noticing how bewildered Rosie was looking.

'Yes, tomorrow. He would like to see you and hear your story himself. What I wanted to tell you is that if he asks you how you manage to live, you must tell him your pension is very low and that it's impossible for you to survive without the support of your children, even though they haven't got proper jobs. The embassy is obliged to help you, but you must ask for it. I understand that you never like to ask for anything, that you're not that kind of person, but don't be afraid to ask, or at least tell him your needs.'

I felt completely lost. 'Oh dear, I wouldn't know where to begin and what to ask for. No one has ever offered me help before. They've always found a way to take whatever they could. I really don't know what I could ask for.'

'Everything,' Mimi said. 'Your rent, your heating, water, electricity, medication, everything!'

'My mother could do with some clothes,' Rosie spoke up shyly.

'Yes, of course, that too,' Mimi assured me.

The next day I'd hardly touched the embassy bell before the door opened automatically.

'Just go down this corridor and you'll reach the consul's department,' the receptionist told me. Miss Morell was waiting and greeted me like an old friend.

'The consul will be here in a minute,' she told me, and sure enough he was, beaming as widely as her.

'Well, well, you are a hero,' he said as he shook my hand. 'After all you've been through. Do you know, you're the only English person who has survived in Bulgaria for so long, and that during the worst regime that has ever ruled here.'

I couldn't think of anything to say. He asked me about my life before the war. For three hours I told my story and Miss Morell stayed to hear the whole thing again. They hardly ever interrupted.

'Now you belong to us,' he said eventually, 'we must help you a bit. Tell me what financial help you would need in a month. I know your pension is a joke. I need you to give me some idea about your essentials.'

'I don't think I could tell you exactly just now,' I said, embarrassed. 'There are so many things I simply do without.'

'You know what,' Miss Morell interrupted to save my blushes. 'I'll have a word with Mimi. She knows very well what a normal citizen's expenses are, so we shall work something out between us, OK?' I nodded. 'Of course the final decision will be taken in England, so it might take a few days, but you needn't worry, you won't lose anything.'

'Thank you very much,' I said. 'I'm sure you'll do your best. You're like a guardian angel to me.'

'I wish I could be,' she said as she gathered up her papers. 'I would change your whole life if I could.'

'You have already,' I assured her.

Chapter Twenty-Three
Going Home

At one o'clock the next day I was told that Mr Short, the ambassador himself, and his wife, would like to meet me over a cup of coffee, and all I could think was how inappropriate my clothes were for such a meeting. It was the first time in many years that I'd given my appearance any thought at all. When you're worried where the next meal is coming from you don't worry about what your clothes look like, only if they're warm enough. Rosie helped me to choose a skirt and blouse that would be decent enough, but the shoes we could do nothing about. I'd noticed how nicely dressed all the embassy staff were.

'You'll just have to keep your feet under the table,' Rosie told me. 'No one will look at your feet or think about criticising your shoes.'

I tried to remember how one was supposed to address an ambassador – was it Your Eminence? I felt so stupid for not knowing such a thing.

When I arrived at the appointed time I waited in Miss Morell's office until she was ready to take me to the main reception hall. As we walked slowly towards it I noticed quite a few staff members were following us, which was puzzling. A wonderful red carpet had been laid on the steps to the reception hall, reaching far beyond the bottom of the stairs.

I began to feel uneasy. Miss Morell led me up the steps and followed the carpet, which led into the reception hall. There at the top stood the ambassador, Mr Short, his face radiating kindness. He welcomed me and invited me in, asking me to sign a book for honoured visitors. His wife embraced me. When I looked around I saw the hall was filled with members of staff, even some journalists who'd come all the way from London for the occasion.

The ambassador opened the first bottle of very special champagne and offered the first glass to me. I took it with trembling hands, unable to find any words as he chatted to me and then raised his glass to wish me a warm welcome back to my home country. Everyone else cheered, wishing me a much happier life from now on. I did my best to thank them all.

A pretty young girl came round with a tray offering beautifully arranged little snacks, which Miss Morell encouraged me to take. But every time I was about to take a bite someone else would ask me a question. Everyone was being so nice and trying not to let me feel uneasy, but I still did. Listening to all of them, I realised I couldn't express myself in the contemporary, intelligent way I wanted. I felt ashamed of myself. I wasn't used to answering questions openly, more practised in giving away as little as possible, always expecting my interrogators to shout at me or to hit me.

'I've gone through all the archives since before the Second World War,' the Ambassador told me. 'There was no letter or message found either from you or your mother. In an old half-destroyed notebook we managed to read some Bulgarian text, which said, "some people will try to get in touch with them, but we will never let them". Maybe you were one of them. Anyway, you're the only British person to have survived here so long without going back to England for even a couple of days. We know that you were never allowed a visa.'

Miss Morell asked me to come back again the next morning as she had some papers for me to sign. I was sure it couldn't be anything bad, but I still felt a tremor of worry at having to do anything so official. The next day, however, I was back and was about to sign the papers she put in front of me when she asked if I didn't want to read them first.

'I wouldn't want to take up too much of your time,' I said, confused. 'I know you wouldn't ask me to sign anything that would do me any harm.'

'You shouldn't be so trustful of everyone. You know that better than anyone. Anyway just look at this.'

She pointed at the place she wanted me to read and I saw the figure of sixty dollars. 'Is that the price I'll have to pay for my passport?' I asked. I must have changed colour because that was more money than I would ever be able to gather together.

'Of course not, read on.'

It gradually dawned on me that what they were saying was that they would pay me sixty dollars a month to help me live a more suitable life. I couldn't say a word and I couldn't stop the tears from running down my face. Miss Morell handed me a tissue.

'You deserve that help,' she said. 'Now you can sign, take your money and go home.'

I signed and she gave me my copy of the papers and the dollars.

'You can change them at any change bureau,' she said, 'but always be very careful and count the money while you're still inside the bureau.'

As soon as I left the embassy I changed ten dollars. It felt so good to hold the money in my hand and to know I would be able to buy something nice for my family to eat. I was no longer going to have to be so dependent on them. By the time I reached home my bag had got rather heavy. Rosie wasn't back yet so I hurried to arrange the table with all the goodies I'd just bought, and a bunch of flowers to finish it all off. When she arrived she had Laurie with her and they just stood and stared at the pretty table.

'Where did you get all this from?' Rosie exclaimed.

'Such wonderful things!' Laurie added. 'I can't believe my eyes.'

We sat down to our tea and I told them all my news. When I finished they both jumped up and hugged me tightly, telling me how happy they were for me and how proud.

* * *

A couple of months later Rosie and I went to a garden party at the embassy to celebrate the Queen's birthday. All the women were wearing hats. Rosie had bought me a nice new skirt and blouse in Germany and I'd bought myself a pair of new shoes and borrowed a hat. The Bulgarian president was there and lots of other distinguished people. After the sandwiches they offered us fish and chips in little cones of rolled newspaper, just like I remembered from my childhood. I loved being able to show Rosie what something in my childhood had looked like. Then they brought on the strawberries and thick cream and I nearly melted, transported back to my childhood once more.

I reminisced about how we all went as a family to Harrods to order everything for our new house in Camrose Avenue. Octave and I were allowed to choose what we wanted for our own rooms. Harrods did everything, even putting the curtains up and arranging the cutlery in the sideboard.

When Christmas came Miss Morell not only gave me an extra sixty dollars, telling me that all pensioners in England got extra at this time of year, she also gave me bags and bags of presents.

'Just a few things to help you have a really nice Christmas treat,' she said. 'Everything is from England. I bet you haven't had a Christmas pudding for a long time.'

When I got home I discovered that as well as a pudding there was a turkey, mince pies, wine, Christmas crackers, everything. I made up some stockings and fixed them to the tree, filling them with goodies.

* * *

In the New Year Miss Morell began to talk seriously about me going back to England for a visit. She warned me that life in the UK was very different to how I remembered it from my childhood.

'There are a lot of asylum seekers now,' she explained, 'and it might take anything up to two years to get you some accommodation. But if you would like to go and see for yourself I'll chat with the representative of British Airways and see if I can get you a free return flight to London.'

A few weeks later I was told I could travel first class to London, with Rosie to take care of me, and stay for a whole month.

Flying was a revelation. I had lived too long in a dark, depressed world. I'd simply forgotten how beautiful life could be. It had been sixty-four years since Mum, Octave and I had set off from England on our adventure.

A car had been sent to pick us up at the airport and when he heard our story, the driver took us on a free sightseeing tour of the city. So much had changed, but still I remembered landmarks like it had only been a couple of weeks since we had left. Piccadilly, Harrods, Selfridges, Big Ben, Buckingham Palace, Trafalgar Square, all so familiar even after so many years. My sixty-four-year-old dream had come true. I was home.

Epilogue

Now I live full time in London, with Rosie caring for me as I grow older. Mickie still lives in Germany and works as a musician and Laurie has retired from the steel factory and lives in Bulgaria, amusing herself by working on a market stall for a friend. Sadly, Hennie died a few years ago, after being an actress all her life. I am blessed with three grand-sons, two granddaughters and one great-granddaughter.

The situation in Europe has changed beyond anything I could ever have hoped for, and now they are all free to move around the world just like anyone else. All of my family come to see me when they are in England. We are still a family of travellers, all speaking many different languages as a result of the countries we have all lived in, but at heart I feel that I am now safely home.

My children and I have tried, by every means we can think of, to trace what happened to my father, my brother and other members of my family after we left England, but every path leads to a dead end. Addresses where my uncles lived were bombed during the war and the residents were either killed or moved away. Even the bank my father worked for has no records for that period, because its City premises were bombed. We have been unable to find anyone with any connection to me or my parents in either England or Canada.

I feel so sad for my mother, who was never able to escape from the poverty and cruelty of life in Bulgaria, and for the many other people who lived through that terrible half-century of bullying, deprivation and repression. Let's hope we never see its like again.

How Robotics Is Changing Society

Don Nardo

ReferencePoint Press®

San Diego, CA

Science, Technology, and Society

About the Author

In addition to his numerous acclaimed volumes on ancient civilizations, historian Don Nardo has published several studies of modern scientific discoveries and phenomena. Among these are *Atoms, Black Holes, Forces and Motion, The Extinction of the Dinosaurs, The Search for Extraterrestrial Life, Biological Warfare, Global Warming*, and biographies of scientists Charles Darwin and Tycho Brahe. Nardo lives with his wife, Christine, in Massachusetts.

For more information, contact:
ReferencePoint Press, Inc.
PO Box 27779
San Diego, CA 92198
www.ReferencePointPress.com

Picture Credits:
Cover: Thinkstock Images; © ABK/BSIP/Corbis: 31; Accurate Art, Inc.: 18, 27; Apega/MCT/Newscom: 59; Associated Press: 67; © Noah Berger/Reuters/Corbis: 39; © Bettmann/Corbis: 14; © Ashley Cooper/Corbis: 43; © Piero Cruciatti/Demotix/Corbis: 22; Depositphotos: 7; © NASA/JPL-Caltech: 35; © Gideon Mendel/Corbis: 9; Friedrich Saurer/Newscom: 71; Shutterstock: 6 (top), 47; Thinkstock Images: 63; Oz un monde extraordinaire Return To Oz de WalterMurch avec Fairuza Balk (Dorothy), Bellina the hen et Tik Tok, 1985/Bridgeman Images: 51; Le Jour ou la Terre s'arreta The Day The Earth Stood Still de Robert Wise avec Michael Rennie, 1951/Bridgeman Images: 54

LIBRARY OF CONGRESS CATALOGING-IN-PUBLICATION DATA

Nardo, Don, 1947- author.
  How robotics is changing society / by Don Nardo.
    pages cm. -- (Science, technology, and society series)
  Audience: Grades 9 to 12.
  Includes bibliographical references and index.
  ISBN-13: 978-1-60152-906-0 (hardback)
  ISBN-10: 1-60152-906-6 (hardback)
  1. Robotics--Social aspects--Juvenile literature. 2. Technology--Social aspects--Juvenile literature.
3. Technological innovations--Juvenile literature. 4. Technology and civilization--Juvenile
literature. I. Title.
  TJ211.2.N36 2016
  629.8'92--dc23
                                                                    2015019765

Contents

"Science and technology have had a major impact on society, and their impact is growing. By drastically changing our means of communication, the way we work, our housing, clothes, and food, our methods of transportation, and, indeed, even the length and quality of life itself, science has generated changes in the moral values and basic philosophies of mankind.

"Beginning with the plow, science has changed how we live and what we believe. By making life easier, science has given man the chance to pursue societal concerns such as ethics, aesthetics, education, and justice; to create cultures; and to improve human conditions. But it has also placed us in the unique position of being able to destroy ourselves."

— Donald P. Hearth, former director of the
NASA Langley Research Center, 1985.

Donald P. Hearth wrote these words in 1985. They appear in the foreword of a publication titled *The Impact of Science on Society*, a collection of speeches given during a public lecture series of the same name. Although Hearth's words were written about three decades ago, they are as true today as when they first appeared on the page.

Advances in science and technology undeniably bring about societal change. Gene therapy, for instance, has the potential to revolutionize medicine and the treatment of debilitating illnesses such as sickle-cell anemia and Parkinson's disease. Medical experts say gene therapy might also be used to treat conditions ranging from obesity to depression and someday, perhaps, even to help extend human life spans.

Although gene therapy offers great hope and promise, it also carries significant risks. The 1999 death of an eighteen-year-old patient taking part in a gene therapy clinical trial in the United States provided a painful reminder of the need for strict safeguards and monitoring. Other risks may be less tangible for the time being, but they are no less serious. The idea of changing the genetic instructions for human beings can be construed in some instances as arrogant, immoral, and dangerous. The possibility of making such changes raises questions of who should decide which traits are normal and desirable and which are to be

4

considered unhealthy. It raises questions about the enhancement of the intellectual and athletic capabilities of individuals and about the potential for discrimination against those judged to be in possession of less desirable or faulty genes.

ReferencePoint's *Science, Technology, and Society* series examines scientific and technological advances in the context of their impact on society. Topics covered in the series include gene therapy, the Internet, renewable energy, robotics, and mobile devices. Each book explores how and why this science or technology came about; how it has influenced or shaped daily life and culture; efforts to guide or control the technology through laws and policies; and what the next generation of this technology might look like. Included in the chapters are focus questions aimed at eliciting conversation and debate. Also included are key words and terms and their meanings in the context of the topics covered. Fully documented quotes enliven the narrative and add to the usefulness of the series as a tool for student researchers.

The study of science, technology, and society—sometimes referred to as STS—has gained significant ground in recent years. Top universities, including Stanford and UC Berkeley in California and MIT and Harvard in Massachusetts, are among the many that offer majors or specialized programs devoted to the study of science, technology, and society. The National Science Foundation, an independent federal agency created by Congress in 1950, even has a program that funds research and education specifically on this topic. For secondary students interested in this field, or for those who are merely curious or just trying to fulfill an assignment, ReferencePoint's new series can provide a useful and accessible starting point.

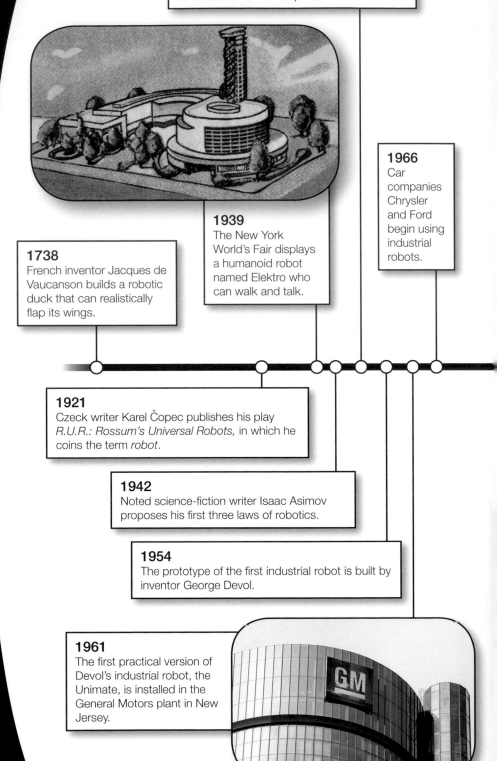

1948
American scientist William G. Walter introduces the first independent electric robot.

1966
Car companies Chrysler and Ford begin using industrial robots.

1939
The New York World's Fair displays a humanoid robot named Elektro who can walk and talk.

1738
French inventor Jacques de Vaucanson builds a robotic duck that can realistically flap its wings.

1921
Czeck writer Karel Čopec publishes his play *R.U.R.: Rossum's Universal Robots,* in which he coins the term *robot.*

1942
Noted science-fiction writer Isaac Asimov proposes his first three laws of robotics.

1954
The prototype of the first industrial robot is built by inventor George Devol.

1961
The first practical version of Devol's industrial robot, the Unimate, is installed in the General Motors plant in New Jersey.

GM

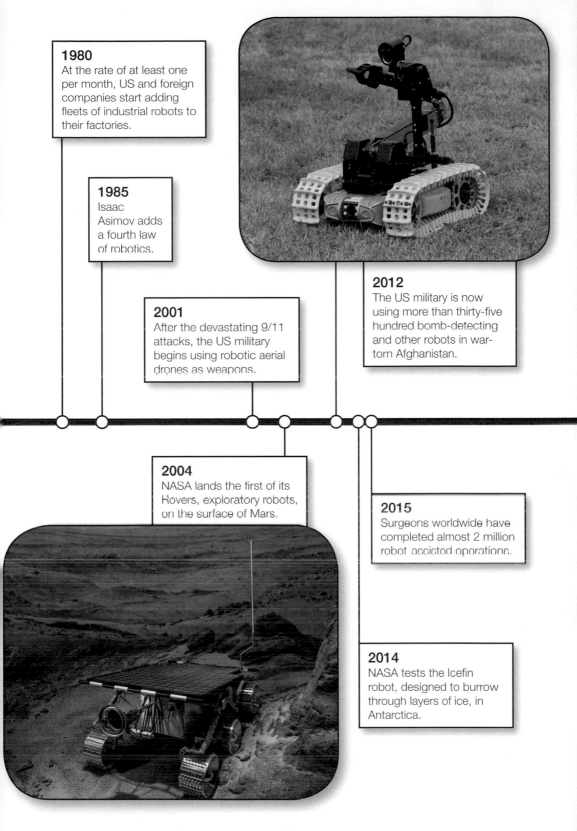

1980
At the rate of at least one per month, US and foreign companies start adding fleets of industrial robots to their factories.

1985
Isaac Asimov adds a fourth law of robotics.

2001
After the devastating 9/11 attacks, the US military begins using robotic aerial drones as weapons.

2012
The US military is now using more than thirty-five hundred bomb-detecting and other robots in war-torn Afghanistan.

2004
NASA lands the first of its Rovers, exploratory robots, on the surface of Mars.

2015
Surgeons worldwide have completed almost 2 million robot-assisted operations.

2014
NASA tests the Icefin robot, designed to burrow through layers of ice, in Antarctica.

Robotics and the New Machine Age

Robots are to humanity's future what cars were to global society's recent past. That is the conclusion that many modern experts on machines and technology have reached. Robots, they say, will help bring about a second machine age even bigger than the one that was largely initiated by the automotive industry. One of those experts, Japan's noted innovator in the field of robotics, Hirohisa Hirukawa, explains, "Automobiles were the biggest product of the twentieth century." Similarly, he says, people will "eventually look back and say that robots were the big product of the twenty-first century."[1]

The Cars of the New Century

In part because cars were such a huge innovation in the 1900s, they and the industry that produced them transformed the economic landscape of that century. The money the car companies made from selling those vehicles was only a small part of the financial boom that occurred, particularly in the decades following World War II. There were also numerous industry spinoffs. One included gasoline, oil, and other kinds of fuel, as well as the oil rigs, trucks, and refineries that produced them. There were also gas stations to dispense these products; replacement auto parts, the factories that made them, and the warehouses that stored them; mechanics and their shops to repair cars; new highways for the cars; tar, concrete, and other products to build the highways; motels, stores, and other amenities built along the highways; the expansion of the banking industry to handle millions of car loans; and much more.

Similarly, according to leading robotics expert Colin Lewis, modern robots are already spinning off numerous related products and services. These range from the thousands of new metal parts required to build the robots, to the creation of the computerized brains that provide them with artificial intelligence (AI), to the thousands of new specialized technicians needed to assemble them. In fact, Lewis says,

the potential uses for robotics, AI, and automation in business are great and ever expanding and helping to move jobs locally. But we must remember technology is here to serve us, not the other way around. It is the tech savvy company that successfully unites robots, automation, and humans that will thrive in the "second machine age."[2]

Sparks fly as robotic arms weld car frames at a Hyundai factory in China. Robotic equipment and devices are used today in all kinds of factories, in operating rooms and medical offices, on battlefields, in cities, and in space and ocean exploration.

Doing the Dirty Work

One important difference between cars and robots is that when automobiles first appeared in the early 1900s, they were a fairly new concept to most people, including most scientists. In contrast, the experts point out, robots are *not* new, either in concept or execution. As far back as ancient times, a few far-sighted individuals described such mechanical devices that might perform a variety of human tasks. At first, no one expected that such humanlike machines would become reality any time soon. Indeed, for a long time robots remained limited to science-fiction and fantasy stories.

In the early 1900s, however, a handful of enterprising inventors began tinkering with the first robots. Soon the field of robotics was in full swing. It is the branch of engineering concerned with designing, building, and operating machines that can assist humans—and sometimes even take their place—in diverse situations. These situations include factory assembly lines, operating rooms, and settings in which it is difficult or dangerous for humans to work. From the ocean bottom, to the battlefield, to outer space, robots are primed to safely expand humanity's reach into all sorts of hostile environments. More than anything else, experts on robotics say, these advanced machines are and will continue to be designed to do human dirty work. That is, they will accomplish those tasks that humans view as too repetitive, complex, boring, difficult, or hazardous. That will free up people to spend their time on more creative or meaningful endeavors.

android

A robot designed to look and act like a human.

The unification of robots and humans will see its most obvious development in the android—the human-looking machine helper. "For human-interactive operations," Japanese researcher Fumio Kanehiro points out, "humanoid robots are the best suited. A robot that has a shape very similar to that of human beings is capable of operating in an environment adjusted for human use, utilizing existing tools without modification and working in collaboration with human workers."[3]

Journalist Daniel Ichbiah, who has written extensively about robots, explains why supplying androids with existing tools will save a great deal of time and money in the coming decades. "All the tools we use on a routine basis," he writes, "from the screwdriver to the automobile, were designed for human use." A robot that looks and acts like a human "should logically be able to use the appliances and apparatuses that crowd our environment." That mechanical being "would be ideally cut out for doing our dirty work."[4]

Chapter One

Robot Origins and Industrial Robots

"If you can develop a robot that's capable of integrating into the human workflow, into the human part of the factory—if it has just a little bit of decision-making ability, a little bit of flexibility— that opens up a new type of manufacturing process."

—Manufacturing and technology expert Willy Shih.

Quoted in Will Knight, "This Robot Could Transform Manufacturing," *MIT Technology Review*, September 18, 2012. www.technologyreview.com.

The exact origins of the concept of the robot, or moving mechanical helper or being, are lost in the shadowy mists of humanity's earliest ages. Indeed, the first examples of what later came to be called robots will likely never be known. What is more certain is that robot-like creatures inhabited the mythologies of some ancient peoples, especially the Greeks. Their myths feature a number of such animate nonliving beings, which the Greeks called automatons (or automata). That word is the derivation of the modern term *automation*, meaning the use of machines to speed up and/or improve various human manufacturing and communications systems.

One of the more vivid of those early depictions of automatons was that of the attendants of Hephaestos, the god of the forge and metallurgy. He was said to have made several female beings from pure gold. Those attendants are the first known examples of the modern vision of the robot—a mechanical servant that frees people from having to do mundane work. According to the famous eighth-century-BCE Greek poet Homer in his great epic the *Iliad*, one day Hephaestos closed down his forge, put on a tunic, took up a heavy stick in his hand, and went to the doorway, limping [because he had a crippled leg]. And in support of their master moved his attendants. These are golden and in appearance like living young women. There is intelligence in their hearts, and there is speech in them, and strength, and from the immortal gods they have learned how to do things. These [metal beings now] stirred in support of their master.[5]

A number of other descriptions of robot-like beings and creatures can be found in ancient mythology. These later inspired several Greek inventors to tinker together various mechanical devices. These included the first simple prototypes of steam engines and some humanoid, or human-shaped, puppets that featured moving parts. Later still, Chinese and Arabic inventors built even more complex moving mechanical humanlike puppets. These puppetlike robots reached their culmination in 1738, when French inventor Jacques de Vaucanson created a mechanical duck so complex that each of its wings featured more than four hundred moving parts. In addition to flapping those wings, the robot duck drank water, ate and digested grain, and even excreted imitation duck poop stored inside a hidden container.

automation

The use of machines to speed up and/or improve various human manufacturing and communications systems.

The First Electric and Industrial Robots

The next major advance in robotics came with the application of electricity to machines and other aspects of society in the early 1900s. The Westinghouse Electric Corporation led the way by developing the first electric-powered robot in the late 1930s. Its introduction was part of the company's effort to convince American consumers to buy electric-powered refrigerators, stoves, and other appliances. At the New York World's Fair in 1939, Westinghouse unveiled the humanoid robot Elektro. Standing 7 feet (2 m) tall and weighing 265 pounds (120 kg), Elektro could walk, talk (with a vocabulary of some seven hundred words), play the piano,

Elektro, the humanoid robot, and Sparko, a robotic dog, were displayed at the 1939 New York World's Fair. Elektro could walk, talk, play piano, and blow up balloons.

and blow up balloons, among other actions. Also, his head, legs, arms, and all his fingers moved separately. These many movements were driven by his power sources, consisting of eleven small electric motors and several photoelectric cells (which convert sunlight into electricity).

Elektro's main drawback was that he was not autonomous, or self-sufficient. That is, he was unable to sense his environment or

14

to navigate using sensed data. Nor could he maintain his power sources on his own. This obstacle was overcome less than a decade later in 1948, when American scientist William G. Walter introduced the first autonomous electric robots. Their names were Elmer and Elsie. Powered by electric batteries, they could sense their surroundings, as well as seek out and hook up to their recharging station when their batteries were low.

With Walter's advances, it was now practical to build robots capable of doing programmed tasks, including in industrial settings. In 1954 American engineer and inventor George Devol created the first industrial robot, called the Unimate. It consisted of a big arm with numerous movable parts. He realized the tremendous potential, both mechanically and financially, for this device and others like it. So in 1956 he and an associate, Joseph Engelberger, opened the first robot-making company, Unimation.

After some initial development, experiments, and testing, in 1961 the Unimate was installed at the General Motors plant in Ewing Township, New Jersey. It weighed a whopping 4,000 pounds (1,814 kg) and cost $25,000, considered a lot of money

photoelectric cells

Devices that convert sunlight into electricity.

in those days. The arm had the ability to put a machine part or other item on an assembly line. It could also be programmed to remove an item from the line. Its first task was to lift and stack metal automobile parts that were too hot for human workers to safely touch.

General Motors was thrilled with the new robotic arm, which clearly saved both time and money. In time the company began rebuilding its plant in Lordstown, Ohio, which eventually became the most automated car factory in the world. It could turn out automobiles at the rate of 110 per hour, twice as fast as any other car plant of that era.

At the same time, Unimation and other companies that had followed its lead in making mechanical arms designed a second generation of robotic machines. These machines were capable of screwing one part to another and performing other somewhat more complex jobs. As a result, in 1966 two other car companies, Chrysler and Ford, installed their own industrial robots. Within

15

a few years, European automakers did the same. By the early 1970s, the car companies Fiat, Volvo, Mercedes-Benz, British Leyland, and BMW were all installing industrial robots at a furious pace. This trend continued nonstop, and today about 80 percent of all the work involved in building cars is done by fairly simple robots. Furthermore, as soon as the car industry paved the way, many other US and overseas companies wanted to have their own robots. As a result, in 1980 the idea of robots in industry really took off, with a new company adopting those specialized devices at least every month.

Typical Robot Tasks

Almost all of the early modern industrial robots, like many of the ones in use today, did only one task at a time. That is largely because most of them were and are used in manufacturing individual, identical products, and not only for car companies. A list of only a few of the other companies that came to use such robots demonstrates the extreme diversity of industrial robots. Those corporations include Motorola (televisions, radios, and recording devices); Pratt & Whitney (aircraft engines); DuPont (chemical, transportation, and construction products); Whirlpool (washers and dryers); Digital Equipment Corporation (computer keyboards); and General Electric (electronic items). These and other manufacturing companies feature assembly lines of one sort of another, and by definition an assembly line is designed to accomplish one task at a time.

Those tasks are extremely diverse. But most have something in common—they require a robotic arm with fingerlike grippers or pinchers at the end. That allows these mechanical devices to perform actions such as grasping, lifting, inserting, or twisting the items moving along the assembly line. Other robots weld or glue two parts together; drill holes in objects; paint items (using spray guns); load finished products onto trucks; test the durability of specific products by making them function over and over again; and inspect work done earlier by both robots and humans.

That last mentioned task, inspection, needs a robot to be equipped with some sort of sensor. Robot sensors have a wide

Who Coined the Term *Robot*?

The term *robot,* along with the widely popular modern image of humanoid robots as menacing beings seeking to overthrow and replace humanity, were the work of Czech writer Karel Čopec (CHOP-ick). In 1921 he introduced his powerful play *R.U.R.: Rossum's Universal Robots.* Before that, such mechanical humanlike creatures were referred to by other names, including automatons. But in the play, Čopec used the Czech word *robata,* meaning "forced labor" or "servitude" to describe them. That fit the theme of the play, which is the inhumanity of slave labor. When translated into English, *robata* became *robots.*

The play starts out on an island where a mentally ill inventor named Old Rossum and his nephew have built a robot factory. The nephew favors using the robots as low-cost forced laborers, so they would become humanity's servants. But a number of the island's other residents feel that slavery is wrong, so they attempt to close down the factory. The robots, which have humanlike intelligence, view this action as an attack on them, however. As a result, they fight back and slaughter most of the world's human population. Čopec's daring and imaginative tale about robots turning on and destroying their makers turned out to have a cultural outcome that he did not foresee. In short, the play gave robots a bad reputation. For the next few decades, most robots in literature and film were depicted as sinister, evil, destructive, or all of these.

array of types and applications in industry, including telling human workers if one or more items are or are not where they belong on the assembly line. For example, a sensor might detect pulses of light reflected by objects on the line. Such sensors might also detect certain sounds or various types of radiation. In addition, some industrial robots have tactical, or contact, sensors, in which case a robot indicates an object is present by very lightly touching it. Once it has been determined that the object is either there or not there, the robot immediately sends a signal to a control panel monitored by a person.

Another more general and extremely important task for industrial robots has been to reduce the considerable danger

Parts of a Robot

Robots come in many shapes and sizes. The basic industrial robot has four major components. The mechanical unit resembles an inverted human arm with a shoulder, elbow, and wrist. The power supply provides energy for the robot to operate. The controller or control systems consist of computers or microprocessors that guide all functions and enable the robot to self-diagnose any problems that arise. The end-of-arm tooling allows the robot to manipulate items during manufacturing or other processes.

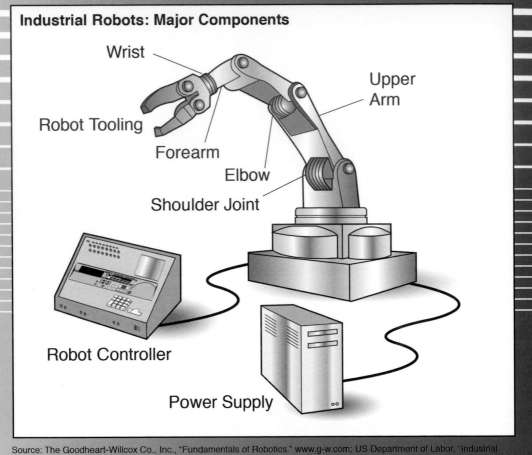

Industrial Robots: Major Components

Wrist

Upper Arm

Robot Tooling

Forearm

Elbow

Shoulder Joint

Robot Controller

Power Supply

Source: The Goodheart-Willcox Co., Inc., "Fundamentals of Robotics." www.g-w.com; US Department of Labor, "Industrial Robotics and Robot System Safety." www.osha.gov.

posed to human workers by a number of industrial jobs. Applying robots to a specific factory typically decreases the incidence of workers' injuries in that workplace. A well-known example is the foundry industry, which makes diverse products from molten, or melted, metals. According to V. Daniel Hunt, an authority on modern robotics:

> The major motivation for robotizing foundry work has been the high risk to human workers. Virtually every foundry process, from pouring molten metal, to the final cleaning of a casting [metal mold], exposes workers to heat, noise, fumes, and dust. Robots have been used to reduce this exposure and also to relieve humans of the fatiguing tasks of manipulating hot, heavy metal parts.[6]

Economic Benefits of Robots

Robots do these and numerous other jobs on assembly lines at high speed and with a degree of accuracy that human workers cannot maintain for long periods. Such advantages result in more work getting done in each factory shift than could be done by human workers doing the same work. This is because the average person cannot work as fast as most robots. Additionally, human workers tire and need breaks to rest and eat. Then, at the end of the workday, they go home, whereas robots can work around the clock. Moreover, human workers receive pay and various benefits (such as health insurance) that robots do not need. All of these factors contribute to the cost of doing business. Some manufacturers have found that they can save a lot of money over the course of a week, month, or year by using robots for assembly-line jobs that workers once held.

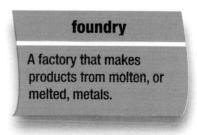

foundry

A factory that makes products from molten, or melted, metals.

Mark Stevens, an expert on how modern factories operate, summarizes some of the principle economic benefits of using robots in manufacturing and other industrial and workplace settings. First, he says, these special machines accomplish work in a very precise way, which turns out products of higher quality. "Once industrial robots have been correctly programmed," he explains, "they are fairly predictable and precise, resulting in high quality without much variation."[7] In turn, better-quality products attract more customers, who buy those items over and over again, a long-term financial plus to the company.

Moreover, Stevens says, the precision work of robots eliminates waste, which saves money during each and every shift a robot works. He lists still other economic benefits of employing industrial robots, saying:

> An industrial robot increases speed for manufacturing processes, in part by eliminating interruptions. Robots run 24/7, without breaks, shift changes or other interruptions. The speed and dependability of robots ultimately reduces the cycle time for an operation and maximizes the [number of products turned out in a given amount of time]. Using robots for repetitive tasks also means fewer risks of injury for workers. Even the people who oversee the robots don't have to be on the shop floor with them. [Instead] they could oversee the process online, even remotely. The cost of having a person handle many operations is probably going to be more expensive than a robot, even with the high initial expense of this technology investment.[8]

Smarter Industrial Robots

Although robots produce higher-quality products overall, increase efficiency on assembly lines, and have numerous economic advantages, they do have some drawbacks. First, they typically take several hours to program. For example, the factory supervisors might need a particular robot to use its arm and pinchers in a different way than usual. If so, each of the robot's individual components must be adjusted so it will do the new job with a high degree of precision. If its new range of motion is off by even a little, the result could be its pinchers grabbing at thin air over and over, hour after hour.

Another drawback of these large robotic arms is that they tend to be dangerous to human workers. Such a mechanism

Making Compliant Industrial Robots

One of the most important desired physical traits for industrial robots has always been compliance, or flexibility, sensitivity, and smoothness of movement. But until recently, most industrial robots were stiff and unable to respond to touch or other physical contact with people. If a person touched such a robot, that machine was not programmed to feel it, so it just ignored the contact and kept on performing its assigned tasks.

That situation has begun to change, thanks to the introduction of a mechanism called a series elastic actuator. It was invented by robotics experts Gill Pratt and Matthew Williamson. They say that in the past, robot parts such as the elbow joints were attached to one another in a rigid manner. So there was little or no flexibility or smoothness of motion, as there is in human elbows. In contrast, newer elbow joints in industrial robots contain a gearbox and motor equipped with the series elastic actuator, which also features a flexible metal spring. The spring makes the elbow much less rigid and more able to measure and respond to human contact with it. The robot's control system interprets the range of different possible pressures on the spring similarly to the way human skin feels the pressure of another person's touch. In turn, the robot is programmed to react accordingly. For example, when it senses a human touch, it slows down or even stops, thereby becoming far less of a safety hazard in the factory.

can weigh hundreds of pounds and produce a great deal of force when it moves. So any human worker who gets in the way of that movement can be seriously injured. (A few of the many recorded accidents have actually been fatal.) To reduce the incidence of such mishaps, many industrial robots are surrounded by protective shielding.

The main reason why these problems persist in many factories in the United States and around the world is that for the most part simple, one-task industrial robots have not evolved much since they appeared in the 1960s and 1970s. Australian robotics expert

Rodney Brooks, founder of Rethink Robotics, a leading maker of industrial robots, explains:

> If you've watched the evolution of industrial robots over the last 50 years, you haven't actually seen much innovation since the Unimate. These machines perform well on very narrowly defined, repeatable tasks. But they aren't adaptable, flexible, or easy to use. Nor are most of these machines safe for people to be around. . . . Go to a car factory in Japan or Detroit, you'll see a body shop full of robots, but with no people. Go to final assembly and you'll find all people, no robots. Industrial robots and people don't mix.[9]

According to Brooks and other leading authorities on industrial robots, these and most other problems with these mechanical

Baxter the robot (left) poses with a robot friend at a 2014 international robotics trade show. Baxter can be taught to recognize objects or perform new tasks quickly.

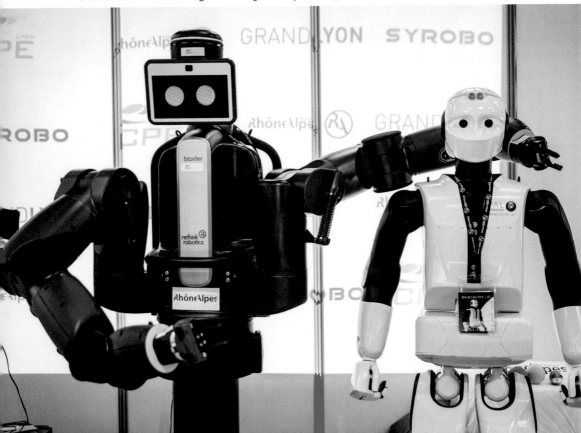

helpers will soon be a thing of the past. More and more factories are installing smarter robots that are easier to program and that pose few or no safety hazards in the workplace. A leading example is Baxter, a robot created by Brooks's company.

MIT Technology Review editor Will Knight describes this innovative machine:

> Much like a human worker, Baxter can be taught in minutes how to recognize a new object or perform a new task. To teach Baxter to recognize something, you just hold the object in front of one of its cameras, which are located in the head, in the chest, and at the end of each arm. To program an action, you can move one of Baxter's two giant arms through the desired motion and select from a number of preprogrammed actions using a pair of dial controls found in each forearm. When you grab one of Baxter's arms, it feels light as a feather. Its motors compensate in response to your touch, making the heavy limb easy to move through the air.[10]

Moreover, Baxter, like other new industrial robots currently under development by various companies, is safe for humans to work with on the factory floor. Brooks says that Baxter

> doesn't need an expensive or elaborate safety cage, and factory operators don't need to put it in a part of the factory where it's segregated from the rest of the workers. It's safe to share a workspace with. If you see a Baxter, you can actually go and hug it while it's in operation. [In fact] interacting with Baxter is more like working with a person than operating a traditional industrial robot. If the robot picks up something it shouldn't on the assembly line, for instance, you can take its arm and move the robot to put the object down. (Don't try that with a current industrial robot.) You don't have to know anything about computer languages. It knows what you mean, and it does what you want.[11]

This new generation of industrial robots is poised to change the way factories work in the same way that the first industrial robots transformed such workplaces half a century ago. Expert observers Erico Guizzo and Evan Ackerman, of *IEEE Spectrum*'s *Robotics* blog, have studied these new machine helpers in detail and are enthusiastic about their potential. They say that modern makers of industrial robots are in the process of unleashing "a revolution in manufacturing with a friendly faced factory robot."[12]

Chapter Two

The Widespread Use of Robots

Focus Questions

1. In your opinion, what are the chief benefits and drawbacks of using robots in warfare?
2. What are your views about using robots as stand-ins for nurses or doctors?
3. Do you think that robotic explorers have greater, equal, or lesser value than human explorers? Explain your answer.

"*Advancements in robotics are continually taking place in the fields of space exploration, health care, public safety, entertainment, defense, and more. These machines—some fully autonomous, some requiring human input—extend our grasp [and] enhance our capabilities.*"

—Alan Taylor, senior editor of the *Atlantic*.

Alan Taylor, "Robots at Work and Play," *Atlantic*, October 21, 2013. www.theatlantic .com.

In 2011 soldiers in a US Army unit fighting in Iraq mourned the death of a member they had nicknamed "Scooby Doo." They were truly saddened by his passing. What made this different from most other battlefield losses in the war was that Scooby Doo was not a human being. He was a robot. Built by the company iRobot, weighing 60 pounds (27 kg), and equipped with four cameras and a mechanical arm featuring small grippers, Scooby Doo was designed to detect enemy bombs intended to kill American fighters. He did this job with distinction, carrying out nineteen successful missions and saving several dozen American and Iraqi lives. Well before a bomb finally took him out of action for good, the human members of the unit had come to think of him as a full member of the group. In gratitude, they dedicated a plaque to him; it listed his battlefield accomplishments, an honor normally accorded only human soldiers.

Scooby Doo was just one of thousands of robots being used in military and other nonindustrial settings. By 2012 more than thirty-five hundred bomb-detecting and other robots patrolled war-torn Afghanistan, for example, and at least twelve thousand were used by US forces in Iraq. Similar military bots, as they are often called, are used by other armies around the globe. Robots have also been put to work in homes, in the medical field, in police work, in the entertainment industry, and in sea and space exploration, to name only a few areas.

Their numbers in the workforce—and their accomplishments— are growing. Indeed, says researcher Duncan Graham-Rowe, "Robots are increasingly marching into our lives."[13] Robots still perform repetitive tasks of all sorts. In addition to that, they do jobs that require high levels of accuracy and, in some cases, pose grave danger to human beings.

Saving Lives

Whereas industrial robots are built to make things in factories and other workplace settings, most of the robots created for the military are intended either to save or take human lives. The majority of military robots, like Scooby Doo in Iraq, aim to protect soldiers and other men and women on the front lines of war. Many of these ingenious devices are small and sit atop mini-tank treads, making them look like toys. Far from a toy, however, each such protective robot is highly complex and sturdy enough to move along extremely rough terrain. It features built-in sensors that can "see," "hear," and otherwise detect the presence of a wide range of the lethal substances currently used in the chemical weapons employed by some armies in warfare. Also, almost all such battlefield robots are "man-portable," meaning that a single

man-portable

Able to be carried by a single person.

The PackBot

The PackBot is a small robot designed to fit into a standard US Army backpack. In Iraq and Afghanistan, PackBots have been used to clear caves and bunkers, search buildings, and defeat IEDs. The lightweight robot is designed to withstand rough treatment. Soldiers often toss it through windows, for instance, so that it can search for hidden enemy combatants. The PackBot is equipped with cameras, a maneuverable arm, and other devices. It relays real-time audio, video, and other data so that soldiers can see and hear what is taking place while remaining at a safe distance. Using treaded flippers, it can climb over obstacles and right itself if it lands upside down.

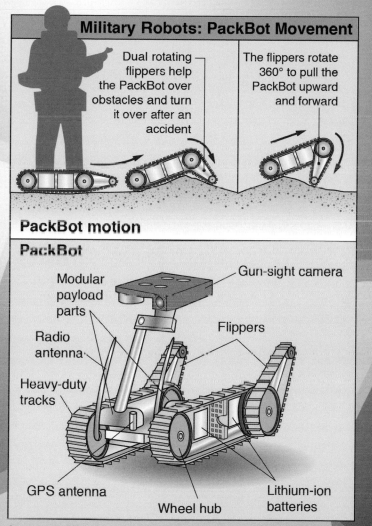

Military Robots: PackBot Movement

Dual rotating flippers help the PackBot over obstacles and turn it over after an accident

The flippers rotate 360° to pull the PackBot upward and forward

PackBot motion

PackBot

Modular payload parts

Gun-sight camera

Radio antenna

Flippers

Heavy-duty tracks

GPS antenna

Wheel hub

Lithium-ion batteries

Source: HowStuffWorks, "How Military Robots Work." http://science.howstuffworks.com/military-robot3.htm; Space Foundation, "iRobot PackBot Tactical Mobile Robot." www.spacefoundation.org

person can carry such a device into a battle situation. This is vital because heavier, bulkier robots must be brought into combat on trucks and other large carriers. These have trouble maneuvering through rubble-strewn streets and are easy targets for enemy snipers and missile launchers.

One of the most useful of these military robots is called Talon. The standard version, including a mechanical arm that can grasp objects, weighs 85 pounds (39 kg); a similar robot without the arm weighs 60 pounds (27 kg). Both versions can move along on their own as swiftly as 6 feet (1.8 m) per second. They have been used extensively on the battlefields of Afghanistan, Iraq, and Bosnia. Using programming that includes advanced image recognition, Talons have repeatedly and safely cleared away objects that threatened soldiers' lives, among them improvised explosive devices, live grenades, and other explosives. In addition, a Talon's sensors can detect the presence of radiation and various chemical weapons. Using sensors capable of detecting the heat given off by human bodies, several Talons were employed to help find survivors and access the damage at Ground Zero in New York City after the terrorist assault on the World Trade Center towers on September 11, 2001.

Another small robot now used extensively by American soldiers and other armies is the PackBot. Scooby Doo was a PackBot. Primarily an exploratory vehicle, it moves through windows and other openings in buildings in war-torn regions. It uses its extensive sensor array to search for and find hidden enemy bombs and fighters. To accomplish such difficult tasks, PackBot is equipped with a wide array of sophisticated sensors. They include multiple high-resolution cameras that can take both photos and video; a digital thermal (heat-sensing) camera; a sensor that detects explosives; and other ultrasensitive detectors that recognize the presence of various dangerous chemical and biological materials.

thermal

Related to heat.

The US military is also developing robots to aid in recovering ships and aircraft lost at sea. Especially impressive is the navy's Deep Drone, which can dive roughly forty times deeper than

More like a Sniper than a Pilot

One of the leading robotic drones used by the US military, the MQ-9 Reaper, has a wingspan of 66 feet (20 m). It flies at a speed of 230 miles per hour (370 kph) and can reach an altitude of 50,000 feet (15,240 m). Because it is an attack drone, it carries deadly weapons, in this case four AGM-114 Hellfire missiles. They are laser guided, which makes them remarkably accurate. The other equipment inside the drone is also highly complex. Included are communications devices that allow the plane to make contact with any of the hundreds of US satellites orbiting Earth. The Reaper also features a Global Positioning System similar to that in modern cars and trucks. The difference is that the robot's version is so accurate it can pick out any spot on Earth's surface with pinpoint accuracy. Meanwhile, the cameras, located in the drone's nose section, can show the target and surrounding objects in extreme detail. One US Air Force pilot said that when flying an ordinary warplane, he could not see the faces of the people on which he dropped bombs. In contrast, a drone pilot explained, when operating the robotic craft from a remote location, like someone playing a video game from a great distance, he could clearly see people beside the target. It made him feel less like a pilot and more like a sniper, he remarked.

unprotected human divers can. It features two mechanical arms (called manipulators) that can work with a variety of tools. Deep Drone can also transmit photos taken with its digital still camera and videos taken with its color television cameras.

Military Robots on the Offensive

Increasingly, such protective, defensive robots have been modified to go on the offensive when the need arises. A Talon, for instance, can be outfitted with weapons ranging from M16 rifles and M240 machine guns to grenade launchers and small missiles. Other military robots have been conceived as attack vehicles from the start.

Most US offensive robots are currently flying machines, unmanned aerial vehicles more commonly known as drones. They have been increasingly prominent in news reports since the September 11 attacks in 2001. Before that, drones were mainly small, lightweight planes equipped with cameras to help map the earth's surface. From that year onward, however, more and more of these robotic craft became offensive robotic devices armed with missiles and other military equipment. According to noted Pentagon correspondent Richard Whittle:

> The Predator [drone] became the first weapon in history whose operators could use it to stalk and kill a single individual on the other side of the planet much the way a sniper does, and with total invulnerability. The Predator's phenomenal flight endurance also made it a powerful new form of overhead intelligence, surveillance, and reconnaissance—a drone that can find and shine a laser beam on targets for manned aircraft, eavesdrop on enemy communications, provide troops on the ground warning of enemy movements, and give commanders an overhead view of the battlefield.[14]

Robotic Surgeons, Nurses, and Orderlies

Robots are also increasingly prevalent in hospitals and other medical settings; they see to a host of medical needs. "Picture R2D2 from *Star Wars* carrying a tray of medications or a load of laundry down hospital corridors," says Timothy Hay of the *Wall Street Journal* in a half-joking, half-serious manner. Thousands of service robots are entering the health care field. Hay adds, "This new robotic breed is boasting features increasingly found in smart phones, gaming consoles, and other consumer electronics, from advanced sensors and motion detectors to powerful microprocessors and voice activation. The service robots are self-aware, intelligent and able to navigate changing environments, even chaotic hospital settings."[15]

Of these medical robots, many are surgical helpers that assist doctors in the operating room. The best-selling version to date is the da Vinci surgical system, made by the American company Intuitive Surgical. Close to two thousand da Vinci systems have

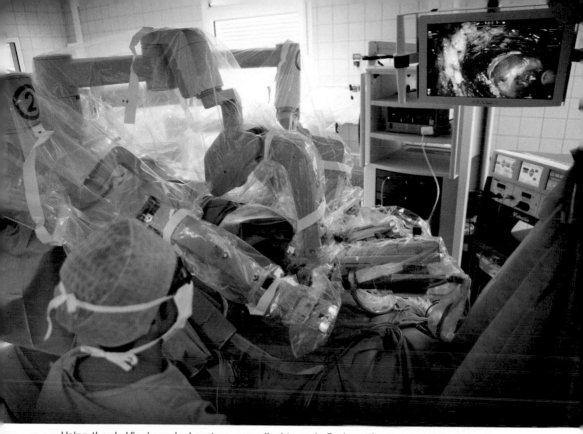

Using the da Vinci surgical system, a medical team in Paris performs a prostatectomy (the surgical removal of the prostate gland). The robotic system allows the doctor to perform minimally invasive surgery with enhanced vision, precision, dexterity, and control.

been installed in major hospitals around the world, including London, Paris, Rome, and Tokyo, along with Boston, New York, Los Angeles, and hundreds of other US cities. Using these robotic systems, by mid-2015 surgeons had completed almost 2 million robot-assisted operations.

During such procedures, the surgeon uses joystick-like hand-grips to guide tiny instruments built into the robotic system. Those miniature tools maintain a rock-hard steady position, as opposed to a human doctor's hand, which sometimes applies slightly too much or too little pressure. The robotic scalpel can make perfect incisions that are much smaller than those a human doctor can produce. The benefits of robotic surgery can be considerable in some cases, according to the world famous Mayo Clinic in Rochester, Minnesota. "Often, robotic surgery makes minimally invasive surgery possible," one of the clinic's spokespeople states. "The benefits of minimally invasive surgery include fewer complications,

Household Robots

Houses and hospitals in the United States lie a long way from the foreign battle-fields scorched by the explosives launched from flying robots. The extreme contrast between these local and distant environments strongly demonstrates the versatility, or flexibility, of modern robots. "Household bots," which can be found in many homes around the world, are smaller, lighter, and far less threatening-looking than military robots.

These home robots perform a variety of household chores. Roomba, designed by iRobot, a leading maker of practical robots, is perhaps the most famous example to date. It is essentially an automated vacuum cleaner. Guided by sensors, it travels over a room's floor in a zigzag pattern. It can be scheduled to "awaken" at any time of the day or night, do its job, and then "go back to sleep." The well-known vacuum cleaner company Electrolux makes a comparable robot called Trilobite. Similar to Roomba and Trilobite is Scooba (also made by iRobot), which both sweeps and washes tiled floors. Still another household bot, named Looj, cleans gutters, and a company called Friendly Robotics, located in Vero Beach, Florida, offers Robomow, a robot that mows lawns. Still other already existing household bots do laundry and warm up food in a microwave, among other jobs.

such as surgical site infection, less pain and blood loss, quicker recovery, and smaller, less noticeable scars."[16]

Many other uses have been devised for robots in hospitals and medical clinics. One example is a robot called the RoboCourier. It carries medical supplies, medicine, and bedding materials throughout the hospital, eliminating the need for many of the orderlies who normally distribute these items. Also, a number of hospitals have already installed units like the Robotic Nurse Assistant, created by Healthcare Robotics, in Atlanta, Georgia. That ingenious device allows nurses to examine patients in any room of the building without actually visiting those rooms. This eliminates the need for nurses to make lengthy rounds and allows them to use that time in more constructive ways. Such a robot is equipped with a sophisticated video system that shows the patient to the nurses, who use a complex remote panel to operate small robotic arms. These take the patient's temperature and record his or her vital signs. The Robotic Nurse Assistant also monitors patients, and experiments have shown that it does this more efficiently than standard monitoring systems.

Robotic Germ-Zappers and Advanced Wheelchairs

Still another new medical use for advanced robots is the destruction of lethal viruses such as those that cause Ebola, hepatitis C, and even the flu. These diseases can linger in hospital operating rooms and patient wards long after patients have been cured of them. New patients can then become infected, perpetuating a vicious cycle of sickness. The Texas-based corporation Xenex recently introduced a robot called Saul, designed to destroy these lethal microscopic bugs and thereby make hospitals safer. Looking much like the famous R2-D2 bot from the *Star Wars* films, Saul has been installed in several military hospitals, including the one at Langley Air Force Base in Hampton, Virginia. The bot zaps viruses, bacteria, and other kinds of germs by hitting them with a beam of high-intensity ultraviolet light. These pulses of light, which are twenty-five thousand times brighter than a florescent light, smash the germs' cell walls, killing them instantly.

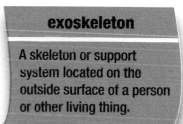

exoskeleton

A skeleton or support system located on the outside surface of a person or other living thing.

In some cases soldiers and civilians who have sustained major leg injuries or even lost legs have benefited from a new breed of robotic wheelchair. Companies like Matia Robotics in Los Altos, California, offer such devices, which it calls "mobility platforms." Employing advanced robotic technology, they allow a badly incapacitated person to maneuver throughout his or her home with surprising ease. Several thousand such advanced robotic wheelchairs were in use in 2014.

Some robot makers are already carrying the same concept a step further by providing people who cannot walk with what are essentially wearable robots. These exoskeletons (or outer skeletons) have already been approved by the US Food and Drug

Administration for home use. One company, Ekso Bionics, based in Berkeley, California, has developed a wearable robotic system that consists of a complex series of metal braces. They support an injured or disabled person's torso and legs and allow him or her to walk. A built-in battery pack provides the power, and the person operates the system via a small computer, also built in.

Robotic Sea and Space Explorers

Medicine is not the only scientific endeavor that is finding uses for robots. Exploration of Earth's seas and the surfaces of other planets and their moons also use complex robotic systems that do jobs humans cannot. In 2014 the US space agency NASA tested its robotic vehicle Icefin in the south-polar continent of Antarctica. A team of scientists from the Georgia Institute of Technology used the needle-shaped Icefin to drill through some 65 feet (20 m) of ice. The robot then descended through another 1,640 feet (500 m) of water to the seafloor, where it took revealing videos of the creatures that dwell in those chilly depths.

Many of those species of sea stars, sponges, and other marine animals were previously unknown to science. According to Britney Schmidt, principal investigator for the Icefin project, "We saw evidence of a complex community" of living things "on the sea floor that has never been observed before." Moreover, the visual images taken during the dive showed "unprecedented detail that hasn't been achieved before." Schmidt added, "Icefin is the most capable small vehicle that's been down there."[17]

Georgia Institute of Technology engineer Mick West, who also worked on the project, explains that

> what truly separates Icefin from some of the other [existing exploratory] vehicles is that it's fairly slender, yet still has all of the sensors that the scientists like Britney need. Our vehicle has instrumentation aboard both for navigation and ocean science that other vehicles do not. Biologists were just amazed at the amount of biology at that location. . . . To have our very first deep-ocean dive happen through a small hole in the ice and go all the way to the ocean bottom and get the video we did was pretty amazing.[18]

Robots have also explored well beyond Earth's oceans and land surfaces. In 2004 and again in 2011, NASA landed its robotic exploratory vehicles—the so-called Rovers—on Mars. Two of those robots, the *Curiosity* and *Opportunity*, were still making their way across that planet's surface in 2015. Their mission is to look for evidence of microscopic life, either alive or dead, in the soil; to determine the mineral and other composition of the soil in various sectors of Mars; and to collect any other facts that might help scientists decide whether the planet might someday be habitable by humans.

To accomplish these goals, the robotic Rovers are equipped with a wide range of mechanical devices, some fairly simple and others extremely complex. They have high-quality digital color cameras, for instance. These feed the electronic data they record into a transmitter, which sends the images back at the speed of light to NASA headquarters on Earth. Each Rover also features a handy robotic arm that moves almost exactly like a human one. Other tools built into the robot can clean dust off rocks to make

Several generations of Mars Rovers can be seen in this photograph. The robotic Rovers have been searching for evidence of life on the red planet.

testing them easier, as well as transfer samples of soil and rocks into small onboard labs for analysis. The information gathered in those labs is also transmitted back to Earth.

NASA has also begun preparations for exploring and analyzing a world even more distant than Mars—Europa, one of Jupiter's four biggest moons. The robot explorer in this case, which is already under construction, is a modified version of Icefin. Earlier flybys of Europa have shown it to be covered by a shell of ice similar to the one that covers Antarctica. Moreover, beneath Europa's icy surface lies a massive global ocean that possibly contains more water than exists in all of Earth's oceans. Thanks to heat generated from Europa's core, many scientists say, it is possible that aquatic life may exist in that faraway extraterrestrial sea. If so, the next generation of Icefin will photograph it, and what most scientists call the single greatest discovery in human history will be made by a robot.

Chapter Three

Potential Problems with Robots

Focus Questions

1. Do you think concern about robots taking jobs from people is a valid concern? Explain your answer.
2. Do you think it is justified for companies to use robots to gather personal information about consumers? Why or why not?
3. Should continuing advances in robotic technology, especially those that involve AI, be subject to additional regulation or monitoring? Why or why not?

"[Robots] will let us focus on becoming more human than we were. Let the robots take the jobs, and let them help us dream up new work that matters."

—Technology expert Kevin Kelly.

Kevin Kelly, "Better than Human: Why Robots Will—and Must—Take Our Jobs," *Wired*, December 24, 2012. www.wired.com.

Modern robots offer many work-saving, time-saving, and other advantages. Yet experts point to a number of possible negative effects and/or consequences of robots that have surfaced over the years. Of these, perhaps the most familiar idea is that employing robots in industry and other workplaces causes some people to permanently lose their jobs.

This is an example of what noted early twentieth-century English economist John Maynard Keynes called "technological unemployment." He defined it as "unemployment due to our discovery of means of economizing the use of labor outrunning the pace at which we can find new uses for labor."[19] As it relates to robots, this means that these mechanical helpers will reduce the amount of human labor required to do certain jobs. Furthermore, this will happen faster than the time it takes to create new jobs to replace the lost ones.

technological unemployment

The idea that machines, including robots, would eradicate existing jobs faster than new ones could be created.

At the time, Keynes and other experts seemed to put into words what most average people assumed was true simply as a matter of common sense. A given number of jobs exist; if a robot or other machine can take the place of four workers, then those four individuals will lose their jobs. So over time, as more and more robots are introduced, the scourge of automation will ruin the economy and destroy the fabric of society. One common social fear of the mid-twentieth century, therefore, was that the onrush of industrial and other workplace robots might eliminate nearly all human jobs.

The "Lump of Labor" Fallacy

This gloomy scenario never came to pass, however. In fact, quite the opposite occurred, as the companies that installed sophisticated mechanical devices, including robots, in their workplaces actually *added* jobs. Colin Lewis, an authority on robotics, reported in 2014, "Our research shows that 76 companies that implemented industrial or factory/warehouse robots actually increased the number of employees by 294,000 over the last 3 years." Also, when the corporate giant Amazon bought Kiva Systems in 2012, Lewis points out, soon afterward Amazon "added more than 89,000 new staff to its payroll." That company

now employs over 117,000 people, more than four times the 28,300 employees it reported on June 30th 2010. Tesla Motors, manufacturer of electric cars, and with one of the most sophisticated robot manufacturing sites, has added over 6,000 new jobs. Hundreds of thousands of new jobs are being created in drone manufacturers, industrial robot makers, and other sectors of the robotic arena. The [European Union] recently announced the world's largest investment in robotics and a target of an additional 240,000 new jobs in [Europe]. It is highly probable that over a million new jobs will be created in the robotics sectors in the coming 5 years.[20]

One reason that the early warnings about robots stealing human jobs was wrong is that in the past many people were quick to fall for deceptive Luddite views of life and labor. The Luddites were mostly lower-class laborers who lived in England and the United States in the early 1800s. As the Industrial Revolution transformed their societies, they came to fear that machines would throw them out of work. So they banded together and wrecked as many machines as they could.

Robotic arms assemble Tesla Model S sedans at the company's California factory. The electric car maker's sophisticated robotic manufacturing facility still employs thousands of human workers.

The Luddites' misplaced fears were based on their unthinking acceptance of a fallacy known as the "lump of labor" theory. It presupposes that only a fixed amount of human work exists in the world. That amount—the so-called lump of labor—consists of a set number of jobs, and if a machine does the labor of several workers, their jobs are supposedly gone forever.

"A Race *with* the Machines"

The opposite argument—explained in recent times by economists like the University of Chicago's Milton Friedman—is that the amount of human work is far from fixed. Instead, people's wants and needs change constantly as new ideas and inventions transform society. Hence, new kinds of jobs are steadily generated, easily making up for those lost in the past. This means that the number of new jobs available will likely always be higher than the number lost to robots.

Moreover, robots are most frequently designed to make human workers more efficient, not to replace them, says Rodney Brooks, founder of the increasingly influential robot-making company Rethink Robotics. "An electric drill makes a home contractor more productive," he explains. "Should we ban electric drills so there are more jobs for home contractors? You ask any home contractor that."[21]

In addition, it has been shown that automation reduces the cost of making and buying products, which in turn increases the standard of living. As Marc Andreessen, cofounder of Netscape, puts it:

> One consequence of a growing robot workforce is that products become less expensive. Indeed, the main reason to use robots instead of people to make something is when robots can make it at significantly lower cost. When we are behaving and thinking as consumers, we rarely

Luddism

In England and the United States during the early Industrial Revolution, a belief by some people that machines would eliminate most jobs. Luddites sometimes destroyed machines in hopes of stopping their expansion.

resist technological change that provides us with better, cheaper products and services even when it costs jobs. Nor should we. This is how we build a better world and provide for our children. Seeking to slow technological change to preserve jobs is equivalent to advocating the punishment of consumers and stalling efforts to improve our quality of life.[22]

Human Creativity to the Rescue

According to Marc Andreessen, cofounder of Netscape, one important reason that robots will raise rather than reduce the number of human jobs is that people possess the gift of creativity, whereas robots do not. "I do not believe robots will eat all the jobs," he declares.

Here is why. For a start, robots and artificial intelligence are not nearly as powerful and sophisticated as some people fear. There are big gaps between what we *want* them to do and what they *can* do. This means there is still an enormous gap between what many people do in jobs today and what robots and artificial intelligence can replace. And even when robots and artificial intelligence are far more powerful, decades from now, there will still be many things people can do that they cannot. For example, creativity, innovation, exploration, art, science, entertainment, and caring for others. Finally, when automation is abundant and cheap, human experience becomes rare and valuable. . . . [Also], just as most of us have jobs that were not even invented 100 years ago, the same will be true 100 years from now. We have no idea what those jobs will be, but I am certain there will be an enormous number of them. To argue that huge numbers of people will be put out of work but we will find nothing for them to do is to short human creativity dramatically. And I am long on human creativity.

Marc Andreessen, "Robots Will Not Eat the Jobs but Will Unleash Our Creativity," *Financial Times*, June 23, 2014. www.ft.com.

In addition, says Kevin Kelly, a prominent lecturer and writer on future society's use of science, an increasing number of the new jobs will be more fulfilling than those in the past. Indeed, he argues, allowing robots to take certain jobs that people used to do is a wise approach. This is because it will free up people to do more creative and constructive things. "This is not a race *against* the machines," he states.

> If we race against them, we lose. This is a race *with* the machines. You'll be paid in the future based on how well you work with robots. Ninety percent of your coworkers will be unseen machines. Most of what you do will not be possible without them. And there will be a blurry line between what you do and what they do. You might no longer think of it as a job, at least at first, because anything that seems like drudgery will be done by robots. We need to let robots take over. They will do jobs we have been doing, and do them much better than we can. They will do jobs we can't do at all. They will do jobs we never imagined even needed to be done. And they will help us discover new jobs for ourselves, new tasks that expand who we are.[23]

The Risk of Losing Privacy

Although robots will continue to multiply in the workplace without crippling or destroying local economies, some experts feel it is worth debating whether these devices might harm society in other ways. For example, the more complex robots increasingly use AI in the form of computer brains. Already, computers equipped with high-quality cameras watch and record people in numerous aspects of their lives, from security cameras in retail stores to traffic cameras located at street corners and elsewhere. Is there a potential, therefore, for computerized robots to use those cameras and their memory chips in ways that threaten human privacy?

Joss Wright of the Oxford Internet Institute in Oxford, England, is only one of many modern computer scientists who think this disturbing possibility should be investigated now rather than later.

Surveillance cameras monitor traffic and pedestrians in London. Some experts warn of the potential for abuse as computer-equipped cameras and other devices merge with robotic technology.

"What we're increasingly seeing now is the existence of computers and sensing devices as part of the infrastructure that surrounds us," he says. Wright calls attention to the wireless Internet that pervades much of the modern world, along with the existence of millions of smartphones at all levels of society. "Ultimately," he states, "what a robot is or what a robot represents is an increasing presence of computers as more physical objects that we interact with. Those interactions are going to be very rich [and] physical and pervasive."[24]

That pervasiveness of computers, coupled with the fact that robotic devices are quickly multiplying in society, concerns some researchers. They worry that these changes have given the companies that own these machines too much access to people's private lives. An often cited example is the household robot. The concern is that such devices might record details about a per-

> **infrastructure**
>
> The basic organization, features, and services of society.

Businesses Uninterested in Safeguards?

Widely respected Hugo Award–winning science-fiction writer Robert J. Sawyer explains why he thinks that people will likely never program robots with safeguards like science-fiction writer Isaac Asimov's ethical laws of robotics:

> We are getting closer to artificial intelligence by small degrees and, as such, nobody is really implementing fundamental safeguards. Take Eliza, the first computer psychiatric program [developed at the Massachusetts Institute of Technology in the 1960s]. There is nothing in its logic to make sure that it doesn't harm the user in an Asimovian sense, by, for instance, re-opening old mental wounds with its probing. Now, we can argue that Eliza is way too primitive to do any real harm, but then that means someone has to say arbitrarily, okay, *that* attempt at AI requires no safeguards but *this* attempt does. Who would that someone be? The development of AI is a business, and businesses are notoriously uninterested in fundamental safeguards—*especially* philosophic ones. (A few quick examples: the tobacco industry, the automotive industry, the nuclear industry. Not one of these has said from the outset that fundamental safeguards are necessary. Every one of them has resisted externally imposed safeguards, and none have accepted an absolute edict against ever causing harm to humans.) Indeed, given that a huge amount of AI and robotics research is underwritten by the military, it seems that there will never be a general "law" against ever harming human beings.

Robert J. Sawyer, "Random Musings on Asimov's Three Laws of Robotics," SFWriter.com. www.sfwriter.com.

son's home life while they innocently appear only to be cleaning the floor or gutters. Certain people behind the scenes in industry and commerce would be happy to get their hands on such information. They could easily sell it to companies that would use it to target the very people who were spied on with tailor-made ads and products.

Some experts warn that household robots may end up posing a *particularly* high risk of invading people's privacy. The reason is that there is a tendency for humans to make personal connections with those devices. As science writer Marcus Woo says, many people "treat robots as something more than another piece of technology, even if they don't look human-like at all." In a 2007 study, he continues, researchers at the Georgia Institute of Technology interviewed thirty owners of the robotic vacuum cleaner Roomba. Most of these individuals had given "their robots names and a gender, with many even considering it as a member of the family as if it were a pet."[25]

Clearly, such attitudes could lead some owners of robotic devices to lower their guards in privacy matters. This is why Wright thinks it is prudent to build certain safety measures into robots to protect human privacy. To this end, he and other like-minded scientists design their robots so that they store only the data needed to perform an intended task. This is very different from numerous existing smartphone apps and web-based e-mail systems that collect a wide range of information, allowing companies to learn a great deal about those devices' owners.

The Laws of Robotics

Another often cited problem related to robots deals with a serious unintended consequence of programming them with large amounts of information. Namely, could they eventually achieve self-awareness and turn on their makers? This unsettling idea was the main theme of Karel Čopec's groundbreaking play R.U.R., which appeared in the early 1920s.

In the decades that followed this bold vision, science-fiction writers tackled the same concept in their short stories and novels. Typically, these works involved robots with computerlike brains complex enough to achieve some sort of self-awareness. Some of those fictional robots decided to continue helping their makers, while others opted to seize control of or destroy humanity.

Most modern robotics experts say that such potentially dangerous superintelligent robots are not likely to be built in the near future. Nevertheless, they agree that much more complex robots will be created over time. Even if the chances of their becoming self-aware are low, there is always the possibility that they might pose some sort of threat to human civilization.

That realization was also addressed in the early twentieth century by science-fiction writers, notably the late Isaac Asimov. In his 1942 short story "Runaround" (part of a collection titled *I Robot*), he introduced his now famous "laws of robotics." Initially, there were three, all designed to protect people from any superintelligent robots that might be built:

1. A robot may not injure a human being or, through inaction, allow a human being to come to harm.

2. A robot must obey orders given it by human beings except where such orders would conflict with the First Law.

3. A robot must protect its own existence as long as such protection does not conflict with the First or Second Law.[26]

In 1985 Asimov added a fourth robotic law: "A robot may not harm humanity, or, by inaction, allow humanity to come to harm."[27]

At first glance, Asimov's robotic laws seem both logical and compelling. After all, no one wants robots to turn on and hurt their builders. However, as late as 2015 no robot makers had yet taken such precautions. In fact, some of those companies and agencies staunchly refused to program their robots with such safety rules.

The most obvious example, award-winning writer Robert J. Sawyer points out, is the US military, which has spent billions of dollars to develop robotic drones. Those flying machines are specifically designed to kill humans, in this case enemies of the United States. In addition, Sawyer says, the military is working on the creation of humanoid robotic soldiers. Clearly, if all those killer robots were programmed to refrain from harming people, they would no longer be killers. Thus, Sawyer concludes, it would be self-defeating for the military to limit its robots' behavior by taking precautions like those Asimov described in his robotics laws.

Very Special Tools

Sawyer and other experts also argue that such built-in safeguards for robots are not likely to be needed anyway. According to this

A Predator drone is displayed at an Illinois air show. Robotic drones are used by the military for surveillance and for killing enemies. The latter would seem to conflict with Isaac Asimov's first robotic law, which prohibits robots from harming humans.

view, *R.U.R.* and other fictional visions of robots turning on humanity make a fundamental error. They assume that self-aware machines would automatically feel that humans are both competitors and a threat to "robotkind."

That assumption is likely to be false, Sawyer says. It is based on the notion that highly intelligent robots will be as mistrustful and paranoid as humans frequently are. "A machine that spontaneously gains self-awareness isn't the product of millions of generations of survival of the fittest," he explains. "And most of our nastiness comes from" that inborn, desperate drive to survive. He adds, "Our selfish genes make us incapable of actually wanting others to do well without a hoped-for benefit for ourselves."[28]

In contrast, this argument goes, future robots, like those that exist today, will not possess such instinct-based fears. Nor is there any evidence to suggest they would feel any *other* human-like emotions. Indeed, nothing in their programming would inform them about concepts like worry, fear, or self-survival. So they would be blissfully unaware of such things, just as they would likely be unaware of the concept that they could become rational beings.

Instead, a majority of computer and robotics experts think, no matter how complex such machines might become, they will simply continue to carry out the tasks they were programmed to do. Hence, there would be no reason for robots to feel threatened by their makers. The idea that these mechanical devices should be programmed with ethical rules is therefore pointless. As the robotics experts within the Engineering and Physical Sciences Research Council, the United Kingdom's chief science agency, put it:

> Asimov's laws are inappropriate because they try to insist that robots behave in certain ways, as if they were people, when in real life, it is the humans who design and use the robots and who must be the actual subjects of any law. As we consider the ethical implications of having robots in our society, it becomes obvious that robots themselves are not where responsibility lies. Robots are simply tools of various kinds, [although] very special tools, and the responsibility of making sure they behave well must always lie with human beings.[29]

Chapter Four

Robots in Popular Culture

Focus Questions

1. Why are worries about robots taking over the world a common theme in literature and film, and do you think these fears are justified? Explain.
2. How do real-world events influence people's views of robots? Provide an example to support your answer.
3. If it were possible to create an entity that is part human and part robot, would that entity be human or robot, and how should it be treated by society?

"[The] depiction of modern robots, cyborgs, androids, and operating systems in film and books may provide a greater window into ourselves than we realize."

—Social commentator Todd Kliman.

Todd Kliman, "Robots and Pop Culture," transcript, *The Kojo Nnamdi Show*, July 31, 2014. http://thekojonnamdishow.org.

Numerous centuries have passed since the earliest stories about robot-like beings became a part of Greek mythology and other ancient lore. These tales inspired inventors like Jacques de Vaucanson in the 1700s. They designed, and in de Vaucanson's case also built, robotic devices. In turn these feats motivated fiction writers such as Karel Čopec, thanks to whom robots became deeply embedded in modern popular culture. Frequently called "pop culture" for short, it includes novels and other writings; toys and video games; music; and plays, TV shows, and movies. For the most part, pop culture focuses on more advanced robots—those with some form of AI and the romantic, adventurous, charming, and/or scary aspects of such "thinking" mechanical beings.

Although concepts and images of advanced robots existed well before 1900, they virtually exploded into society in the twentieth century. In part this was because pop culture itself expanded enormously in that century. Radio, film, television, video games, and other electronic media were invented and rapidly became popular worldwide in the 1900s. Those means of creative, artistic, and trendy expression joined already existing plays, short stories, and novels as colorful platforms on which to present stories about robots.

Early Twentieth-Century Robots

Thus, with so many means of exploiting the concept of intelligent mechanical beings, robots became extremely plentiful in pop culture after 1900. One of the century's first widely popular robots appeared in several of the fourteen Oz books penned by popular American author L. Frank Baum. The character, named Tik-Tok, was introduced in the third book, *Ozma of Oz*, published in 1907. Baum described Tik-Tok as having a round body made of copper and thin metal arms and legs. He moved and spoke thanks to a complex set of clockwork springs and gears and had no original thoughts. Still, he proved very loyal to the main character, Dorothy, who found him likable and useful.

Thus, the twentieth century began with a well-known robot that was constructive, good-natured, and friendly. That positive image of the intelligent robot did not last long, however. Karel Čopec's 1921 play *R.U.R.: Rossum's Universal Robots,* in which the mechanical beings wipe out most of humanity, soundly established the negative image of such creatures. It was soon reinforced by several more "bad" robots. One notable example was a mechanical brain invented by a fictional scientist in novelist Edmond Ham-

The character Tik-Tok, a robot made of copper, was first introduced in a 1907 book by L. Frank Baum. This robot was both likable and helpful—an image that changed in a matter of decades.

ilton's *The Metal Giants* (1926). That brain runs amok and constructs several enormous robots that destroy a town.

Another important harmful robot of the 1920s was the sinister female android in Fritz Lang's movie *Metropolis* (1927). Because large numbers of people attended the film, the visual image of its humanoid robot became well known. As a result, it established a pattern and was widely copied in the decades that followed. That is, most pop culture robots of the twentieth century featured a roughly human-looking torso topped by a head of some sort, along with two arms and two legs. Typical was Robbie, a humanoid household robot in Isaac Asimov's 1940 short story of the same name.

Robbie not only looked like a metallic person. He also possessed a positronic brain, a fictional device employed by Asimov in most of his many fictional robots. It was a precomputer version of the software that today in a sense brings a computer to life. Asimov pictured it as a complex assembly of tiny parts made from an alloy of the exotic metals iridium and platinum. As a storage unit for a robot's memories and brain functions, the positronic brain was so logical and compelling that most other science-fiction writers and filmmakers subsequently copied it in one form or another.

positronic brain

First imagined by noted science-fiction writer Isaac Asimov, it is an electronic, computerlike source of a robot's intelligence.

A Constructive but Frightening Figure

The concept of a robot with both humanoid form and intelligent brain functions was burned into the public consciousness as never before in 1951. That year Twentieth Century Fox released its first big-budget science-fiction film, *The Day the Earth Stood Still*. It was loosely based on a 1940 short story, "Farewell to the Master," by Harry Bates.

The movie version was so well made that today it is hailed as a classic film, and when first released it was extremely popular with the public. Moviegoers flocked by the millions in large part to see its widely advertised 10-foot (3-m)-tall and visually startling robot, Gort. Made of a silvery metallic substance, Gort is able to shoot a lethal laser-like beam from a visor covering the area where his eyes should be located. That "death ray" melts human weapons, including tanks, into harmless puddles in only seconds.

As the movie's audiences discovered, however, Gort is far from a mere mechanical menace. Indeed, it turns out that he is a mechanized policeman built by a race of extraterrestrials who have been warily watching humanity for some time. As summarized by Daniel Ichbiah:

The story begins when a flying saucer arrives in Washington D.C. and out steps Gort, accompanied by an extraterrestrial, Klaatu, who bears a message of peace to all the peoples of the Earth. But hardly has he stepped outside his craft, when a panic-stricken soldier shoots and wounds him. Gort has to use force to ensure that peace prevails, so he destroys all the military's weapons. Klaatu finds shelter in the home of a widow, Helen, but is denounced [to the authorities] by the man who hopes to marry her and assassinated by the U.S. army. Gort retrieves his body and brings him back to life. Klaatu then delivers an address to all the scientists of the world and warns them that unless the human race renounces nuclear weaponry and agrees to live in peace, the Earth and all life on it will be destroyed.[30]

The Transformers Follow a Unique Path

Among the many robot toys that have hit the market over the course of close to a century, by far the most popular have been those associated with the *Transformers* TV shows and films. Interestingly, these gizmos followed a path completely opposite to that of most toys linked to film projects. Usually, the robot character appears first on film and is later made into a popular toy. In contrast, the Transformers started out as original robot toys and over time inspired the creation of films based on them. The initial toy versions, made by the Japanese company Takara, first appeared in stores in 1984. Not long after that, Takara signed a contract with the American toy company Hasbro to sell the robots in the United States and other countries outside Japan. Their great success was in large part driven by their main marketing slogan—"Robots in disguise!" It was based on the fact that the user could rearrange a Transformer's numerous plastic parts into more commonplace objects and machines, such as cars, ships, airplanes, and animals. These toys became so fashionable that they inspired a TV show that ran from 1984 to 1992. Its robot characters enjoyed various adventures, all the while attracting huge audiences of children around the world. Two spinoff shows followed—*Transformers: Generation 2* (1992–1994) and *Transformers: Universe* (2003–2006). Because of their tremendous success, the first big-budget *Transformers* movie opened in 2007, and the hugely popular film series continues.

Gort, a robot made of a silvery metallic substance, and Klaatu, an extraterrestrial, greet frightened inhabitants of Earth when they exit their spacecraft in The Day the Earth Stood Still. *Gort's programming and goals are complex, marking a change in pop culture portrayals of robots.*

Gort represented a major milestone among modern pop culture robots. In part this was because his programming and goals were both complex and controversial. The movie was released only six years after the United States ended World War II in the Pacific by dropping atomic bombs on Japan in 1945. Many people were disturbed and even fearful that those superweapons now existed. Gort and Klaatu's mission—to neutralize such deadly devices—therefore struck a powerful chord with the public. Complicating matters was the fact that most people who saw the film viewed Gort as a robot with both good and bad qualities. He had been built for a constructive purpose—to bring about and maintain peace—but his ability to destroy the Earth at will and at a moment's notice also made him a frightening figure.

The Convincing and Endearing Robby

In every literary and artistic genre, original and outstanding creations are typically followed by many spinoffs and knockoffs. This happened with filmed robots following the strong cultural impression made by Gort in *The Day the Earth Stood Still*. A long series of cheaply made, easily forgettable robots, all of which supposedly posed a threat to Earth and/or humanity, plagued movie and TV screens in the 1950s.

In 1954 alone, for instance, audiences endured no less than four such uninspiring robot films, prominent among them *Devil Girl from Mars* and *Gog*. In *Devil Girl* a 15-foot (4.6 m) robot tries to kidnap Earth men so they can be taken to Mars to breed with that planet's females. *Gog* featured two American-made robots—Gog and Magog—both under the control of a central, computerlike brain. Predictably, they run amok until the hero manages to defeat them. The silly radio, TV, and newspaper ads for *Gog* billed the robot of that name as "a Frankenstein of steel."[31]

Fortunately for film audiences of the 1950s, the rest of that decade was not a total loss in regard to pop culture robots. In 1956 the prestigious MGM movie studio released a big-budget, visually spectacular science-fiction film based on William Shakespeare's *The Tempest*. Titled *Forbidden Planet*, it featured one of the most compelling and memorable mechanical beings ever conceived—Robby the Robot. He was designed by widely respected American movie art director Robert Kinoshita. Although basically humanoid in shape, Robby featured a host of original and clever details—in both looks and personality—that made him very convincing and endearing to audiences. As noted American film critic Tim Dirks explains:

> Robby had a cone-shaped, clear-domed and jukebox-like head (with twirling lights and rotating motorized antenna ears), a lighted chest panel, gripping hands (with thumb and two fingers), bulbous segmented legs, and a pot-belly stove-shaped body. Robby stood 7 feet 6 inches tall, and had a charming, often smug sense of humor (for example: "Quiet please. I am analyzing" and his excuse for being late: "Sorry, miss, I was giving myself an oil-job"). Robby was language-fluent. He could speak English and "187 other languages along with their various dialects and sub-tongues." Robby was also very domesticated as a butler (chauffeuring, cooking, cleaning, and performing heavy lifting tasks).[32]

In the film, set several centuries in the future, an Earth space cruiser comes across Altair-4 (the fourth planet orbiting the star Altair). There the crew discovers a brilliant Earth scientist, Dr. Morbius, who had arrived on the planet many years before. Along with his grown daughter, Morbius lives with the incredible Robby, who sees to the humans' needs and protects them. The new arrivals eventually learn that Morbius built Robby himself, aided by designs left behind by the Krell, the highly advanced and now extinct race of aliens that had evolved on Altair-4.

Later Movie and TV Robots

Robby was so beautifully designed, effective, and popular that filmmakers decided to use him, bearing different names, in many later movies and TV shows. Among the films were *The Invisible Boy* (1957), *Gremlins* (1984), and *Earth Girls Are Easy* (1988). The television shows included *The Thin Man* (in which Robby appeared in 1958), *The Addams Family* (1966), *Columbo* (1974), *Mork & Mindy* (1979), and *The Big Bang Theory* (2014), among many others.

Robby was also a model for other pop culture robots that looked and acted in a similar manner. Of those, by the far the most famous example was the B9, which appeared in the iconic TV se-

A Robot Police Force?

Canadian science writer George Dvorsky here recalls the potent impact the robot Gort, in the film *The Day the Earth Stood Still*, had on public fears and hopes about the future when the movie was released in 1951. The alien being Klaatu, he says, brought with him

Gort—the intimidating robotic presence who patiently lurks in the background. Gort is the stick with which Klaatu can enforce his ultimatum. "There's no limit to what he could do," he says of the robot. "He could destroy the Earth." Klaatu stresses the Importance of law and the need to enforce it. "There must be security for all, or no one is secure." [Klaatu's] plea for world security on film acts as a call for international co-operation in the real world. A number of observers of the day, Einstein included, believed that the advent of nuclear weapons necessitated the creation of more powerful global bodies. . . . Today, with the threat of bioterrorism [and] ongoing nuclear proliferation, [the] call for increased global co-operation can once again be heard. Driven by the rational desire for self-preservation, Klaatu's society has given the robots police-like powers. "In matters of aggression, we have given them absolute power over us. This power cannot be revoked," says Klaatu, "At the first signs of violence, they act automatically against the aggressor. The penalty for provoking their action is too terrible to risk." [Gort's] power is analogous to the nuclear bomb itself. They are both ultimate deterrents.

George Dvorsky, "Revisiting *The Day the Earth Stood Still*," *Sentient Developments* (blog), January 9, 2007, www.sentientdevelopments.com.

ries *Lost in Space* (1965–1968). That robot served and protected a family of future spacefarers, the Robinsons, just as Robby had done for Dr. Morbius and his daughter. The B9 was most famous for wildly waving its arms and yelling warnings whenever danger threatened its masters.

While various unremarkable spinoffs of Gort and Robby continued to appear in the 1970s, 1980s, and 1990s, those decades also witnessed the pop culture exploitation of some different and more advanced robot types. One was the cyborg, short for "cybernetic organism." Essentially, cyborgs are fictional beings having both organic (living) and mechanical parts. This part-flesh, part-machine version of a robot achieved widespread public popularity thanks to the 1970s TV adventure series *The Six Million Dollar Man*. It featured a lead character—an astronaut—who had almost died in an accident. Doctors working for the US government secretly saved him by replacing several of his body parts with special mechanical ones, making him freakishly strong and fast.

cyborg

A shortened version of "cybernetic organism," a cyborg is a fictional being having both organic (living) and mechanical parts.

Another famous cyborg of the period was the black-cloaked villain of the first three *Star Wars* films, Darth Vader. One of the later movies in that renowned science-fiction film series showed how he was originally a handsome young man who was transformed into a menacing cyborg after being damaged beyond repair in a space war. The *Star Wars* films also featured many standard robots, notably two of the most famous of all pop culture robots—R2-D2 and C-3PO. Interestingly, the tall, gaunt, brass-colored C-3PO bore a strong resemblance to the famous robot in Fritz Lang's 1927 masterpiece *Metropolis*.

Not long after Darth Vader terrorized C-3PO, R2-D2, and their human friends, an entire race of cyborgs repeatedly menaced the crew of the starship *Enterprise* in the highly popular TV series *Star Trek: The Next Generation* (1987–1994). These original and truly creepy creatures were appropriately called the Borg (from *cyborg*). Each Borg was a member of a hive-like collective society made up of former humans and other organic beings. The collective transformed each into a partial robot through the addition of a complex of electronic devices connected to their brains, spines, and various organs.

That same long-running series also featured one of the best-known and most entertaining modern pop culture androids—Data, who is the *Enterprise*'s chief operations officer. In a number of series episodes, it is revealed that he was created by a mechanical genius, Dr. Noonien Soong. The latter outfitted the quick-witted and good-natured Data with a positronic brain. This was a purposeful tip of the hat by the series' producer and writers to Isaac Asimov, who had earlier invented that device for his own literary robots.

Even more advanced than Data among pop culture androids were the Cylons in *Battlestar Galactica*. That gripping big-budget science-fiction series ran from 2004 to 2009 and attracted legions of fans in countries around the world. Extremely lifelike, as well as ruthless and powerful, the Cylons were initially constructed by humans as robotic workers and servants. Those formidable androids turned on their makers, however. They wiped out most of humanity, leaving only a few thousand survivors, who must continually fight for their lives against their own creations.

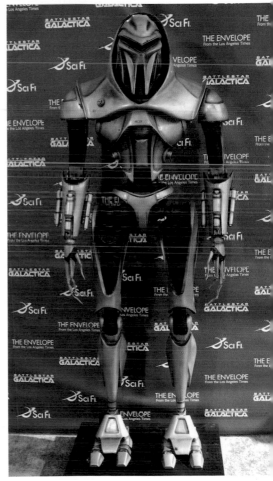

Battlestar Galactica, *re-created for television in the mid-2000s, featured Cylon robots like this one as well as Cylons that resembled humans in every way. Both types of Cylons were built by humans, but ultimately, they turned on their makers and wiped out most of humanity.*

Toy Robots

The unrelenting popularity of movie and TV robots over the course of many decades made it almost a given that they would have other kinds of spinoffs in popular culture. The Cylons from *Battlestar Galactica*, as only one example, generated toy robots, coloring books, Halloween costumes, lunch boxes, card games, board games, video games, graphic novels, and numerous other ancillary, or secondary, consumer products. The same was true for the *Star Trek* android Data; the *Star Wars* characters Darth Vader, R2-D2, and C-3PO; the B9 on *Lost in Space*; *The Six Million Dollar Man*'s astronaut-cyborg; Robby the Robot; and others. Similarly, the more recent and ongoing series of huge-budget *Transformers* movies (about giant metallic robots that can drastically alter their physical form in seconds) continues to spawn all sorts of robot games and toys.

Some of the most popular robot toys were not spinoffs from films and TV, however. The items in question were original toys that became broadly popular all on their own. Among the earliest of these unique products were Atomic Robot Man and Robot Lilliput. Each had a boxlike torso made of thin sheets of tin, was assembled in Japan in the late 1940s, and became a big seller in the United States. Atomic Robot Man stood 5 inches (13 cm) tall, whereas Robot Lilliput was 6.5 inches (16.5 cm) high. Both were painted in bright colors that appealed to children.

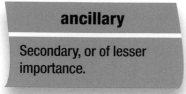

ancillary

Secondary, or of lesser importance.

Another widely popular original robot toy, Robert the Robot (not to be confused with Robby the Robot), was a product of the Ideal Toy Company. He moved via power from a remote control device connected to his back by a wire. Robert hit US stores in 1954 and immediately caught on with children. The medium of television was fairly new and fast growing at the time, and TV commercials proved a potent way to advertise him to young people. One big selling point was his voice. Thanks to a built-in miniature and rather crude phonographic record, he said, "I am Robert the Robot, the mechanical man. Drive me, steer me wherever you can."[33]

The widespread popularity of toys, comic books, video games, and other products featuring robots demonstrates how much these artificial beings have wormed their way into almost every area of modern pop culture. Surely one reason for this is that many people find the concept of AI fascinating. Also, robots are by their very nature mechanical. So they fit seamlessly into the constant expansion of modern technology that is helping drive humanity into an increasingly mechanized future.

Chapter Five

The Future of Robotics

Focus Questions

1. What do you think about the idea of creating fully intelligent machines? Is this a worthy goal? Explain your answer.
2. Under what conditions, if any, would use of military superrobots capable of destroying human armies be justified? Explain your answer.
3. Should robots be built to look and act like humans? Why or why not?

"[As] robotic machines enter our lives in relatively transparent ways, we will cease to think of them as robots. It is merely a question of time. They will submerge into our environment and gradually become invisible to us."

—Robotics expert Will Wright.

Quoted in Daniel Ichbiah, *Robots: From Science Fiction to Technological Revolution*. New York: Abrams, 2005, p. 7.

Robots are already involved in industry, business, medicine, the military, exploration, and home life. The future of robots lies in continuing to expand not only the number of robots in society and their degree of usefulness, but also the degree to which they mimic humans, both physically and mentally. First, many scientists and other experts are trying to create robots that look more or less like people and that can duplicate human movements as realistically as possible. Second, they are trying to increase robotic intelligence. In this respect, AI is one of the fastest-growing sectors of robotics.

As robots become more and more sophisticated, they will also steadily grow in number, and the amount of money spent to design and build them will also increase. Several experts predict that the amount of money spent in advanced robotics will grow 10 percent a year in the world's twenty-five largest export nations until at least 2035. In comparison, between 2010 and 2015 the amount of money spent on new robots grew at the rate of only about 2 to 3 percent a year.

Also, as AI becomes more prevalent and complex in some robots, experts point out, these mechanical beings will increasingly be able to sense their environment and make independent decisions based on changes in that environment. To make that happen, conventional robots will more and more need to fuse with computers, making those robots smarter and smarter.

A few experts worry that this ongoing trend might result in a new race of nonbiological, fully intelligent machines, possibly by the middle of the current century. If so, they ask, could those super-robots become even more intelligent than people? Those who fret over this possibility suggest that such intelligent machines might feel that they no longer need humans. They recall the words of the great twentieth-century British mathematician I.J. Good, who said:

> Let an ultra-intelligent machine be defined as a machine that can far surpass all the intellectual activities of any man, however clever. Since the design of machines is one of these intellectual activities, an ultra-intelligent machine could design even better machines. There would then unquestionably be an "intelligence explosion," and the intelligence of man would be left far behind. Thus the first ultra-intelligent machine is the last invention that man need ever make.[34]

Many Future Uses

The majority of robotics experts feel that such worries about robots surpassing humans in the near future are unfounded, or at least exaggerated. In their view, an important part of robotic re-

Robotic helpers might one day be found in many areas of daily life. They might someday harvest produce, dispense pills at pharmacies, clean offices and schools, and drive trucks on long-distance routes.

search has been and will continue to be ensuring that robot designers learn how to control their creations as they develop them. So robots are likely to remain human helpers for the near term.

Nevertheless, these automated servants will be far more complex and efficient than today's robots. So the industries and workplaces that already rely on robots will gradually become still more automated. "After robots finish replacing assembly line workers, they will replace the workers in warehouses," says science writer Kevin Kelly.

> Speedy bots able to lift 150 pounds all day long will retrieve boxes, sort them, and load them onto trucks. Fruit and vegetable picking will continue to be robotized until no humans pick outside of specialty farms. Pharmacies will feature a single pill-dispensing robot in the back while the pharmacists focus on patient consulting. Next, the more dexterous chores of cleaning in offices and schools will be taken over by late-night robots, starting with easy-to-do floors and windows and eventually getting to toilets. The highway legs of long-haul trucking routes will be driven by robots embedded in truck cabs.[35]

Linda, the Robot Security Guard

Researchers from six European universities are working together on developing a robot security guard for rest homes where elderly people spend their final years. The project aims to perfect the device, named Linda, for use within a few years. The developers think that Linda, who looks much like a human-sized chess pawn, could solve one of the biggest problems patients in such homes face—falls. According to English journalist Nick Collins, who investigated the project:

> Nurses in homes are typically so busy that when residents fall and injure themselves in their own rooms, it can be several hours until the accident is discovered—when they fail to appear for breakfast, for example. Continuously sweeping the building in search of distressed residents would be far too demanding on a nurse's time, but is exactly the kind of repetitive task to which robots are ideally suited. Not only could robots like Linda patrol corridors for 24 hours a day, providing much more continuous surveillance than any human, but they could save nurses valuable time by performing additional tasks such as carrying messages or escorting patients to appointments. . . . Operating without any input from humans for up to three months at a time, the robots should be able to tell the difference between a normal situation, such as someone leaving their room during the day, and [an] abnormal one, such as doing so in the middle of the night.

Nick Collins, "Meet Linda, the Robot Security Guard," *Telegraph* (London), August 26, 2013. www.telegraph.co.uk.

Other robots of the near future will do jobs that since ancient times were accomplished by people aided by animals. Herding is a good example. Throughout Africa, the Middle East, and parts of Asia, most sheep, goats, cattle, and other domesticated beasts continue to be moved and cared for by human shepherds, often along with their trusty dogs. However, that age-old scenario may become fairly rare within a few decades. Researchers at the University of Sydney in Australia have designed and tested a four-wheeled robot they call Rover. It has successfully rounded up cows in a field and moved them to a nearby dairy. Companies on every continent have already expressed interest in Rover, and it is only a matter of time before it and similar robots become familiar in fields and on farms worldwide.

Robotics engineers in several countries are also experimenting with four-legged robots that walk and even trot like dogs or horses. As time goes on, these "walking bots" and more advanced versions of them will carry water, gear, and other supplies for traders, explorers, mountain climbers, and other people who travel by foot or horse in remote inland areas. In 2015, for example, Google-owned robotics company Boston Dynamics introduced Spot, a four-legged robotic dog. This ingenious device can walk for long distances, climb stairs, and trot over rough terrain, all in a manner almost identical to that of a dog. This artificial beast runs on electric power and contains a series of hydraulic pumps, valves, and other complicated mechanical parts. It is able to carry 160 pounds (73 kg) of gear. Boston Dynamics has also developed other walking bots, among them a larger version of Spot, appropriately named BigDog.

Robotics designers think that more human-looking versions of such service robots will eventually become cooks, waiters, and waitresses in some restaurants; security guards for factories, sports stadiums, rest homes, and prisons; and drivers of automated transportation buses in many cities. The challenge in making this dream a reality, those experts say, will be in building those machines so that they physically act just like human helpers and exhibit fluid, realistic-looking movements. To meet that challenge, engineers in robotics companies are already experimenting with a range of new bendable materials. These will hopefully make initially hard, rigid metal arm, leg, and hand parts move with the necessary flexibility and smoothness, yet remain strong enough to do the job. These materials include new and at times exotic forms of rubber, plastic, and even artificial proteins (the natural building blocks of life on Earth).

Still other robots—some shaped like humans and others like animals—will help rescue people during natural disasters. One of several such robots now on the drawing boards is the so-called mole digger, which will burrow beneath debris and dirt to save trapped people. Engineers in the United Kingdom are working on such a mechanical digger that they hope will use mole-like movements to push aside bricks and other rubble piled up during an earthquake.

Robotic Explorers

Another major area in which robots *are* playing and will *continue* to play important parts is exploration—both on Earth and in space. For years NASA has employed robotic arms on its space shuttles and several of its orbiting satellites. Also, the agency's more sophisticated exploratory robotic device, Icefin, which burrows into sheets of ice, began testing in 2014 in Antarctica.

Later, more sophisticated versions of Icefin will almost certainly explore many of the planets and their moons in our own solar system. These more advanced robotic explorers will need more than the ability to dig through ice and photograph what lies beneath. Such future devices will not, as the existing Icefin does, have the luxury of human handlers to carry them to test sites and retrieve them using safety lines. Future versions of such robots will require the ability to make their way on their own from a spaceship orbiting a planet to that world's surface. They will also need to be outfitted with extremely advanced onboard labs able to analyze any living materials they may discover in those remote subterranean regions.

Even further into the future, such robotic probes will explore planets and moons in other star systems. Those machines will need to have the ability to survive extremely long trips in the far reaches of interstellar space (the space lying between stars). Because all stars lying beyond our own star, the sun, are so far away, even the fastest spaceships on the drawing boards will take dozens, if not hundreds, of years to reach their targets. Current robotic explorers do not come with guarantees that they will wake up on time and operate flawlessly after "naps" lasting fifty or more years.

Some scientists project that a probe bound for the planets circling a nearby star will be launched within thirty to forty years. Once in orbit around a faraway planet, the probe will launch robots that will study and explore that world's surface, along with any seas. Perhaps these future robots will find and photograph living things that developed eons ago far beyond our solar system.

Because of the nature of the jobs they do, these particular exploratory robots will not be humanoid in form. Icefin, for example, looks like a big, elongated bullet, and when it opens, several complex robotic arms extend outward. Nevertheless, NASA has been developing a human-shaped robot named Valkyrie (after the

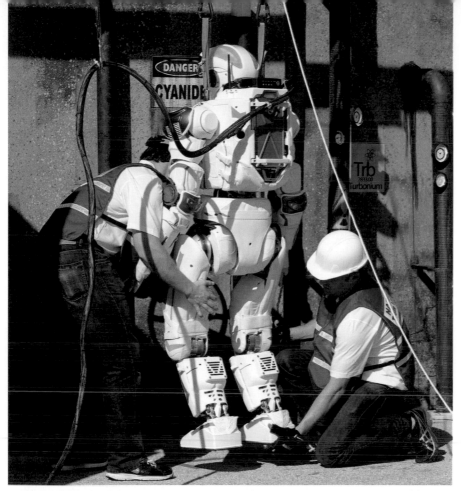

NASA engineers make adjustments on Valkyrie, the humanoid robot. Valkyrie is able to walk and pick up objects; in the future, the robot might be able to help in natural disasters or on missions to the moon or Mars.

flying goddesses of Norse mythology) to accomplish other sorts of tasks. It stands more than 6 feet (1.8 m) tall. The current version of the robot is able to walk and pick up objects from the floor. NASA officials plan to adapt her for use in helping disaster victims both on Earth and eventually on the moon or Mars.

Still another robot built for exploration is the Polaris Prospecting Bot, designed by roboticists at Astrobotic, a spinoff division of Carnegie Mellon University. Powered by solar panels, when fully operational it will dig down into the surfaces of the moon, Mars, and other planets or their satellites. It will also be able to find and extract water ice lying at the poles of some of those celestial bodies. That water could then be used to support human bases and perhaps even cities built on those bodies in the future. On the moon, states science writer Rebecca Boyle, "Polaris would drill up to 100 holes in [ten] days as it searches for water ice deposits. If it survives the lunar night, it could recharge again as soon as the sun comes up, and continue drilling for ice as long as its drill bit lasts."[36]

Future Military Bots

Polaris will likely first reach the moon sometime in the mid-2020s. Well before that, the US military will begin deploying an advanced version of the robotic drones it has been using for more than a decade. Up until 2015, military drones tended to be fairly small as

How to Get into Robotics

On his website, Rich Hooper, a successful robotics engineer, gives the following advice to the many young people who ask him how to get into the field of robotics in the near future:

> Building, deploying and maintaining robots could be very interesting. You would be on the "ground floor" working with robots every day. To get started a person might consider a technical college degree. Networking with people you know or have worked with in the past is always a good idea. Somehow you will need to demonstrate by experience or training that you are qualified. To get a job designing robots or robotic systems you are almost certainly going to need a four-year engineering degree. Many robotics professionals have [a] Master's degree and there are plenty of PhD's around. You also need to understand that when you first graduate college, even with a Master's degree, you will be a very junior engineer. Robotic systems are typically the most complex systems a company will make. You will need to first focus on a subsystem, such as the mechanical, electrical, computing, or software systems. Once you have become an accomplished engineer in one of those fields, you can move up to the more advanced systems engineering role.

Rich Hooper, "Robotics Engineer," Learn About Robots. www.learnaboutrobots.com.

aircraft go, with wingspans of 45 to 55 feet (14 to 17 m). The military is now developing far larger drones, including the Triton, which will have a wingspan of 125 feet (38 m), similar to that of a Boeing 757. The robotic Triton will fly so high and have such advanced sensors that it will be able to watch enemy operations as far away as 2,300 miles (3,700 km), almost the width of the continental United States. That is dozens of times larger than the area that current drones are capable of watching. Moreover, the Triton will carry missiles that will be capable of doing damage over a region far bigger than the area that today's drones can manage.

On battlefields lying below such flying robots, meanwhile, in the years to come human ground troops could steadily be replaced with humanoid robotic soldiers. Mike Adams, an expert on developing technologies, likens them to the scary android and cybernetic warriors in the *Terminator* movies. The Petman robot, currently under development by the US Department of Defense, he writes, is indeed "like something ripped right out of a sci-fi movie." This mechanical fighter "sweats to regulate body temperature, and it can be dressed in chemical suits" or other outfits "to resemble humans." Adams continues:

> The Pentagon wants to develop and deploy a robotic army of autonomous soldiers that will kill without hesitation. It's only a matter of time before these robots are armed with rifles, grenade launchers, and more. Their target acquisition systems can be a hybrid combination of both thermal and night vision technologies, allowing them to see humans at night and even detect heat signatures through building walls. This is the army humanity is eventually going to face.[37]

Initially, Adams and other expert observers say, these robots, many of them humanoid in shape, will be used to carry weapons and gear, remove wounded soldiers from the battlefield, and so forth. But as time goes on, the "robotic soldiers will serve on the front lines while humans only serve support roles to keep the robots running," Adams writes. "Such a transition will take decades, of course, but it's coming."[38]

Another military use for robots will be to create deceptions to mislead enemy forces. Rebecca Boyle uses an interesting analogy with some familiar furry little animals. "Squirrels have a habit of storing acorns and other nuts in various spots, then patrolling those stashes," she explains. "But what happens if another opportunistic squirrel shows up to steal the bounty? The stash-owning squirrel fakes out the would-be thief, 'checking' fake cache sites to throw the invader off the trail."[39] She adds that researchers at the Georgia Institute of Technology are designing robots with the same ability.

Those researchers predict that most of these deception devices will be nonhumanoid. They will more often resemble R2-D2 from the *Star Wars* films, who moved along on wheels. Each bot will be programmed to guard something—an ammunition store, for instance. If it detects some sort of threat, including an enemy robot, it will deceive the intruder by changing its normal routine. That will buy time until human reinforcements arrive or the enemy retreats.

Medical Uses

The military also plans to use various types of robots to help and if possible heal or better the lives of wounded soldiers. This is one area, therefore, in which future military and medical uses of robots will converge. One very promising, and in some ways bizarre, aspect of that convergence will be the employment of nanorobots. The prefix *nano* means "small," and nanorobots will be very small indeed. Each of these miniature bots, which are now in the research phase of development, will be about 1.5 nanometers across. To get an idea of how tiny that is, when placed side by side, 25.4 million nanometers equal a single inch.

nanorobot

A very tiny robot that can be seen only through a microscope.

Most of the medical uses of nanorobots will involve a patient swallowing a fluid containing several million of them. Those bots will be engineered to do specific tasks. Some will identify cancer cells, for example, well before doctors can find the cells using

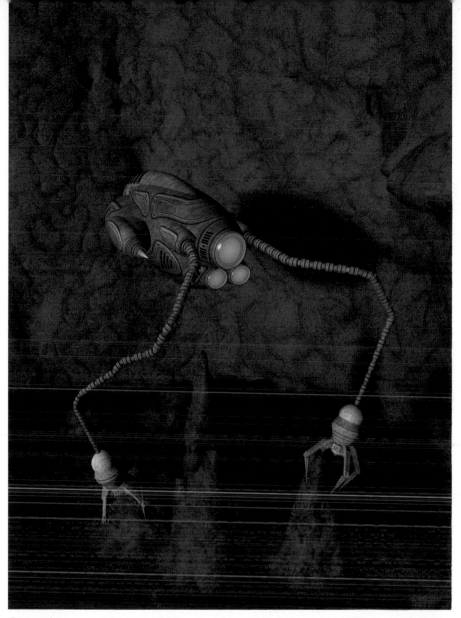

Researchers are working toward the day when nanorobots might be able to remove an obstruction in a blood vessel (as depicted in this illustration) or carry out other delicate procedures. Nanorobots might someday even be able to identify and kill cancerous cells.

standard medical techniques. Other nanorobots will be designed to kill those abnormal cells. Still other nanorobots will detect the presence of toxic chemicals in a person's bloodstream. Researchers say that in addition, some of these tiny probes will monitor the growth of diabetes and other similar diseases and maybe even repair microscopic tears in human tissue.

Based on existing research and experimentation, future medical robots will also likely leap from the microscopic to the macroscopic realms. That is, some medical applications of robots will involve doing large-scale menial tasks. In hospitals, for instance, mundane tasks like cleaning floors, lugging heavy equipment from room to room, lifting and moving patients, and so forth must be done daily.

macroscopic

On a large or larger-than-normal scale.

Perhaps the most exciting development in robotics in the medical arena is using robots to help perform surgery. It has been established that such operating systems have a number of immediate benefits. They give surgeons a maximum level of mobility, provide them with enlarged images of the operating area, and allow for a faster recovery period for patients.

In the future these systems will become even more exacting and specialized, medical experts predict. For example, they will allow surgeons to perform complex surgical procedures from very long distances. Using advanced robotic equipment connected to fiber optics, a doctor could operate on a patient in another city, another state, or even a faraway country. The use of such advanced robotic surgical systems would allow patients living in rural areas with few experienced doctors to have their surgery done by the world's foremost specialists working in New York, Boston, Paris, or Tel Aviv. "In the future," states Michael Palese, a surgeon at Mount Sinai Hospital in New York City, "there will be tele-medicine, where you can operate on someone somewhere else in the world. I don't think that's far-fetched science fiction anymore. I think that I'll see it in my lifetime!"[40]

Introduction: Robotics and the New Machine Age

1. Quoted in Daniel Ichbiah, *Robots: From Science Fiction to Technological Revolution*. New York: Abrams, 2005, p. 115.
2. Colin Lewis, "More Jobs in Companies That Employ Robots," *RobotEnomics* (blog), July 2, 2014. http://robotenomics.com.
3. Quoted in Ichbiah, *Robots*, p. 116.
4. Ichbiah, *Robots*, p. 116.

Chapter One: Robot Origins and Industrial Robots

5. Homer, *Iliad*, trans. Richmond Lattimore. Chicago: University of Chicago Press, 2011, p. 386.
6. V. Daniel Hunt, *Understanding Robotics*. San Diego: Academic Press, 1990, p. 96.
7. Mark Stevens, "Pros and Cons of Using Robots in Your Manufacturing," *Manufacturing Tomorrow Blog*, Wipfli, October 16, 2014. www.wipfli.com.
8. Stevens, "Pros and Cons of Using Robots in Your Manufacturing."
9. Rodney Brooks, "Robots at Work: Toward a Smaller Factory," *Futurist*, May/June 2013. www.wfs.org.
10. Will Knight, "This Robot Could Transform Manufacturing," *MIT Technology Review*, September 18, 2012. www.technologyreview.com.
11. Brooks, "Robots at Work."
12. Erico Guizzo and Evan Ackerman, "How Rethink Robotics Built Its New Baxter Robot Worker," *Robotics* (blog), *IEEE Spectrum*, September 18, 2012. http://spectrum.ieee.org.

Chapter Two: The Widespread Use of Robots

13. Duncan Graham-Rowe, "Introduction: Robots," *NewScientist*, September 2006. www.newscientist.com.
14. Richard Whittle, "The History of the Predator, the Drone That Changed the World," CNET, September 20, 2014. www.cnet.com.

15. Timothy Hay, "The Robots Are Coming to Hospitals," *Wall Street Journal*, March 15, 2012. www.wsj.com.
16. Mayo Clinic, "Robotic Surgery." www.mayoclinic.org.
17. Quoted in Brett Israel, "New Robotic Vehicle Provides Never-Before-Seen Look Under Antarctica," Georgia Tech, April 2, 2015. www.news.gatech.edu.
18. Quoted in Israel, "New Robotic Vehicle Provides Never-Before-Seen Look Under Antarctica."

Chapter Three: Potential Problems with Robots

19. Quoted in Lewis, "More Jobs in Companies That Employ Robots."
20. Lewis, "More Jobs in Companies That Employ Robots."
21. Quoted in Knight, "This Robot Could Transform Manufacturing."
22. Marc Andreessen, "Robots Will Not Eat the Jobs but Will Unleash Our Creativity," *Financial Times*, June 23, 2014. www.ft.com
23. Kevin Kelly, "Better than Human: Why Robots Will—and Must—Take Our Jobs," *Wired*, December 24, 2012. www.wired.com.
24. Quoted in Marcus Woo, "Robots: Can We Trust Them with Our Privacy?," BBC, June 5, 2014. www.bbc.com.
25. Woo, "Robots."
26. Quoted in Chris Willis, "Isaac Asimov Page," Android World. http://androidworld.com.
27. Quoted in Willis, "Isaac Asimov Page."
28. Quoted in Nick DiChario, "Interview with Robert J. Sawyer," *Philosophy Now*, June/July 2015. https://philosophynow.org.
29. Engineering and Physical Sciences Research Council, "Principles of Robotics." www.epsrc.ac.uk.

Chapter Four: Robots in Popular Culture

30. Ichbiah, *Robots*, pp. 63–64.
31. Quoted in Tim Dirks, "Robots in Film, Part 2," AMC Filmsite, 2015. www.filmsite.org.

32. Dirks, "Robots in Film, Part 2."

33. Quoted in Robots and Androids, "Robert the Robot Toys." www.robots-and-androids.com.

Chapter Five: The Future of Robotics

34. I.J. Good, "Speculations Concerning the First Ultra-intelligent Machines," *Advances in Computers*, vol. 6, 1965, p. 32.

35. Kelly, "Better than Human."

36. Rebecca Boyle, "Meet Polaris, the First Ice-Drilling Lunar Prospector-Bot," *Popular Science*, October 10, 2012. www.popsci.com.

37. Mike Adams, "Meet Your Future Enemy: Pentagon Developing Humanoid Terminator Robots That Will Soon Carry Weapons," Natural News, April 8, 2013. www.naturalnews.com.

38. Adams, "Meet Your Future Enemy."

39. Boyle, "Meet Polaris, the First Ice-Drilling Lunar Prospector-Bot."

40. Quoted in Jennifer Polland, "Watch: This Robot Is Poised to Change Surgery Forever," Business Insider, August 1, 2012. www.businessinsider.com.

Books

Kathy Ceceri, *Making Simple Robots*. Sebastopol, CA: Nakermedia, 2015.

Ruth Owen, *Robots in Space*. New York: Ruby Tuesday, 2015.

Behnam Salemi, *Robot Building for Teens*. Boston: Cengage, 2012.

Melissa Stewart, *Robots*. Washington, DC: National Geographic, 2014.

Marne Ventura, *The 12 Biggest Breakthroughs in Robot Technology*. North Mankato, MN: Peterson, 2015.

Christine Zuchara-Walske. *Robots at Home*. Minneapolis: Lerner, 2015.

Internet Sources

Michael Franco, "Icefin Robot: Today, Exploring Antarctica's Depths. Tomorrow, Jupiter's Moon?," CNET, April 3, 2015.www .cnet.com/news/icefin-robot-today-exploring-antarcticas -depths-tomorrow-jupiters-moon.

Tom Harris, "How Robots Work," HowStuffWorks. http://sci ence.howstuffworks.com/robot.htm.

Rich Hooper, "Law Enforcement Robots," Learn About Robots. www.learnaboutrobots.com/lawEnforcement.htm.

Chris Hutton, "R2-D2 Gets Real: 'Star Wars' Droids Already Exist," LiveScience, October 9, 2014. www.livescience .com/48209-star-wars-droids-drones.html.

InformationWeek, "10 Medical Robots That Could Change Healthcare," 2015. www.informationweek.com/mobile/10 -medical-robots-that-could-change-healthcare/d/d-id/11 07696.

Elizabeth Palermo, "Meet Spot: New Breed of Robot Dog Climbs and Trots," LiveScience, February 10, 2015. www.livescience.com/49760-robot-dog-boston-dynamics.html.

Alan Taylor, "Robots at Work and Play," *Atlantic*, October 21, 2013. www.theatlantic.com/photo/2013/10/robots-at-work-and-play/100612.

Websites

B9 Robot Builders Club (www.b9robotbuildersclub.com). The club's members are fans of the *Lost in Space* show and periodically exchange information and/or get together to discuss the show and trade information on how to reproduce their own versions of the B9 robot.

IEEE Robotics and Automation Society (www.icee-ras.org). The group seeks to foster the development and facilitate the exchange of scientific and technological knowledge in the field of robotics. The website includes information for student members and a digital library with articles on all aspects of robotics.

International Federation of Robotics (www.ifr.org). The federation is a nonprofit organization made up of robotics companies, groups, bloggers, and others from more than fifteen countries, all having the goal of strengthening the robotics industry around the world.

The Robotics Alliance Project, NASA (http://robotics.nasa.gov/students/students.php). This site for students provides information about robotics and artificial intelligence. It includes interviews with roboticists, links to other worthwhile sites, and information about robotic projects.